Ray Balkwill's
EXE ESTUARY

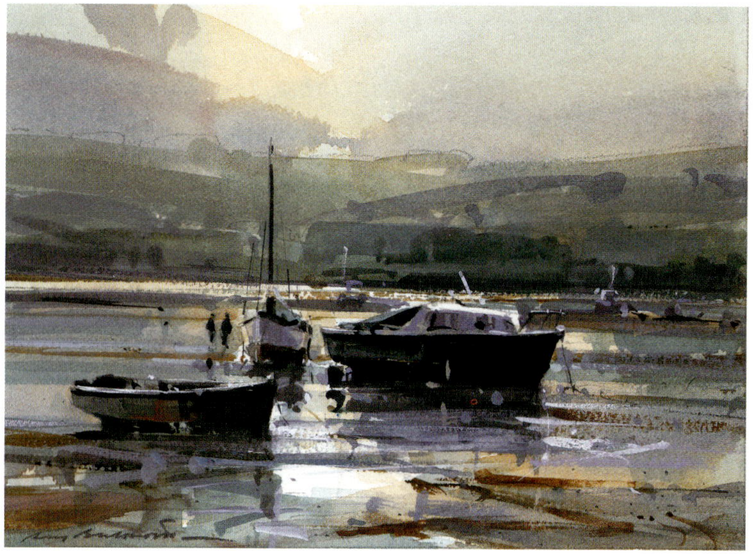

HALSGROVE

First published in Great Britain in 2004

Title page illustration: *Late Afternoon Light.* Watercolour 7x8in (18x20cm).
Contents page illustration: *Head of the Creek.* Charcoal Sketch 10x14in (25x36cm).

British Library Cataloguing-in-Publication Data
A CIP record for this title is available from the British Library

ISBN 1 84114 384 7

HALSGROVE
Halsgrove House
Lower Moor Way
Tiverton, Devon EX16 6SS
Tel: 01884 243242
Fax: 01884 243325
email: sales@halsgrove.com
website: www.halsgrove.com

Printed and bound by D'Auria Industrie Grafiche Spa, Italy

Contents

Acknowledgements	4
Foreword	5
Introduction	7
Portrait of the Artist	11
Painting Methods	19
Past Painters of the Exe and its Estuary	23
Location Map	28
The Paintings	29
Bibliography and Further Reading	144

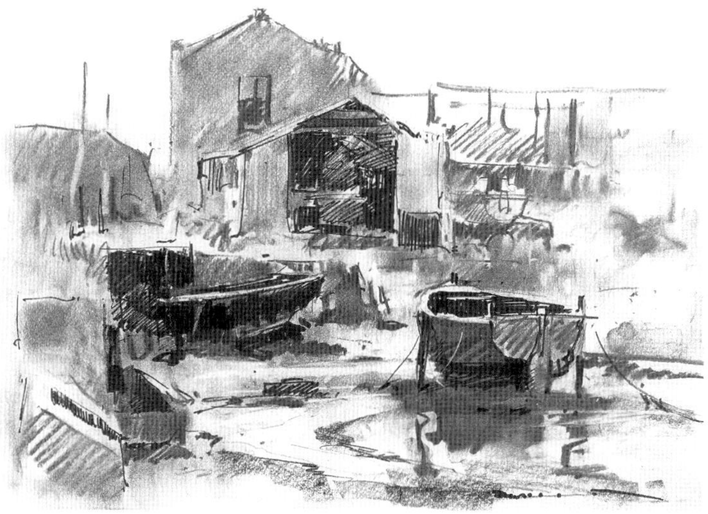

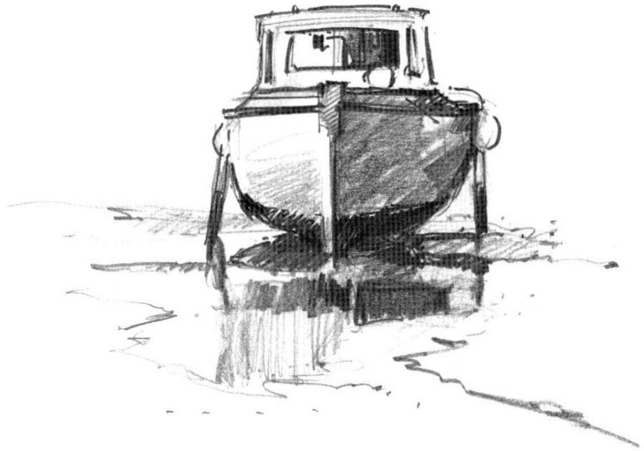

DEDICATION

This book is dedicated to my wife Jane, and sons Sam and Tom, my Mum and in memory of my dear Dad. They all in turn enabled me to realise my ambition and to make the dream a reality. Without them this book would not have been possible.

ACKNOWLEDGEMENTS

The preparation and production of this book has involved many people and I am grateful to them all for their cooperation. In particular, my special thanks to my friend and well respected painter Alan Cotton for writing the foreword. Jane Baker for her expertise and helpfulness with my research of past painters. Also to Brian Le Messurier, Gryff Thomas, Alan Frood, and Catriona Batty. John Biggs (of J. Collins & Son, Bideford), and Nicholas Toyne for the loan of photographs featured on pages 24–25. Geoff Holman, Ron Lavis and Daniel Trout for their assistance in my research on the maritime history of the Exe. Nigel Cheffers-Heard for producing the necessary superb quality transparencies of my paintings. Rose and Jim Brady for casting their expert eyes over my words. Directors and Staff at Halsgrove in particular; Simon Butler, Denise Lyons and Karen Binaccioni. David Walker and Joanna Stroud-Lewis of the Walker Galleries, Honiton, for hosting the book launch and solo exhibition. Finally, a big thank you to my patrons who have supported me in the past and to those who have allowed the reproduction of paintings from their private collections.

Ray Balkwill

Picture Acknowledgment Page 22:
'Dead Calm – Sunset at the Bight of Exmouth' by Francis Danby (1793–1861).
Royal Albert Memorial Museum, Exeter, Devon, UK/ www.bridgeman.co.uk

Foreword

by Alan Cotton

Ray Balkwill's knowledge and genuine affection for the Exe estuary has spanned almost his whole lifetime and his paintings of this very special stretch of water are renowned. Underlying all his work is a deep understanding of the river in all its moods and there is a real awareness of the seasons and of changing weather conditions, of cloud movements, of sunlight and shadow. His observations of the movement of water and of the relationship between sky and earth are skilfully interpreted in his chosen medium, watercolour, with a spontaneous fluency that also extends to his work in gouache, pastel and oils

Ray traces the journey of the estuary from Exmouth to Exeter, from dawn to dusk, throughout the seasons of the year. His paintings of moored boats as they lie in the shallows or rest on wet mud banks, with light shimmering across the water, are classic Balkwill's. The joy of this book lies not only in Ray's close observation and interpretations of the landscape but also from a very personal rapport with the estuary and an intimate knowledge of its history, resulting from conversations with others who have lived and worked along its banks. His commentary on so many aspects of the river, descriptions of his working methods and memories of various experiences, add considerably to the visual delight of his paintings

Not only is Ray a talented artist but he is also a most gifted teacher – in fact one of the best tutors of landscape painting I know, giving much time to his students, analysing the work and showing genuine concern for the development of their paintings. His demonstrations in watercolour, both with students on location and with art societies, are enlightening and extremely popular. Ray and I have been friends for many years and have shared some very memorable experiences. We have twice taken a group of painters to the hills of the Langhe in Piemonte in Northern Italy, where his easy manner and great sense of humour made him popular with both the students and with our Italian hosts, who showed us remarkable hospitality. Ray, after a few glasses of Italian vino, dancing on a hillside to the strains of an accordian, was a sight to behold!

A couple of years ago Ray and Jane invited me to open their new spacious studio-gallery at Thistledown, where he runs painting courses and holds regular and extremely popular exhibitions, giving the public an opportunity to view some of his latest work and from time to time, the work of other invited artists.

This delightful book of the estuary of the River Exe shows the range and diversity of a most popular artist and will be a lasting record of this romantic Devon river in all its moods, from the water's edge to the stunning vistas across the valley from Haldon Hill, of the towns and villages along its banks to the far distant views over Woodbury Common. I hope you enjoy this sumptuously illustrated edition of Ray Balkwill's Exe Estuary.

Painter, and President of the South West Academy of Fine and Applied Arts.

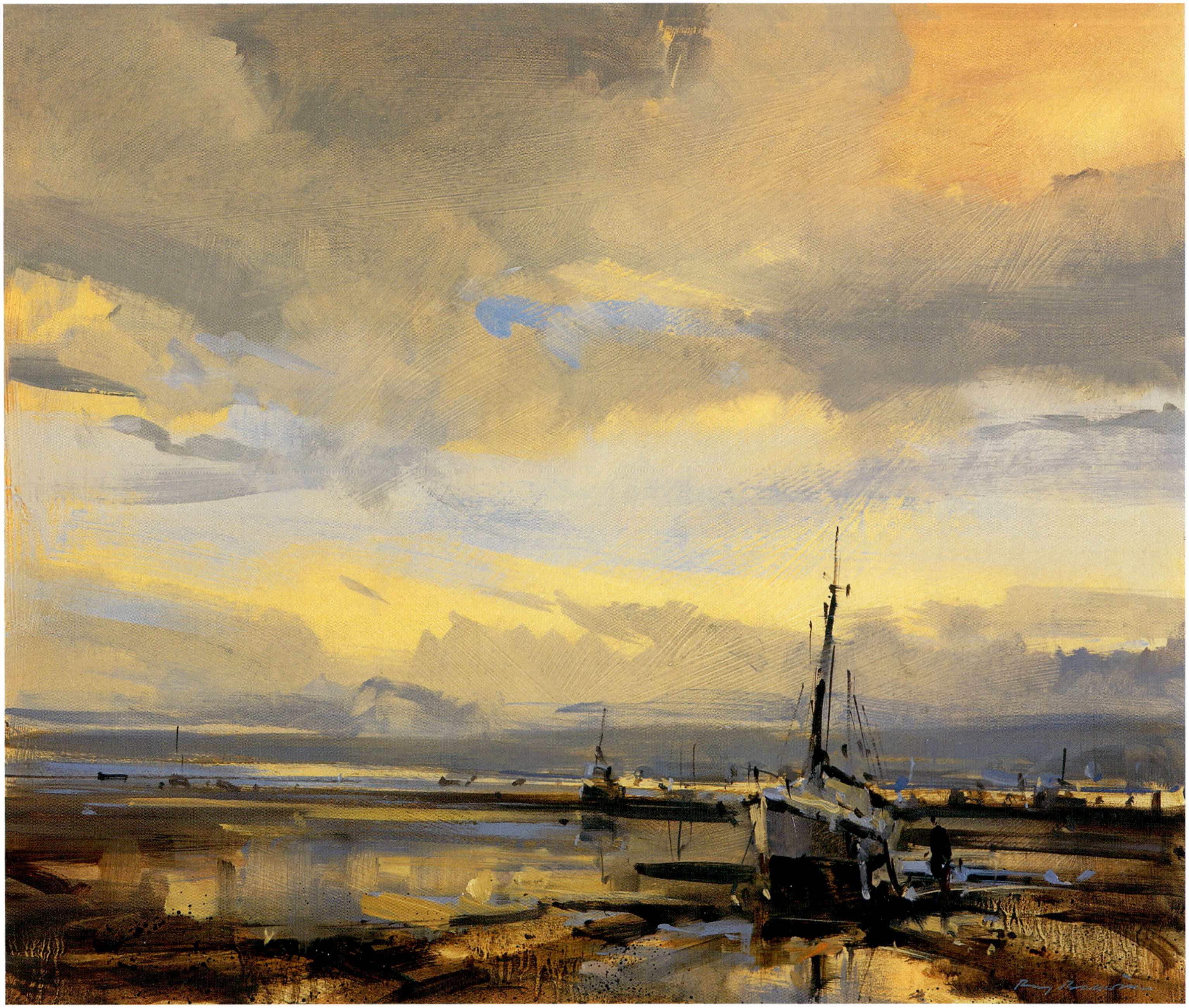

Evening Fanfare
Oil 12x14in (30x36cm)

Introduction

If you have ever sat on the banks of the Exe marvelling at its beauty as the sun slowly sets behind the Haldon Hills, perhaps you will understand why I am so passionate about the place and why I constantly have to try and capture it in paint. Although they are always the same hills, the light and colour of the sky continually cast a new aspect on both land and water, always dominated by the tide as it sweeps in and out to meet the sea. The Exe has much to offer the painter and as each season changes, so too does its mood. Whether it is in the calm balmy evenings of summer, when the gently-flowing waters seem to blaze with sunset reflections, or in the autumn and winter months, when the river is shrouded in mist and storm clouds.

First Encounters

The earliest memory I have of the Exe was when I was about 12 years old. My grandparents, James and Elsie Hosegrove, lived in St Leonards, just a stone's throw from the river. During the long summer holidays, my sister and I often stayed with them and 'Grandum' as we affectionately called him, would take us on walks down to the river and canal, or on the bus to Topsham. The canal up to the late 1960s was a much busier place than it is today and we would often sit for hours watching the coasters navigating the locks at Turf, or unloading their cargoes in the Canal Basin. The *Guidesman, Esso Jersey* and *Alf Everard* were to become familiar names to me and on each visit I would look for them. For a small boy it was a real adventure, but not so exciting for my sister! I can still see my grandfather now, dressed in cloth cap and pinstripe suit, pocket-watch and chain tucked in his waistcoat and nearly always with a Woodbine in his hand. I think those early memories of the river and its shipping made a lasting impression on me, but although boats and water have always fascinated me, I have never had any interest in actually being in either. The river has been the mainspring of my art for two decades and although I have travelled throughout the UK and abroad I don't think there is anywhere I would rather paint. I have always believed that painting should be more than just a literal interpretation – it should also convey emotions – and *'a sense of place.'* This wonderful corner of Devon is my homeland and being born in Exeter and having lived near the river for so long, the *'spirit'* of the Exe is very real to me. As D.H. Lawrence once said *'the spirit of place is a great reality.'* I think it is this personal, as well as physical relationship with the landscape that provides such an important element in my work. I find there is a profound and overpowering sense of character,

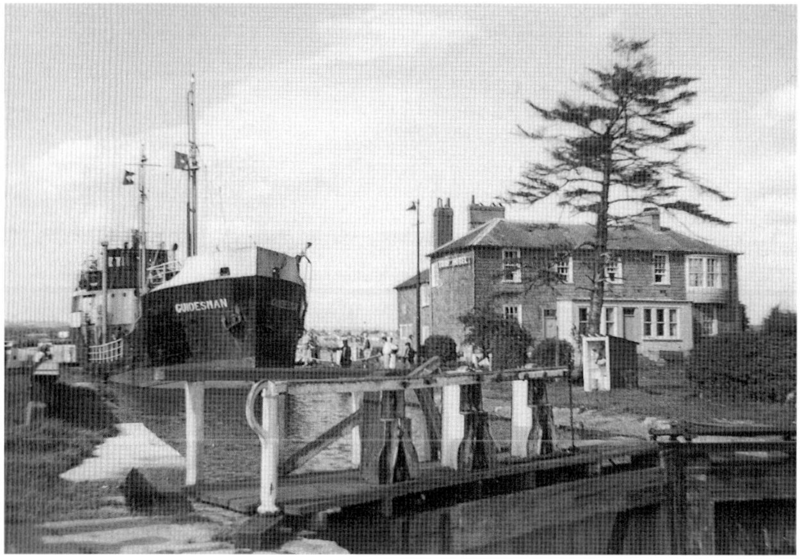

The *Guidesman* at Turf Lock, taken on my Brownie camera in the early 1960s.

history and belonging to be found here and getting *'under the skin'* of a place is as important to me as the painting process itself. Although my early career in advertising led me away from the county, the human instinct to set down roots and return to the scenes of one's childhood can be very strong indeed. I know this is how it was for me.

About the Estuary

The River Exe is 70 miles long and rises high on Exmoor, flowing through some of Devon's most glorious countryside before reaching the sea between Dawlish and Exmouth. It is tidal as far up as Countess Wear, nine miles from the mouth, and this is the area known as the Exe estuary. It is the largest estuary in Devon and derives its name from the Celtic word *'Eisca'* meaning 'fish' – almost certainly salmon, as since prehistoric times it swarmed with them, sadly no longer the case. Centuries ago the Exe was much wider, lapping at the walls of Powderham Castle, while Kenton was a busy trading port. The ancient ferry from Starcross once came right into the very heart of Exmouth at

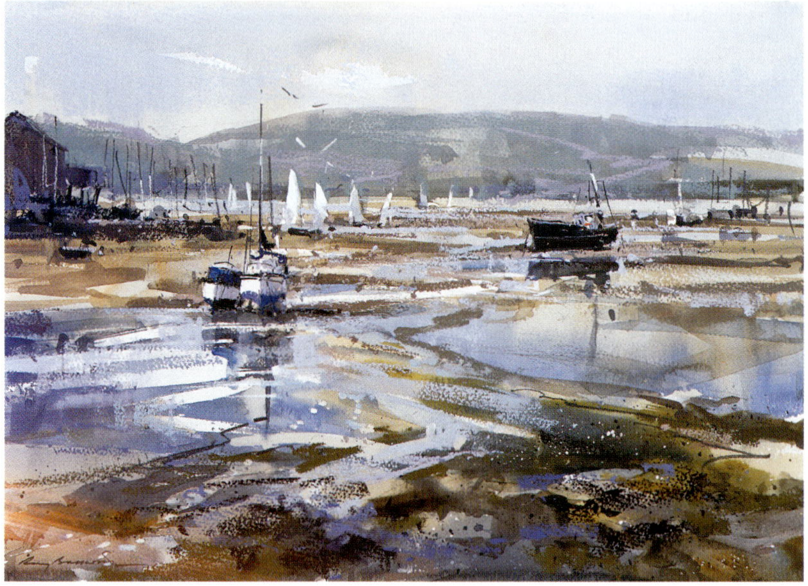

Across the Cockle Sands, Exmouth
Mixed Media 13.5x19in (34x48cm)

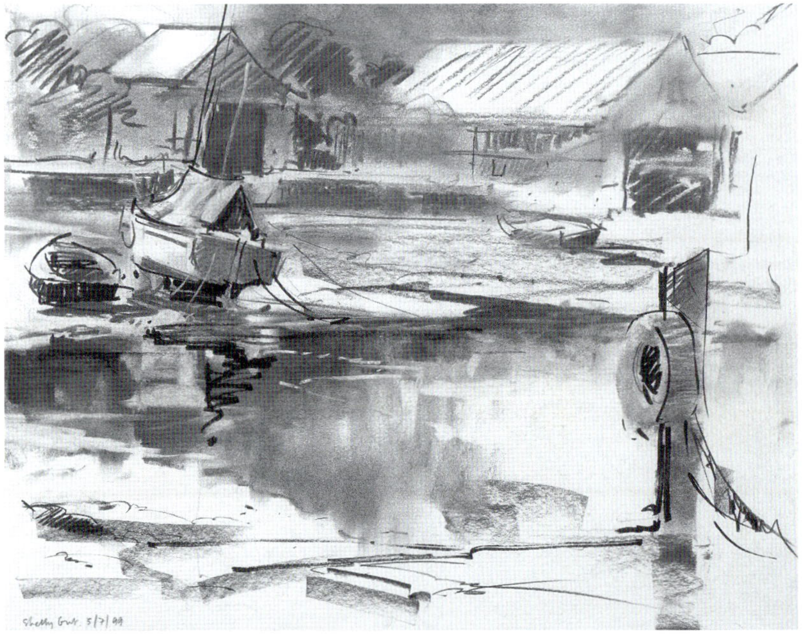

Camperdown Creek, Exmouth
Charcoal Sketch 12x15in (30x38cm)

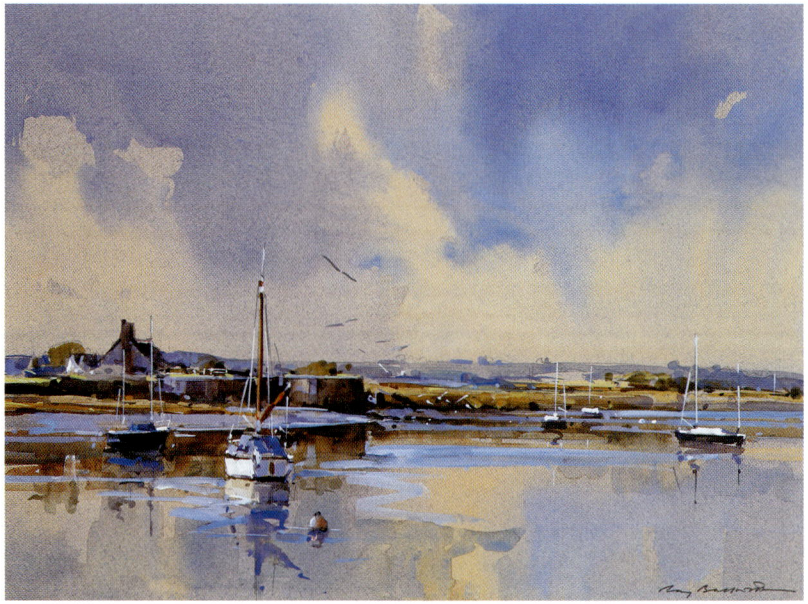

Up River, Topsham
Watercolour/Gouache 10x14in (25x35cm)

Mona Island on the Exeter Road. Just as the shape of the river has changed, so too has its fortunes and travelling upstream, one can find a thousand years of man's history along its banks. Its castle, stately mansions, follies, red sandstone churches, as well as its rich maritime connections are still visible all along its shoreline. At Topsham you will pass the Exeter Ship Canal, claimed to be the first English lock canal, dating back to 1563, which made Exeter such an important trading port. There is also a reminder of a glorious failure too, the red sandstone pumping-tower of Isambard Kingdom Brunel's doomed Atmospheric Railway at Starcross. Over the centuries, the river has witnessed many of man's bloodier events, from marauding Danish raiders, who pillaged Exmouth and sailed up the river to Exeter, to a rebellion at Clyst St George and Civil War skirmishes on both sides of the river. In more recent times, during the Second World War, the river was used as navigation for German bombers to target Exeter. There is a reminder of this with the hulk of *South Coaster,* a steam tramp that ran aground off Cockwood in 1943 avoiding a U-Boat encounter. For two thousand years, the river has been the life-blood of Devon's prosperity, with trading, shipbuilding and fishing all playing major roles in its importance. Today, that has all changed and now tourism, recreation and conservation have replaced the traditional skills. In summer, the Exe attracts thousands of visitors, but in winter, when most of them have gone, it takes on quite a different character, with the estuary playing host to over 20 000 wading birds and wildfowl. The sandbanks, mudflats and nature reserves make the estuary a nationally, as well as internationally, important area for nature conservation.

Your impression of the Exe estuary will of course depend on your viewpoint – both from your own interests as well as from where you are standing. From the top of Woodbury Common, or on the Haldon Hills, one can look down on the estuary like an eagle from its eyrie. The river stretches below like a ribbon of light leading from Exmouth at its mouth, to the gleaming towers of Exeter cathedral in the north. If you are on the Imperial Recreation Ground at Exmouth, you will gaze over a vast expanse of mudbank, or water, depending on the state of the tide. However, to fully appreciate its beauty one must be on the river itself. For it is here – with the *'tang of salt and seaweed'* in the air – that it not only touches all of the senses, but one can also truly appreciate why the river and her surrounding countryside is so revered. Devon's heritage is rich – her red soil and sandstone churches, her deep-cut lanes and thatched cottages and her stalwart sons – so many of whose lives have been bound up with the sea. As Sir Walter Raleigh, Devon's most famous seadog, once said: *'the country of red earth, ruddy apples, rosy cheeks and, honest men.'*

The oyster-catchers still call across the mudflats as yet another sun paints its unique colours in the sky over the estuary. It could be anywhere in the world, but I am thankful it is my home. Who would have thought that the river, which first kindled my interest all those years ago, would form such a quintessential part of my life? If there is a moral, then perhaps it is this: that the real voyage of discovery lies not in seeking new horizons, but in opening one's eyes to the rich heritage and beauty we have right here on our doorstep. Something none of us should ever take for granted.

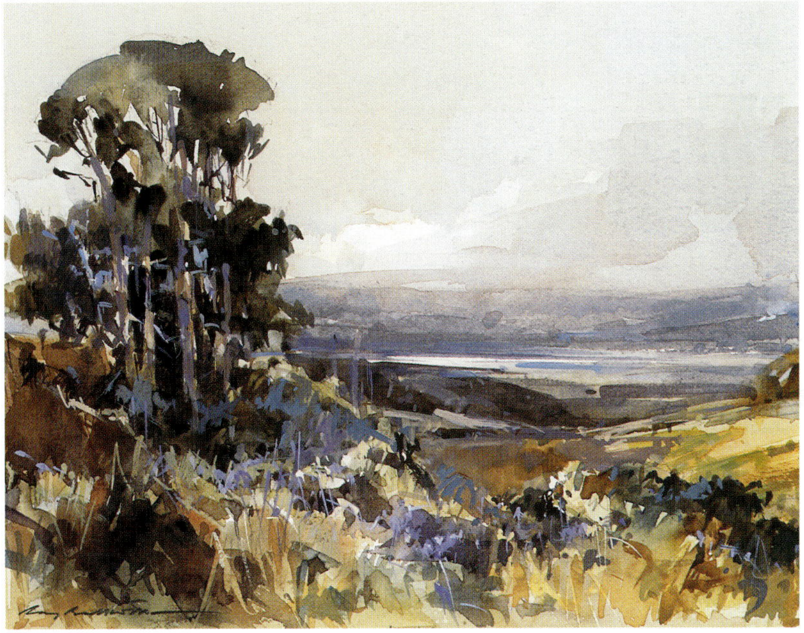

From Woodbury Common
Watercolour/Gouache 9.5x12.5in (24x32cm)

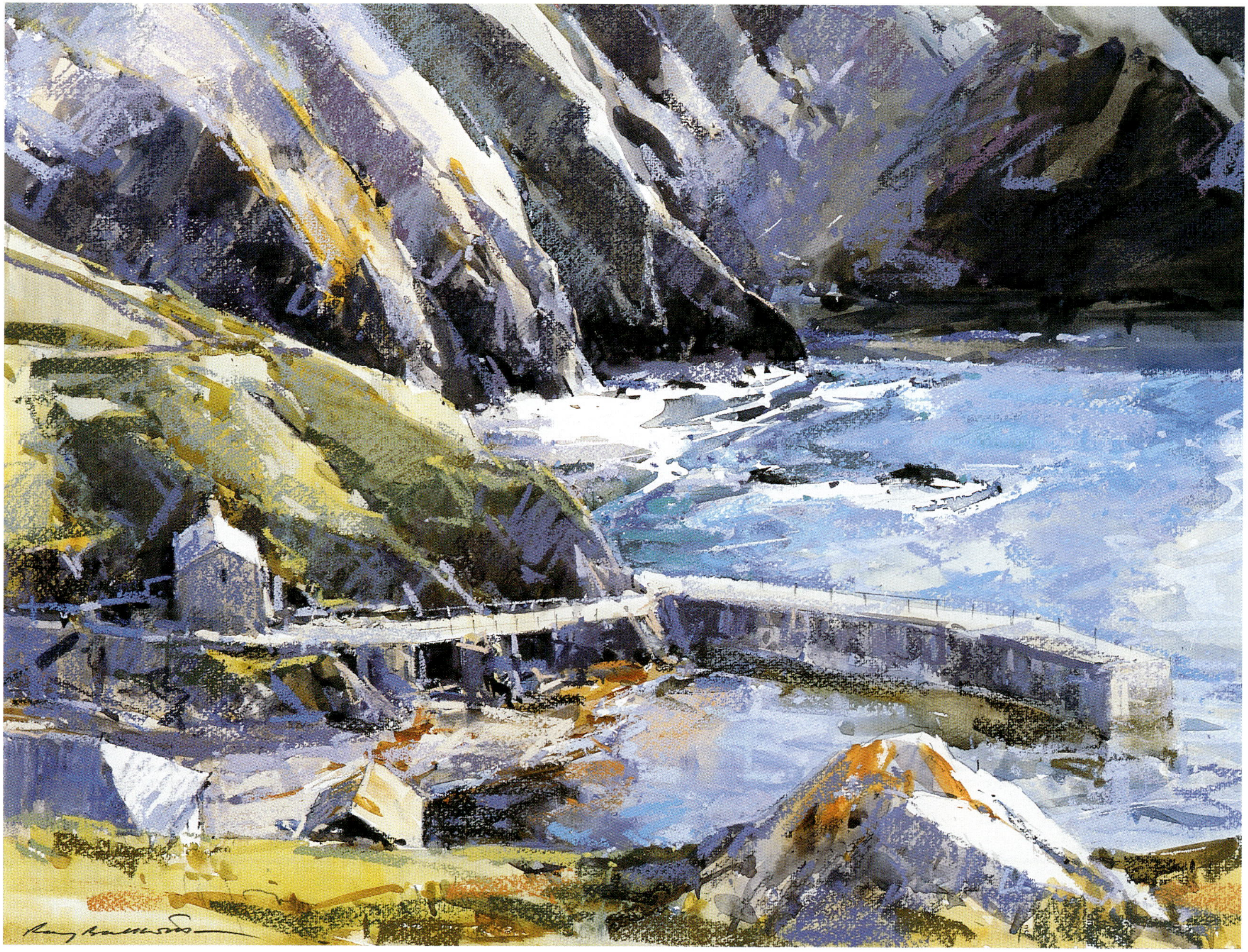

Mullion Cove, Cornwall
Mixed Media 13.5x18in (34x46cm)

Portrait of the Artist

The Early Years

From a very early age, making art a career was always my ambition. I remember my dear old dad saying to me once that it didn't matter what I did, as long as it was a 'PROPER' job! I don't think he thought my later painting career was ever in that category, but perhaps if he had lived to see this book, he might have changed his mind! Nevertheless, he was always a proud father and I know that he would have been thrilled with the result. He spoke with a warm, rich Devonshire accent, which belonged to a less self-conscious age than today and I am sure he would have said something like: *''tis 'ansome bae ...a proper job!'*

As a boy growing up, drawing and painting were always two of my first loves and I remember one day in particular, which was probably my first painting lesson. One wet afternoon, I asked my grandfather if he would paint me a picture. Taking a sheet of thin notepaper and using my inexpensive box of watercolours and an old squirrel-hair brush, he produced a small but impressive painting of Dartmoor. Now of course, I know that those materials were not ideal for that most difficult of all painting media, but that did not matter, as I found this short introduction totally inspiring. Neither of my parents painted, but they always encouraged me in my pursuit of an artistic career. There was a creative

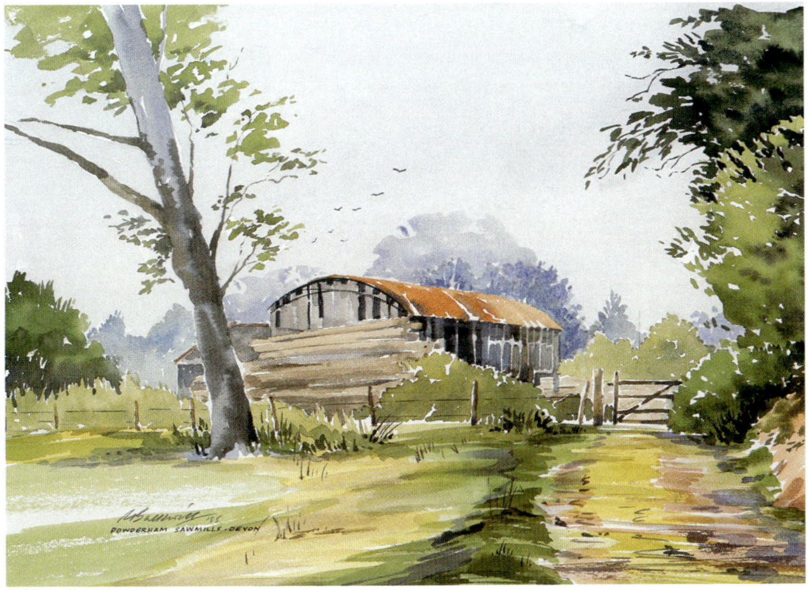

Powderham Saw Mill
Watercolour done in the early 1980s. 10x14in (25x 36cm)

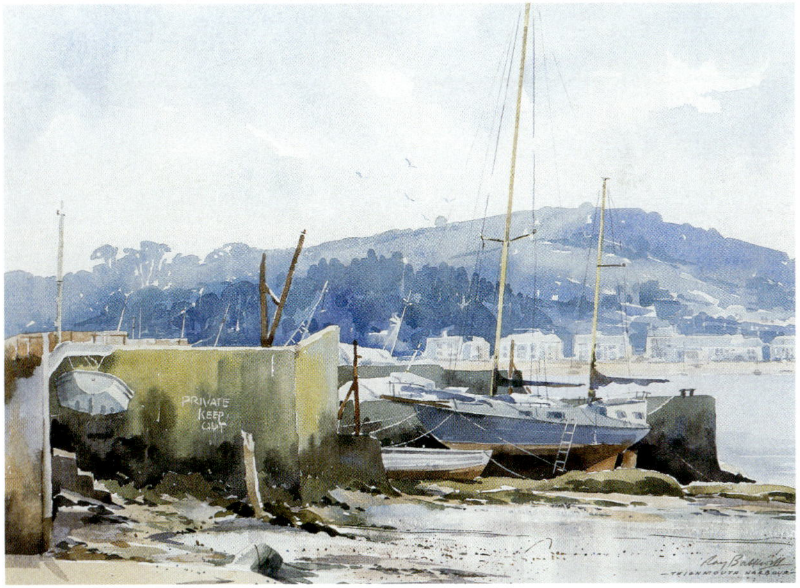

Teignmouth Harbour
Watercolour done in the mid 1980s. 9.5x14in (24x36cm)

link though, as Uncle Henry, my mother's brother, painted as a hobby and the few paintings I have seen of his work are very professional. In fact he sold paintings in Worth's Art Gallery (later the Fred Keetch Gallery) in the Cathedral Close, Exeter. Sadly, he died before I really got started with my own career, as he would have been pleased to know that I was to follow in his footsteps by having many solo exhibitions myself in the Fred Keetch Gallery during the 1990s.

I was born in Exeter on 7 October 1948 and soon afterwards, my parents moved to Okehampton, where my father became manager of Eastmans, the butchers, where he worked all his life – 50 years in total. His father had also been a butcher and both were masters of their profession. I think perhaps he would have liked me to follow him, but seeing the long hours he worked as well as the plasters on his huge hands soon put me off that idea! In any case, my interest was in art, so it seemed a natural progression on leaving school to apply to Exeter College of Art, where I was accepted on a three-year Design and Graphics course. Clifford Fishwick was principal then and the college had an enviable reputation. I have fond memories of many of the tutors who taught me design, typography, printing, illustration and photography. Despite graduating in 1968 with honours, I was unable to get work locally so I moved to London with a fellow student. Eventually I managed to get a job in the art department of Scholl, but after only a year I decided that London was not for me and returned to the West Country, finding work in an advertising agency in Bath. Between 1969 and 1978 I worked for further agencies in Bristol and Bath, before deciding to return to Devon. I think the Exe was calling me, even then! I enjoyed my stay in Bath and whilst there joined the Bath Light Operatic Group, performing in a number of shows at the Theatre Royal. The most memorable was *'Waltzes from Vienna'* as I was understudy for quite a big part and had to step in at the last moment. As if that was not enough, I had also just started a new job at the same time in Bristol! The show ran for a week, including evenings as well as two afternoon matinées, at the end of which I was exhausted. A week later I was rushed into hospital with septicaemia, which resulted in a stay in hospital for six weeks on a course of penicillin and a further three months off work. It was in Bath shortly after my illness that I met Jane quite by chance as she was actually training to be a nurse in South Africa at the time. Anyway to cut a long story short, she had returned to her parents for a few weeks' holiday when we met and fell in love – across a crowded room! We spent a joyous two weeks together before she had to return to Durban to complete her course, and we were apart for over a year, except for my short holiday over there. This was a painful time for us both, but when Jane returned to Bath in March 1978, we were determined not to delay things further, so we were married in June. Later that year, we moved to Exeter, where I started a new job as a Publicity Designer for Wheatons, the book publishers. Our first home was in Starcoss, a short distance from the river where we lived for about 18 months. My next move was to an advertising agency just starting up in Exmouth owned by Tony Corbett, where I worked as Art Director for nearly 10 years. Jane was now expecting our first baby, so we decided to move to the 'sunny side' of the estuary and it was here that Sam and

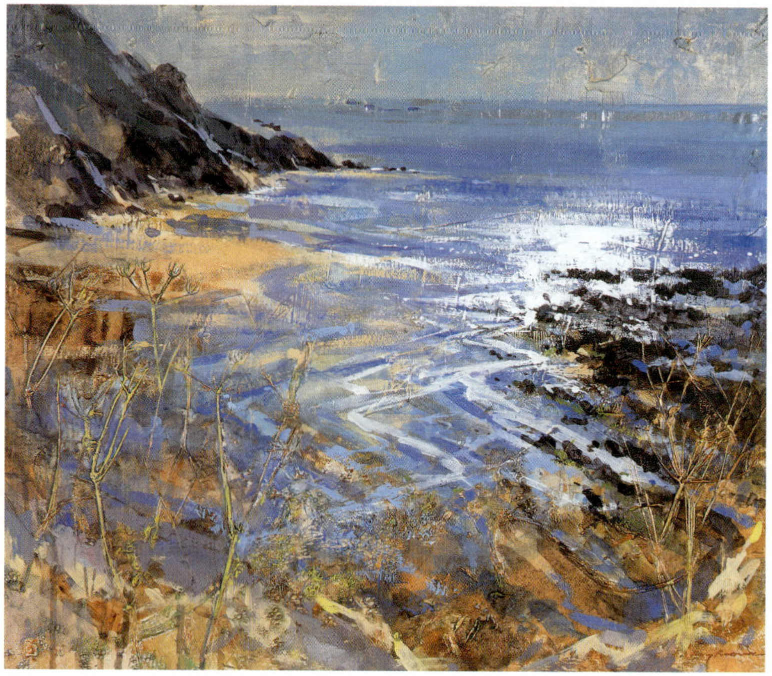

Silver Sea, Hope Cove
Mixed Media 17.5x20in (44x51cm). Prize-winning painting exhibited in the first South West Academy Exhibition in 2000.

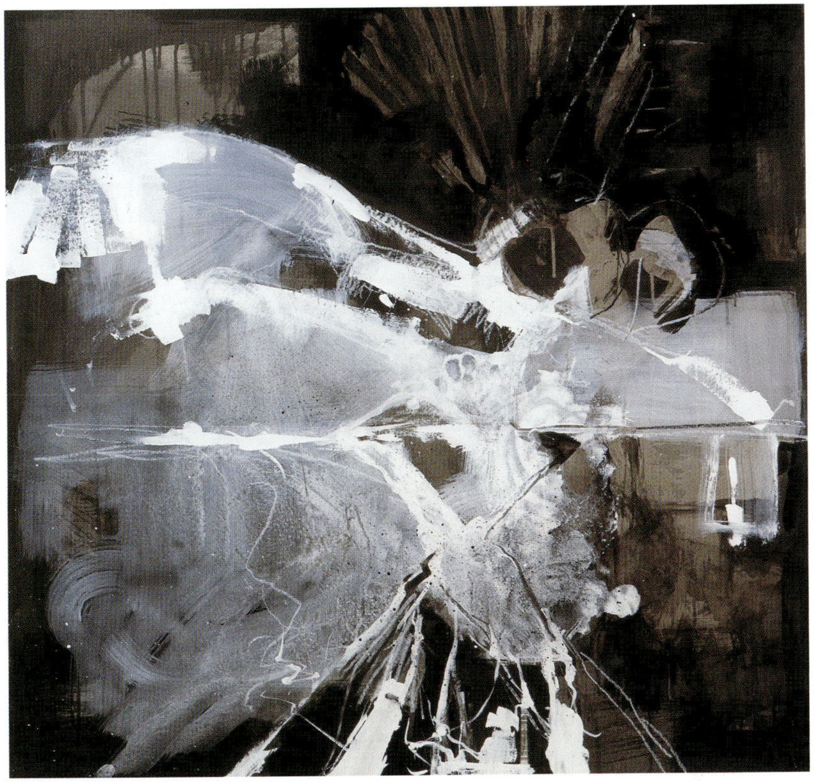

Nature Cupboard
Mixed Media 36x36in (92x92cm)

Tom were born. My career in advertising finally came to an end in 1990, although I did continue freelancing for a while. Since 1983 I had been painting local scenes in watercolour and supplying galleries, in addition to my job. However, demand for my work became so great that I had to make a decision – stay in advertising, or embark on a new career in fine art. Then early in 1989 I entered a painting in the prestigious Royal Institute of Painters in Watercolour, at the Mall Galleries in London, which was selected, hung and subsequently sold. This confirmed to me that it was now or never, so in January 1990 I left my job and began painting professionally despite having a young family to support and the country being in the grip of a recession. At the time, I wondered whether I had made the right decision but I soon realised that I should have done it much earlier.

Development as an artist

My first solo exhibition *'Devon Estuaries'* was held in November 1986, at The Picture Workshop in Topsham, which was the perfect location as the gallery looked out over the river. The show featured over 40 watercolours and was a great success. Further solo and mixed exhibitions followed at galleries in Newton Abbot, Dartmouth, Kingsbridge, St Austell, Bristol, Bath, Exeter, Taunton, Honiton, Burford and Blackheath, London. I continued to enter paintings in the major open

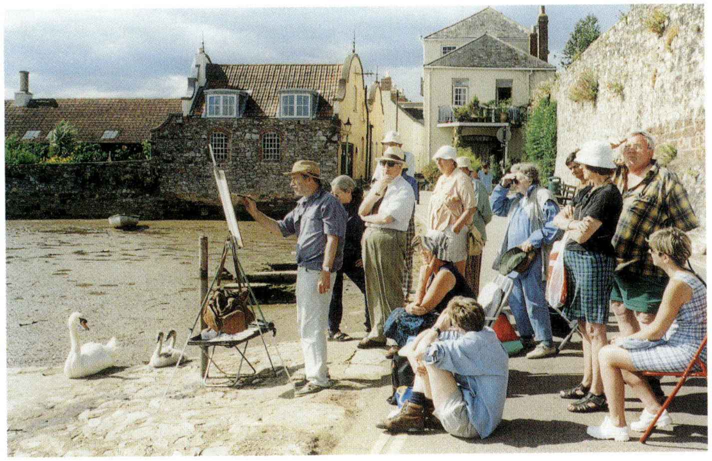

Demonstrating to a group of students at Topsham.

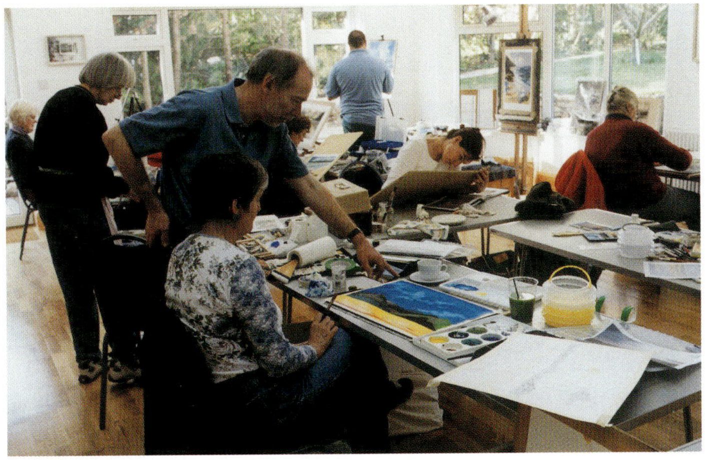

Members of Pilton Art Group during a workshop in the studio at 'Thistledown'.

exhibitions with further successes at the Royal Institute of Painters in Watercolour, the Royal West of England Academy, and the South West Academy of Fine and Applied Arts. At the first South West Academy Open Exhibition in 2000, my painting *'Silver Sea, Hope Cove'* was joint-prize winner voted by the public as the most popular painting, and in 2001 I was runner-up. With a growing family and the need for a larger studio we moved to an Edwardian house in the Broadway, Exmouth and it was here that I held my first studio exhibition in December 1994. This was the start of what was to become a regular event, with exhibitions held twice-yearly, the first during June as part of the Exmouth Summer Festival and the other in December. These exhibitions were sometimes mixed shows that included other painters, as well as potters and wood-turners, and continue to be very popular events. In the same year *The Artist* magazine published my first article, which was so well received that it resulted in my articles being published on a regular basis. Further articles have also been published in *Artist International* and *Pastel Artist International* magazines, which ultimately led to contributing to a number of art instruction books and eventually editing a book myself (these are listed in Further Reading on page 144).

I gave my first painting demonstration in November 1989 to a local art group and I must have done something right, as before long other groups were contacting me to give demonstrations and workshops. Since then I have done literally hundreds all over the West Country – and so the teaching side developed. I have also led evening courses with Devon County Council, painting holidays with HF Holidays, as well as more recently workshops with Exeter University Summer Academy. During this time I also tutored courses in South Devon, Cornwall, Somerset and North Wales. Following the success of my own weekly courses held in local church halls, I decided to develop these even further by organising painting holidays in Exmouth. However, with all this teaching, I now felt the need for fresh inspiration myself! So in September 1997 I went back to college again – this time to do a five year part-time Fine Art Degree Course with the University of Plymouth. Unfortunately, I was only able to complete two years, before our next house move in September 1999 intervened! However,

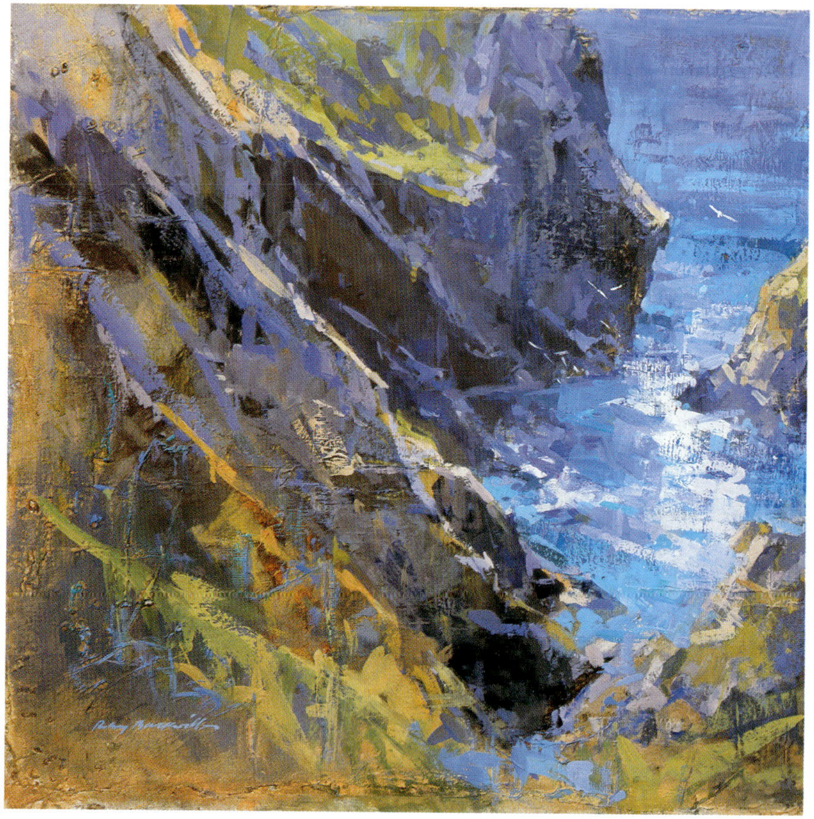

Rugged Coast
Mixed Media 19x19in (48x48cm)

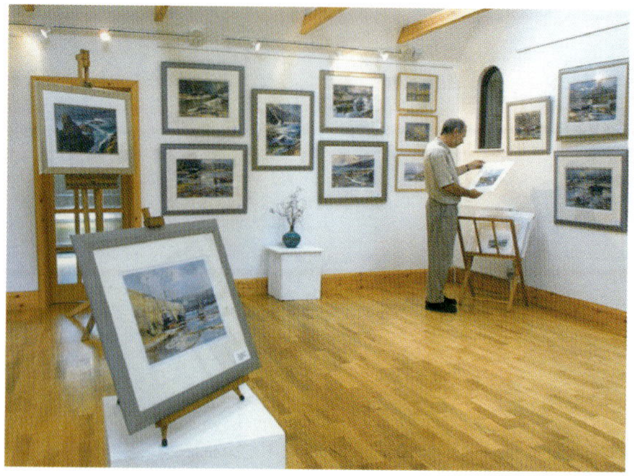

The Studio Gallery, 'Thistledown'.

I found even an abbreviated course a very rewarding experience, as it made me think about my art in a different way, as well as encouraging me to experiment and explore new directions for my work. Some of these influences can be seen within the pages of this book.

The move to 'Thistledown'

The painting courses at Exmouth were really taking off and students were coming from all over the world and I felt the ideal situation would be to have a purpose-built studio at home. My current studio was not large enough for this so, after only four years at the Broadway, we decided to move yet again. We were extremely fortunate in finding the ideal house in 'Thistledown' and the move took just thirteen weeks from start to finish! 'Thistledown' was perfect – set in a large garden, with a view of the estuary and the space to build a north-facing studio on the back of the house. Work on the studio was started in the summer of 2001 and completed in the spring of 2002, and on 3 March renowned artist Alan Cotton performed the official opening, at a party attended by fellow artists and friends. The studio not only provided a base for my painting courses, but also an ideal space for my twice-yearly exhibitions. My first book *Watercolour Plus...* published by David & Charles was successfully launched here on 26 October 2002, with an exhibition attended by contributing artists. The book also featured the work of Mike Bernard, Martin Decent, John Hoar, Wendy Jelbert and Liz Seward Relfe. I was delighted when it was shortlisted by Artists' Choice Book Club for Art Instruction Book of the Year, 2002. It has been well received and has sold well in the UK and USA as well as being reprinted in Dutch.

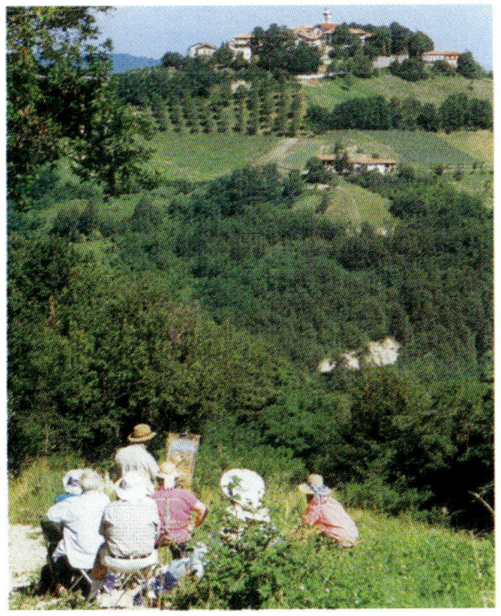

Demonstrating to a group of students on a hot summer's day in Piemonte.

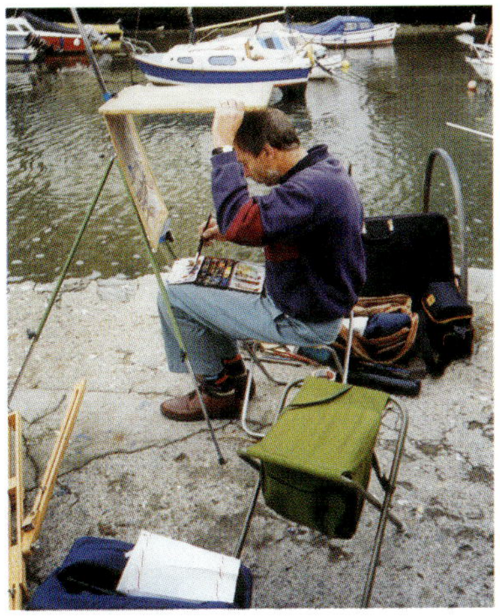

Caught in a shower at Polperro.

(Below) 'Thistledown'.

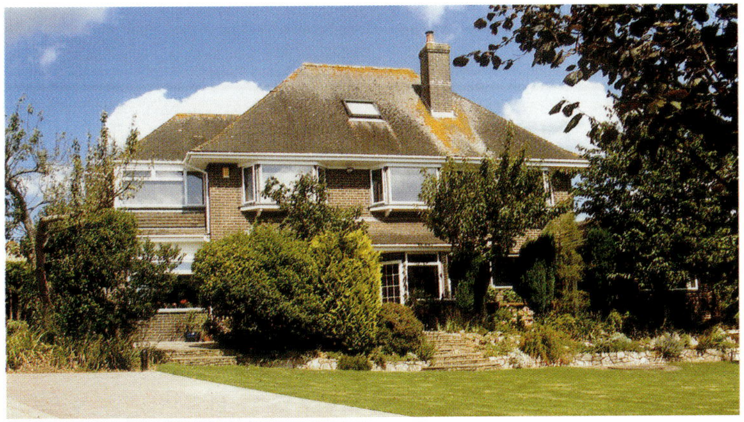

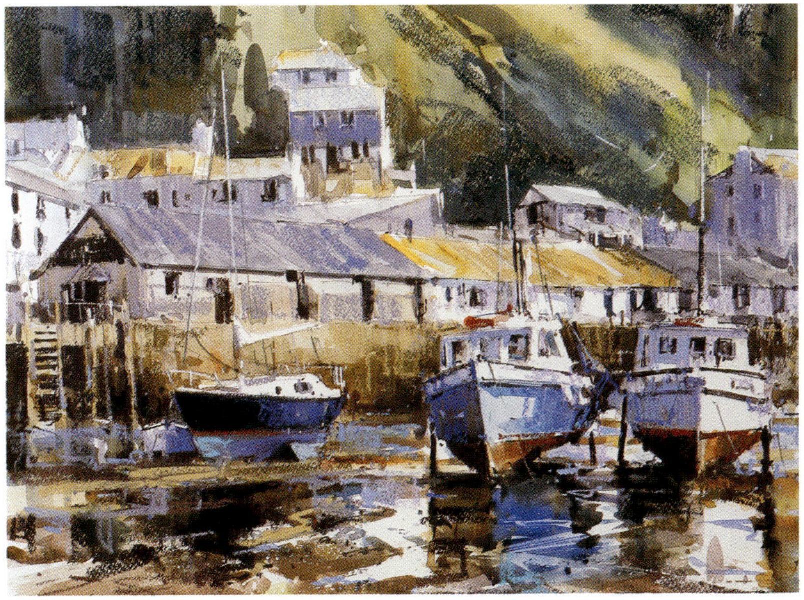

Polperro Harbour
Mixed Media 13.5x 18in (34x46cm)

Painting further afield

Seeking out new subjects and experiencing the vastly different qualities of light and landscape to be found further afield has always played an important part in painters' lives. Although not far away in miles, I have always found Cornwall to be a world away from Devon in the fresh challenges it offers the painter. Its ruggedness and clarity of light demand a more bravura technique for which I prefer to use oils, or mixed media. Consequently, I have enjoyed leading painting courses here for over ten years now, firstly at the Talland Bay Hotel, near Polperro, and more recently at the Tredragon Hotel, near Newquay. I also tutored courses for a number of years in St Ives, for HF Holidays, and in 1999 I was elected a member of the St Ives Society of Artists, so I am pleased to have strengthened my connections with this charming town. I have also tutored courses at such diverse locations as Snowdonia, Southern Brittany and Italy. In July 1998 I joined Alan Cotton in tutoring a painting holiday in Piemonte, Northern Italy, at Serravalle Langhe, the home village of Mario Gerlotto, who then ran a very successful restaurant in Budleigh Salterton. It was a week never to

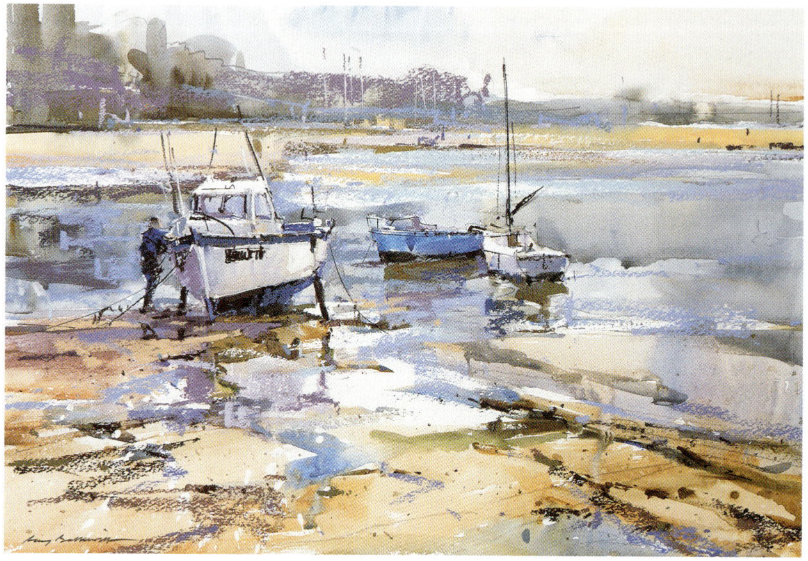

Awaiting the Tide, La Foret Fousenant, Brittany
Mixed Media 13x20in (33x51cm)

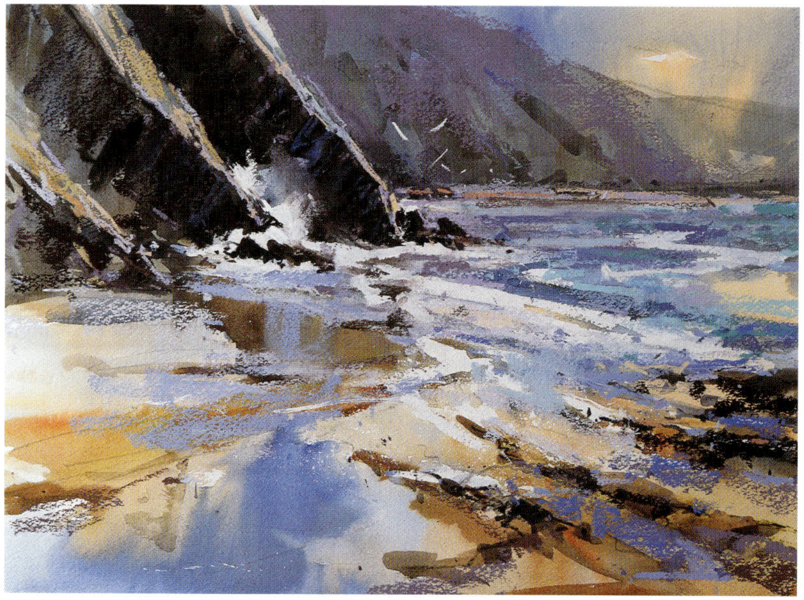

Rocky Headland, Talland Bay
Mixed Media 13.5x18in (34x46cm)

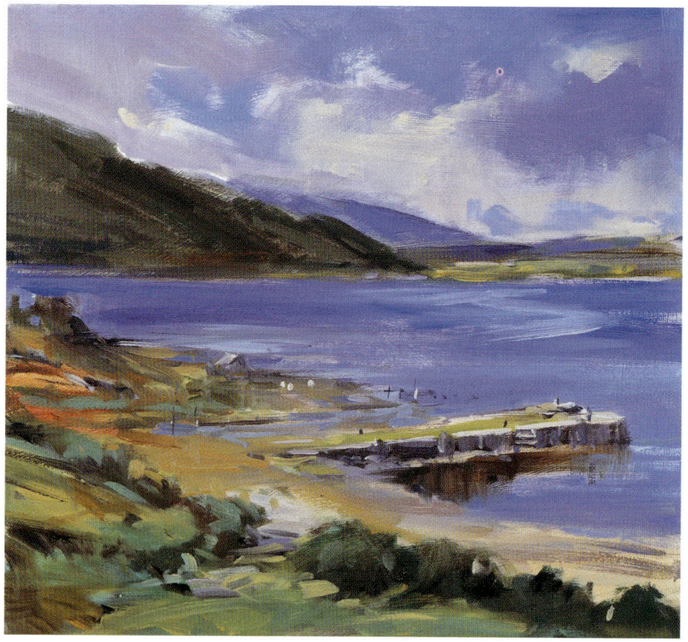

Lough Corrib, Connemara
Oil 14x14in (36x36cm)

be forgotten. The warmth and generosity of the local people was overwhelming and, needless to say, we returned yet again in July 2000. In May 2001, friends David and Anne-Marie Rouse organized a wonderful week in Benodet, Southern Brittany and here I tutored a group of 15 students, painting the creeks and rivers of this attractive part of France. Another memorable trip on my own was to Connemara, Ireland, where, armed with my oil paints, I discovered a world of inspirational scenery, a quality of light similar to Cornwall, big skies, brooding mountains and a palette of greens never before encountered. Two recent painting trips to Snowdonia with its own excitement and challenges, have also added to a diversity of subject material. The grandeur of its mountains, tumbling rivers and waterfalls all contribute to its own unique character. Nearer to home, Dartmoor has also some of those qualities, but on a much more intimate scale. Having spent my childhood at Okehampton on the fringe of the north moor, places like Belstone, Yes Tor and Sourton were my playgrounds, and the freedom, mystery and unpredictability of the place have never ceased to inspire me. In particular, I enjoy the romance of the boulder-strewn rivers that tumble through the ancient woodlands and lush valleys on the edge of the moor.

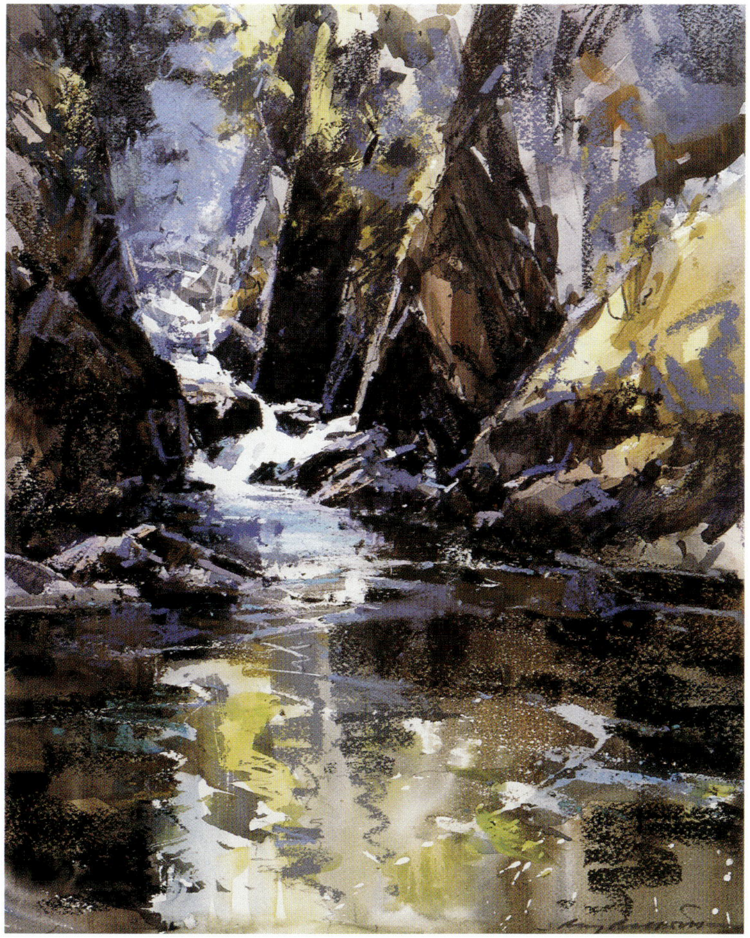

Fairy Glen, Betws-y-Coed, North Wales
Mixed Media 20x16in (51x41cm)

I consider myself fortunate to be earning a living from my painting, especially in this beautiful part of the country. It is very rewarding, as well as humbling, to hear the many complimentary comments from patrons who have bought my paintings and students who have attended my art courses over the years. Peter De Wint, one of the great early English watercolourists once said that he had a *'beautiful profession'*. So he had and I heartily agree with him. Although perhaps in the case of this Devonshire lad an *'...'ansome profession'* might be more apt!

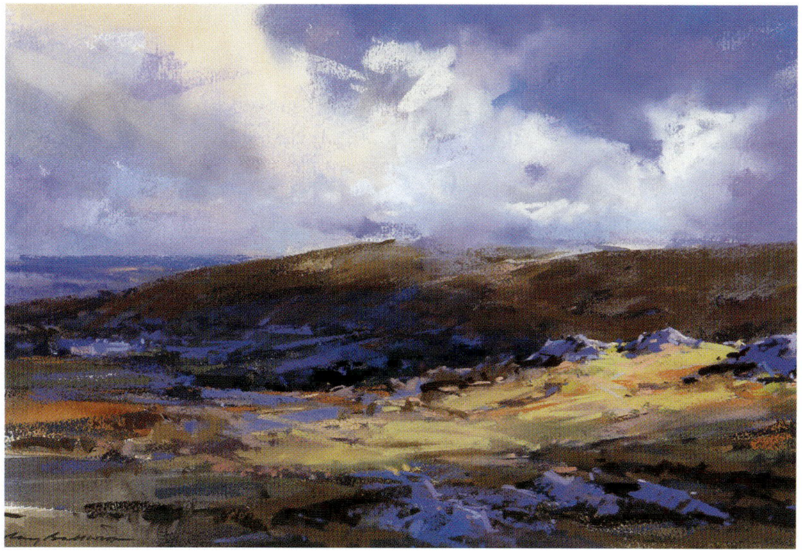

Sunlight and Shadow, Dartmoor
Mixed Media 14x21in (36x53cm)

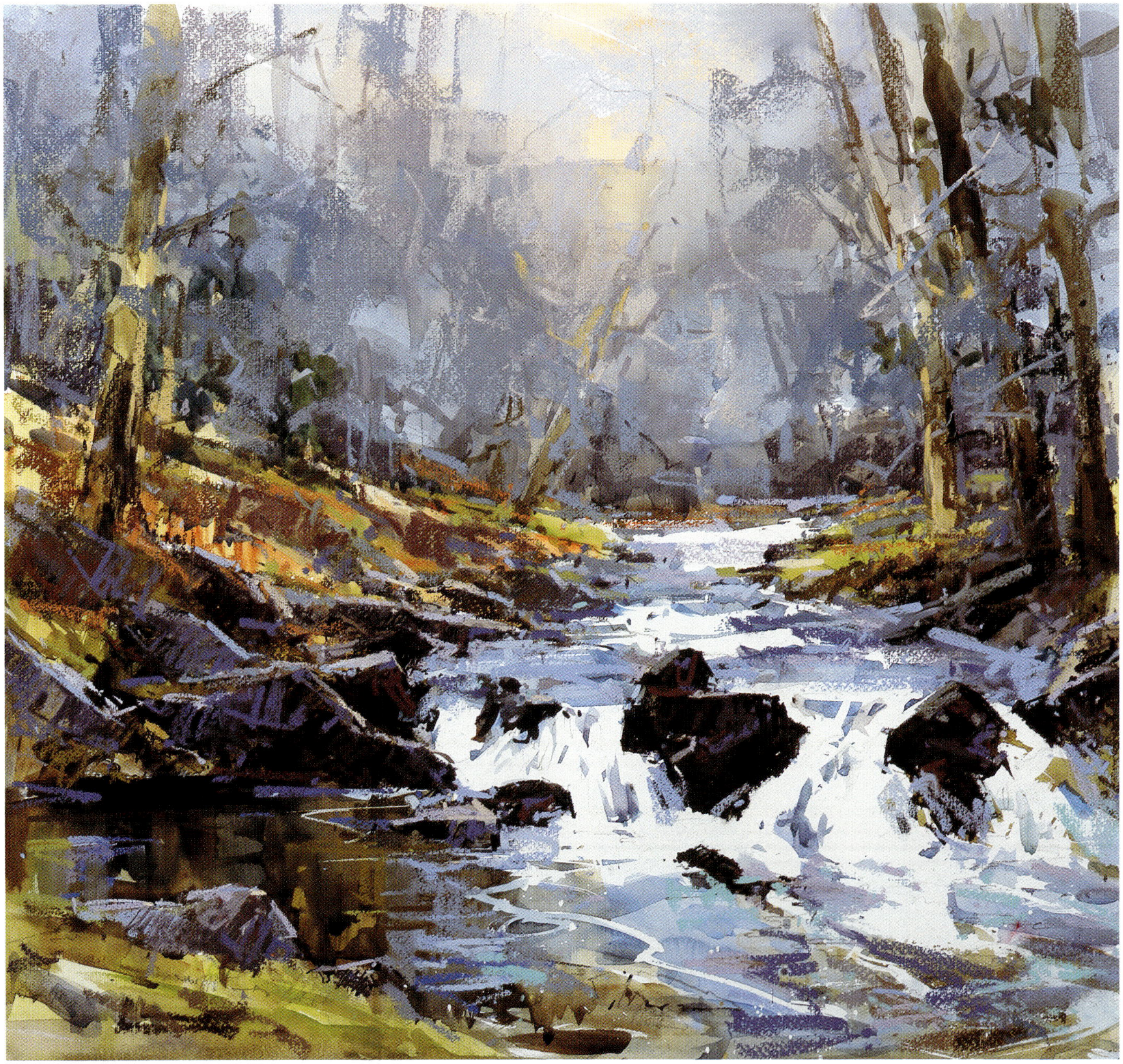

Moorland Falls, Dartmoor
Mixed Media 19x18in (48x46cm)

Painting Methods

These days, there is a wider choice of drawing and painting materials available to the artist than ever before and I am often asked which is my favourite. My answer is 'the one I am using at the time,' and I find it exciting to change from one to another quite frequently. Early on, I worked solely in watercolour, striving to master its elusiveness and soon learned that one needed to 'take risks' for it to remain exciting. Nevertheless, once I felt I had mastered the basic technique, I began to look for new creative challenges, and that was when I decided to devote some time to combining watercolour with other media. One artist whose work influenced me at this time was Aubrey Phillips. During the early 90s, I took off on a rare painting holiday by myself and joined him for a week near Evesham. I returned totally inspired by this incredibly talented and expressive artist. Like him, I am a strong advocate of painting *en plein-air*, although of course some of my work is done in the studio. Mood and atmosphere play a big part in my paintings and the directness of approach and creating a sense of energy in the painting is my main aim, whatever medium I am using. Working quickly helps to create that excitement, but it must be backed up with keen observation and sound drawing. From this the ideas will follow. I often tell my students that Nature is the greatest teacher, with her vast storehouse of ideas and material, so one must get out there to experience it at first hand. Working on location does have its problems, with constantly changing light and weather conditions being the most obvious. Nevertheless, despite these obstacles, the pleasures of painting directly from Nature and taking in the sights and sounds far outweigh them. When I work in the studio, the excitement and

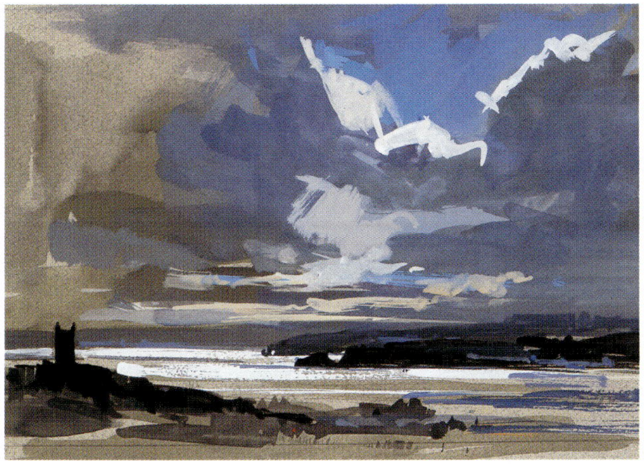

The Estuary from the Studio
Gouache Sketch 7.5x9.5in (19x24cm)

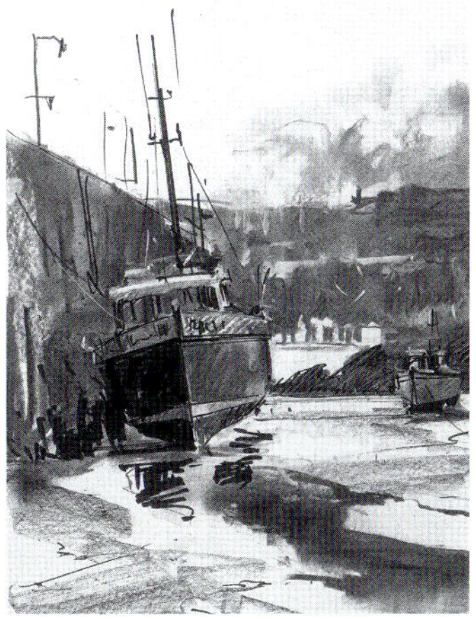

St Ives Harbour
Charcoal Sketch 14x11in (36x28cm)

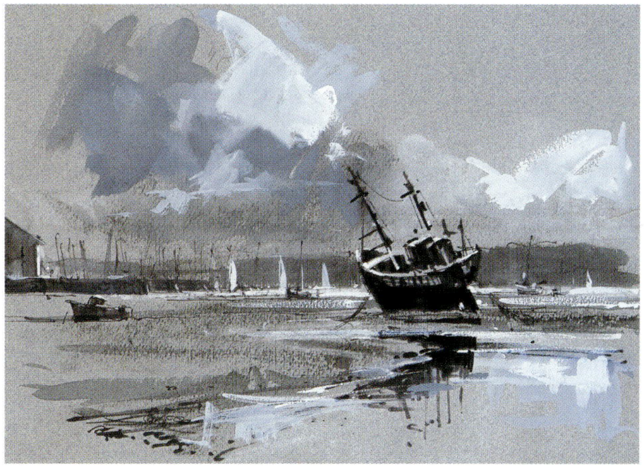

Low Tide, Exmouth
Felt-Tip Pen and Gouache Sketch 8.5x12in (22x30cm)

emotion is much harder to capture, particularly when working from photographs, which is why sketching is so vitally important.

Sketching

When I sketch I like to draw in a broad, loose manner, using a combination of felt-tip pen, charcoal, Conté crayon and putty rubber. Charcoal is a wonderfully expressive medium and invaluable for working quickly and capturing mood and atmosphere. It is the perfect medium for simplifying the scene and, ideally, I try to complete a sketch within thirty minutes if possible. Occasionally I sketch in colour, using watercolour combined with white gouache on a tinted support, such as pastel paper. These are what I call 'location studies', which I use as colour references for painting back in the studio. There is also much to be learnt from studying the sketches and paintings of the masters such as Constable and Turner. In particular, I find their evocative sketches an inspiration as they not only record the facts, but also their feelings in relation to them. They are sometimes controlled and descriptive, but often wild, excited and inspired. In order to appreciate the paintings in this book fully, here is a short description of each the mediums used.

Watercolour and gouache

When one thinks of the traditional English landscape, then it is usually watercolour that springs to mind first. Today, it remains the most popular medium used, yet it is also the most difficult to master. Its characteristics of translucency, expressiveness and unpredictability demand much forward planning by the artist. Nevertheless, it is also the most exciting despite its difficulties. I paint watercolours in the traditional way, building up washes from light to dark, reserving the whiteness of the paper for the highlights. I use several different papers, but my favourite support is Whatman. I particularly like the whiteness of the paper, which allows the colours to 'sing' in subsequent washes. I use a small number of brushes, my favourite being a one-inch hake, filbert and a rigger. I use Artists' Quality paints, preferring tubes to pans and select my colours from a palette of the following: Raw Sienna, Naples Yellow, Aureolin, Burnt Sienna, Permanent Rose, Light Red, Burnt Umber, French Ultramarine, Cerulean Blue, Cobalt Blue and Monestrial Blue. Gouache is also a water-based paint, but has a filler added which makes it more opaque than watercolour. I often add permanent white gouache to my watercolours, particularly when I use tinted paper for a location study.

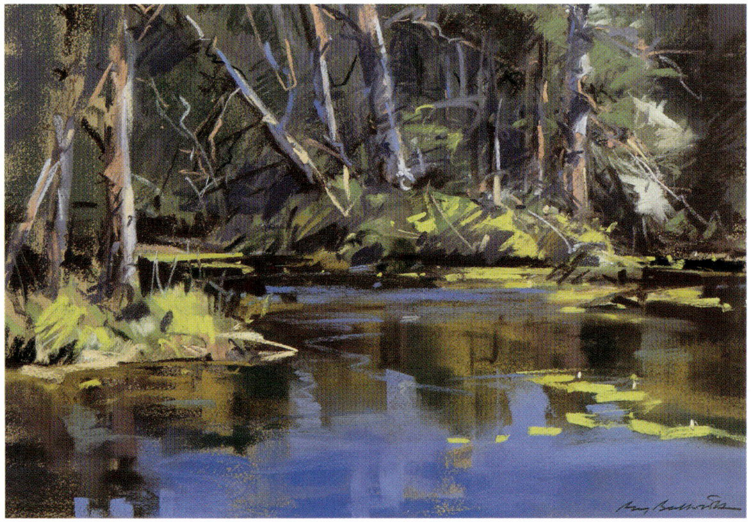

Reflections, Bystock Ponds, Exmouth
Pastel 10x14in (25x36cm)

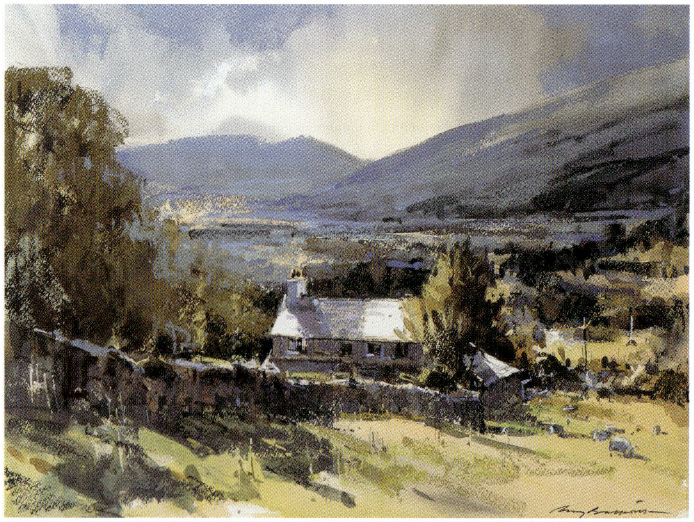

Snowdon from Dolwyddelan, North Wales
Mixed Media 14x18in (36x46cm)

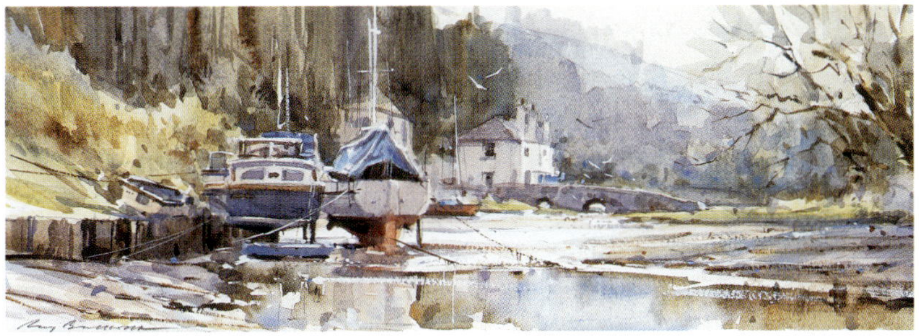

Old Mill Creek, Dartmouth
Watercolour 5x14.5in (13x37cm)

Painting with pastels in the studio.

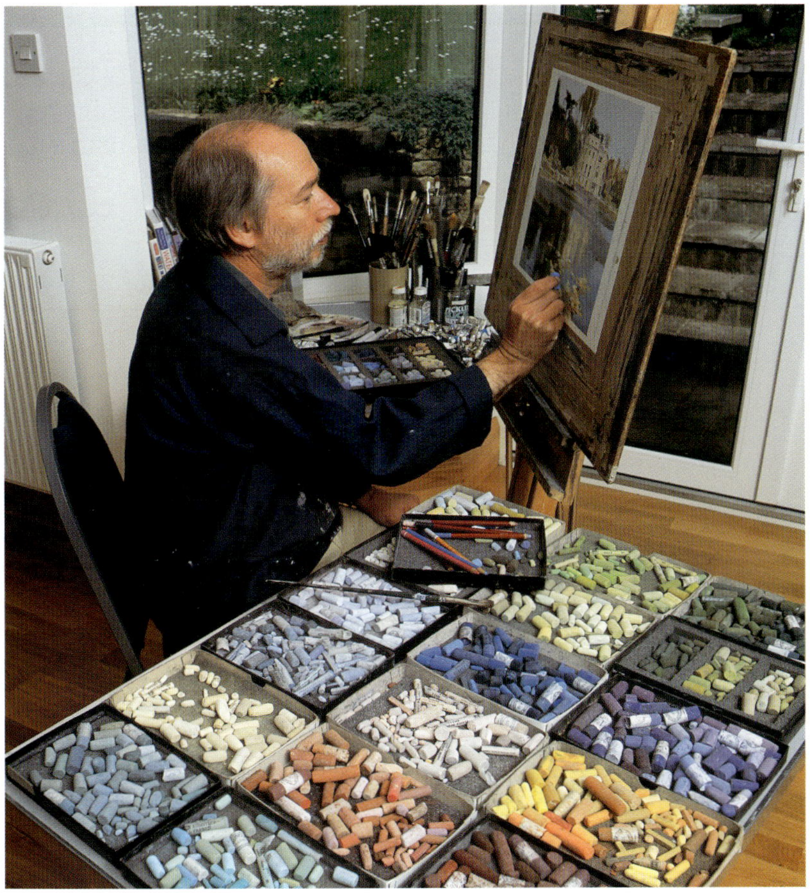

Soft pastel

The equipment needed is conveniently light and portable and the immediacy of pastel lends itself to a quick and direct response, without the problems of drying speed or colour mixing on the palette. I never use fixative with my pastels as it darkens the lighter colours. This makes transporting paintings difficult, particularly those created outside. When this is the case, I simply tape a piece of newspaper over the picture to protect it by preventing any movement. Each pastel manufacturer produces a vast number of colours from which to choose. My own pastel box is made up of all the well-known brand names, but a particular favourite is Unison. Supports vary from pastel paper such as Canson Me-Teinte to sandpaper.

Mixed media (watercolour and pastel)

With watercolour being a transparent medium and pastel being opaque, I like to explore the contrasts between the two when they are combined in the same painting. The variety of technique, such as hard marks against soft, light against dark, and warm colours against cool can produce some exciting results. I use the watercolour to block in the basic structure as an underpainting and when this is dry, I apply the pastel. However, I sometimes go back into the pastel with further watercolour, or gouache. The support I use for this is 140lb(300gsm) watercolour paper, such as Bockingford, Fabriano, Saunders and Arche.

Oils

The smooth, buttery consistency of oils gives the medium a sensual richness unlike any other. The slow drying time means that oils can be manipulated freely to produce a wide range of marks and effects, from transparent washes to thick impasto. When working in oils, I use the method of using a thin 'turps wash' to block in the main shapes and then build up the picture using the principle of 'fat over lean'. The equipment I use on location is a box easel, which carries everything I need, and the support is prepared MDF (medium density fibreboard), which I prime with gesso and texture paste. This gives the surface an interesting texture. I use Artists Oil Colours and my palette consists of Raw Sienna, Cadmium Yellow, Lemon Yellow, Cadmium Red, Alizarin Crimson, Light Red, Viridian, Cerulean Blue, French Ultramarine, Cobalt Blue, Burnt Umber, Burnt Sienna and Titanium White.

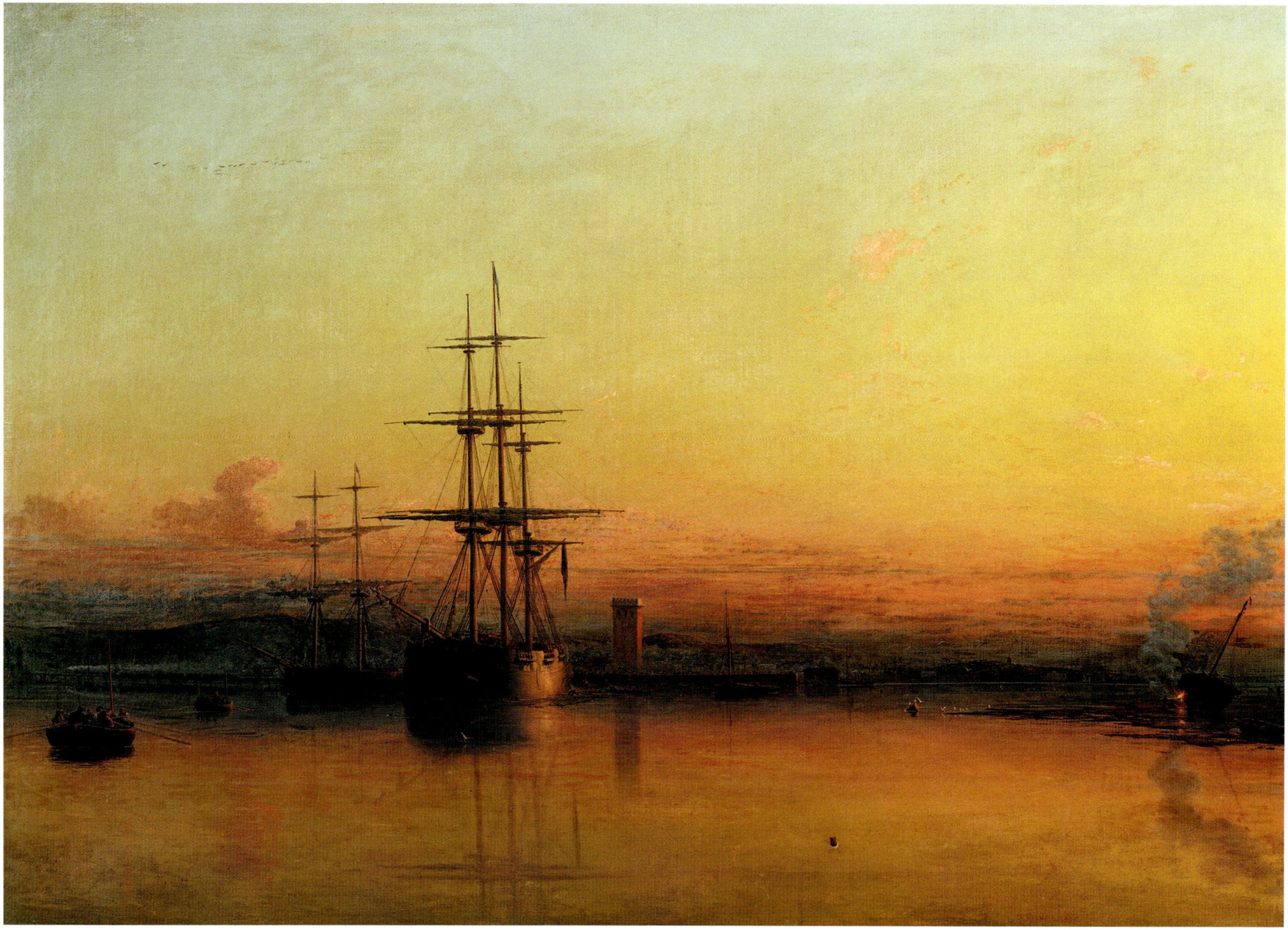

Francis Danby. *Dead Calm – Sunset at the Bight of Exmouth*
Oil 30.5x42in (77x107cm) c.1855 courtesy: Royal Albert Memorial Museum

Past Painters of the Exe and its Estuary

Devon has proved an attractive source of subject matter for landscape artists for over 200 years. Some of these were native Devonians, others settled here for various lengths of time, whilst many came on shorter visits, often with commissions for specific subjects.

Thus, **Joseph Farington R.A. (1747–1821)** made extensive tours of the West Country in 1809 and 1810 making sketches for planned illustrations in his own volume *Britannica Depicta, or a Series of Views in Great Britain*, and Daniel and Samuel Lyson's *Magna Britannia*. **F.C. Lewis (1779–1856**) was another early nineteenth-century visitor whose studies of the various Devon rivers were published in volumes including his *Scenery of the River Exe* which appeared in 1827. **William Payne OWCS (1760–1830)** came to Devon to work on plans to extend the fortifications of the dockyard at Plymouth but found time to draw and paint many aspects of the local scenery, both in Plymouth itself and elsewhere in Devon and Cornwall. So numerous were his delightful and detailed paintings of West Country scenes that it was assumed he was Devonian until David Japes' impeccable research revealed him to be a Londoner. Amongst his varied subject matter he portrayed several of the stately homes in the Exeter area including Oxton, Mamhead, Haldon, Bickham and Powderham Castle. Oxton, near Kenn, was the home of the **Reverend John Swete (1752–1851)**, inherited from a generous grandmother on condition that he changed his name from Tripe to Swete! He also acquired a substantial income and was therefore able to indulge himself making leisurely excursions throughout Devon recording the various aspects of its scenery in a series of scholarly essays accompanied by numerous fascinating, if somewhat amateurish, illustrations. When complete, the total work amounted to twenty bound volumes. He met and entertained many of the artists visiting Devon including Farington and Payne. Payne like most of his fellow artists worked mainly in pencil and/or ink and watercolour, which had become accepted as a medium in its own right, rather than being thought suitable only for preparatory sketches. The subtle vagaries of the English climate, resulting in the gentle greens, greys, blues and golds of the country landscape, makes the delicacy of watercolour paints the perfect medium to convey such subjects. Payne was to add to the range of available colours with his 'Payne's Grey' still in use today. Most of the noted nineteenth century watercolourists were to visit Devon in their travels around the British Isles, including such eminent artists as **J.M.W. Turner RA (1775–1851)** who produced a fascinating view of Exeter and the River Exe, and one of Okehampton, amongst his Devon paintings**.** **Thomas Girtin (1775–1802)** with several depictions of the river Exe; for example *'Rainbow; A Scene on the River Exe'*, and **Peter de Wint (1784–1849)**, remembered for his Lincolnshire subjects, also worked around Exeter and on the River Dart in 1848. One of his last major works was to be a large panorama of Exeter from the river, based on his initial sketches of the city. **Harold Sutton Palmer RBA, RI (1854–1933)** was a Devonian, born in Plymouth, but also travelled throughout Britain. His paintings were used to provide the illustrations in many books, including one on his native county. Views of the River Exe at Countess Wear, and further downstream at Topsham, featured in *The Rivers and Streams of England* published in 1909. The local art scene in Exeter had been enriched in the latter years of the eighteenth century by the arrival of the gifted watercolourist **Francis Towne (1739/40–1816)** as tutor to the Merivale family. Not only did **John Merivale (1752–1831)** himself prove a very able pupil, producing at least two sketchbooks filled with charming drawings of local scenery, but Towne was probably also mentor to the talented local amateur artist**, John White Abbott (1763–1851**). White Abbott particularly delighted in drawing trees, detailing every nuance of gnarled trunks, bent boughs and lush foliage, but he also produced many attractive views of Exeter and other aspects of the West Country landscape including several Exmouth scenes. Most of these were in pen and wash or watercolour but he also painted in oils. Towne himself was more preoccupied with commissions for the aristocratic owners of Powderham Castle and Ugbrooke Park. Some of his studies, were to provide a basis for large oil paintings such as *'Exeter from Exwick.'* **John Gendall (1789–1865)** born and brought up in Exeter developed into a very promising artist who, in turn, worked throughout Britain and abroad, his drawings being used in the popular magazine, *Ackermann's Repository of Arts*. He later returned to Exeter and was in partnership with Charles Cole in his carving and gilding business before setting up his own business in the building known as Mol's Coffee House in Cathedral Yard. This included teaching art as well as painting himself in oil and watercolour. His real skill lay in the latter medium where his subtle and atmospheric use of colour is often akin to that of J.M.W. Turner. One of the more important local artists of the late nineteenth century was **William Widgery (1826–1893)** whose speciality and preference was for the scenery of Dartmoor. However, it was to be his son, **Frederick J. Widgery (1861–1942)** who was to journey more widely across Devon and Cornwall and whose subject matter embraced not only Dartmoor and Exmoor but also many coastal and county scenes. A number of these works were used as book illustrations. The simple, sweeping planes provided by the open spaces of sea, beach and sky seemed to hold a special appeal for him and were admirably suited to his pristine draughtsmanship. His loose sketches and sketchbooks include many studies of skies under different weather conditions (a fascination shared by his great predecessor John Constable). Born in Exeter he was also mayor of the city and one of Exeter's best-known and respected figures, so much so that when car licensing was introduced his initials FJ were chosen to identify the city's number plates. During his lifetime, he enjoyed great commercial

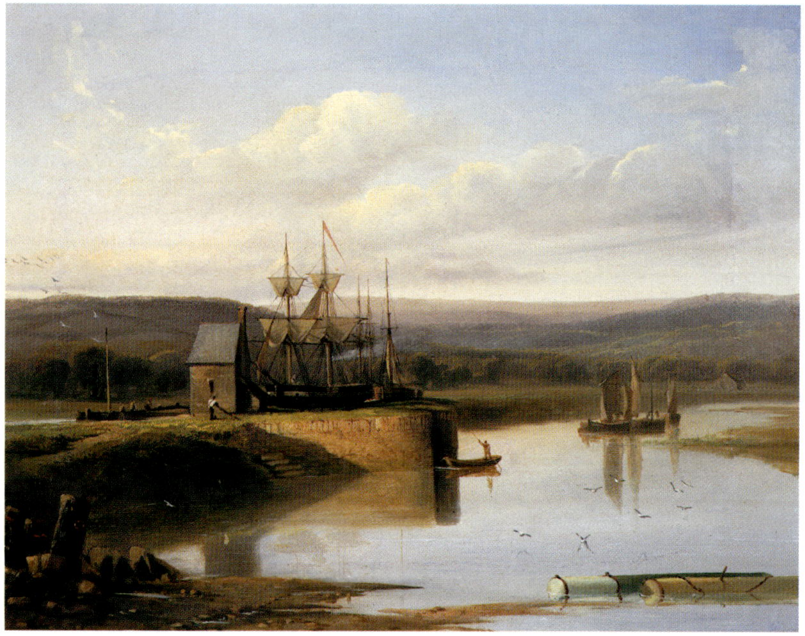

E.H.Hurdle. *Topsham Lock*
Oil 15x18.5in (38x47cm) c.1840 courtesy: Nicholas Toyne

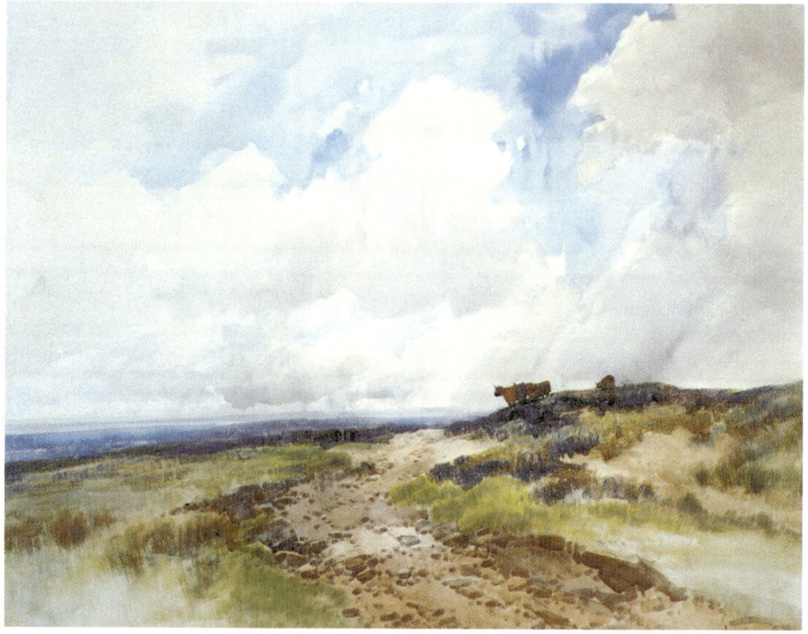

F.J. Widgery. *Woodbury Common and the Estuary of the Exe*
Watercolour 25.5x31.5in (65x80cm) courtesy: J. Collins & Son

success and his paintings were well known in this country as well as abroad. A close contemporary of F. J. Widgery was another local artist, **John Shapland (1865–1929)**. Much less gifted, but capable of producing some very attractive watercolours, he painted many views of the Exe estuary and West Country coastline. He was born in Dawlish, but lived nearly all his life in Exeter. Another well-respected local figure, he had six sons and six daughters and also operated a retail outlet in Exeter where he sold hand-tinted postcards. **John White RI, RBA, ROI (1851–1933)** also painted a number of attractive watercolours both of the coast and inland. **William Williams (1808–1895)** of Plymouth, was later to move to Topsham in 1850, until his death. Here he recorded many aspects of the river in oil and watercolour and it was said that he had chronicled 'every peep' that was possible to put on canvas, a tradition continued by his son **Roscoe Williams (1852–1935)**. He also lived in Topsham and often signed his work S.G.W. Roscoe, rather than using his actual surname. **Edward H. Hurdle (1821–1857)** lived at Topsham, directly across the river from Topsham Lock – the scene depicted in his painting shown opposite. This fine oil was painted around 1840 and shows the recently built lock, a coal boat on the canal, and lighters carrying limestone up the river. His work was also exhibited at the Royal Academy, but he died of consumption at the young age of thirty-six. Another artist strongly associated with Topsham was **Hester Frood (1882–1971)** a fine printmaker as well as watercolourist, who lived in The Strand, overlooking the river. Her superb draughtsmanship can be clearly seen from the etching *'Under the Church Wall, Topsham'* illustrated on page 27. At a time when women artists were seldom taken seriously, she went on to gain international recognition as the county's most outstanding woman artist. As for Exmouth itself, a short-term resident was **Conrad Martens (1801–1878)** who moved there with his mother in 1822 where he lived in Elm Cottage, now the site of the present library. He became ships' artist on the *Beagle* from 1833–34 and subsequently corresponded with Charles Darwin for many years. Afterwards he settled in Australia where he secured a reputation as a talented watercolourist. However, more notable still was **Francis Danby ARA (1793–1861)** who settled in Exmouth in 1846 and was to remain there to his death. He had been born in Ireland and worked in Bristol, London and on the Continent before moving to Exmouth which inspired some of his best

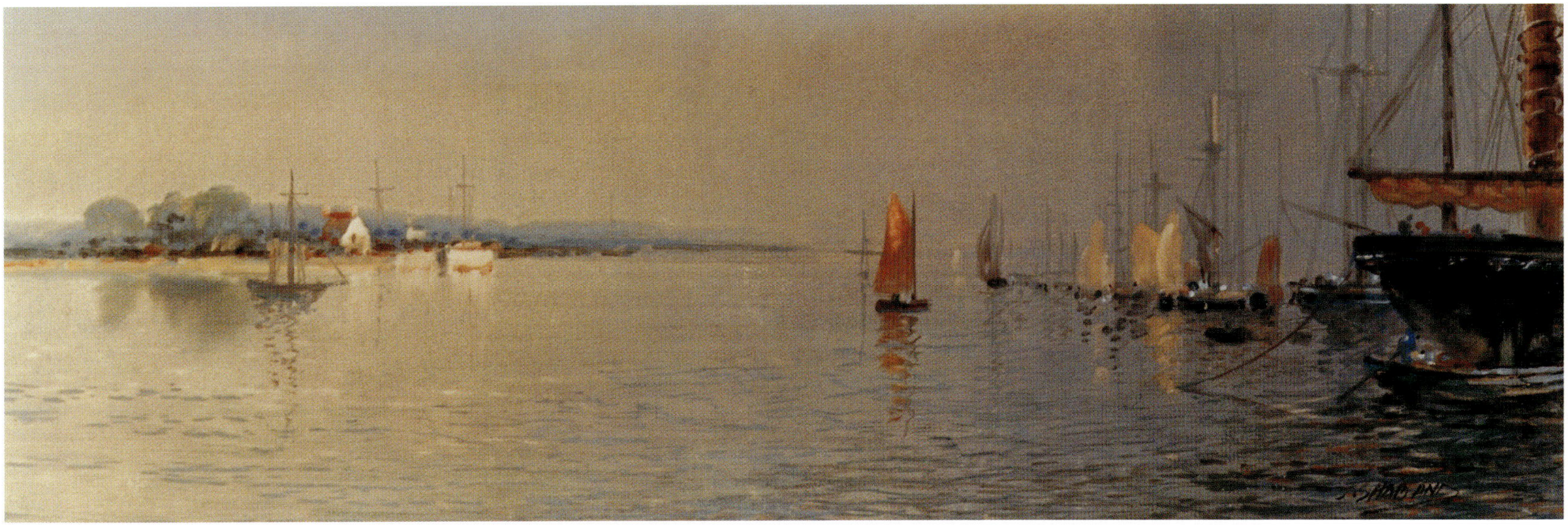

John Shapland. *Misty Morning, Topsham Lock*
Watercolour 7.5x21in (18.5x53.5cm) c.1922 courtesy: J. Collins & Son

pictures of his later years. His first residence was Rill Cottage in North Street, adjoining the road since called Danby Terrace, but in 1856 he moved into Shell House on the Maer (both now demolished). This was ideally situated for observing the changing aspects of sea and sky, including the magnificent sunsets for which Exmouth is famous. One such is depicted in his brilliantly-hued oil painting *'Dead Calm – Sunset at the Bight of Exmouth'* exhibited at the Royal Academy in 1855. Starcross, on the opposite side of the estuary is seen in the distance with the pumping-station tower of Brunel's Atmospheric Railway clearly visible just left of centre. Danby was also a talented boatbuilder, constructing his yacht *Dragon Fly* on the Maer. The boat subsequently sank in a storm and, although rescued, Danby died shortly afterwards in Shell House and was buried in the churchyard of St John-in-the-Wilderness, Withycombe. Alongside all these painters, a considerable number of amateur and semi-professional artists have recorded aspects of the Devon coast and landscape over the same period and continue to do so today. Two typical examples of such artists have work in the collections of the Royal Albert Memorial Museum, Exeter: one is an unknown artist who produced a series of slight but charming sketches during August and September 1846, mostly of Exmouth, and a further group in 1860, two of which are inscribed intriguingly 'with Atty, Alf and Johnny.' The other artist is **George Townsend (1813–1894)** whose work is mainly of Exeter buildings, but who also painted two delightful vignettes of Exmouth life *'Salvaging a Wreck on Exmouth Beach'* and *'A Sale of Wreckage on Exmouth Beach'*, a salient reminder of the sea in its more powerful and turbulent guise.

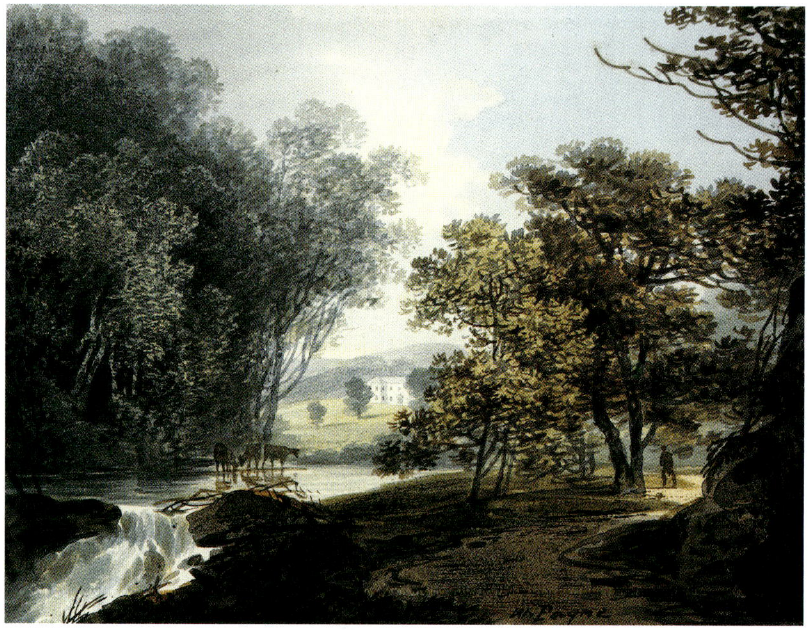

William Payne. *Oxton House*
Watercolour 5x6.5in (13x17cm) courtesy: Devon Record Office

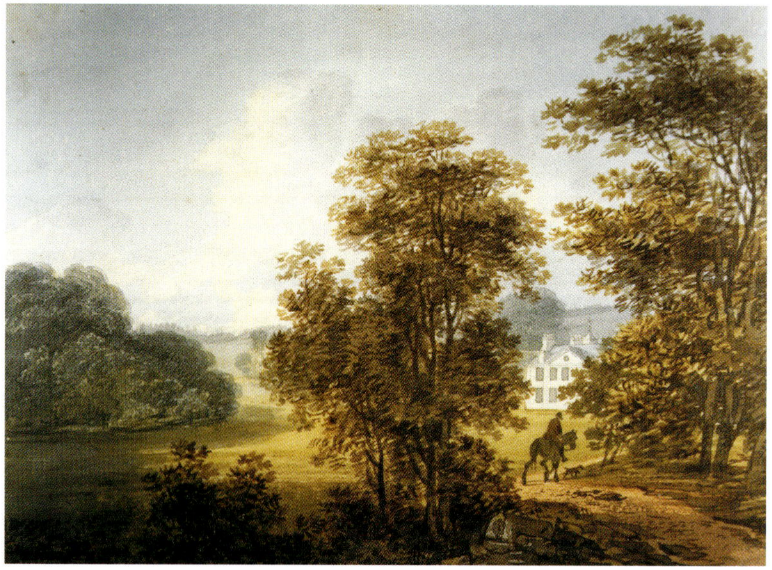

Reverend John Swete. *Bickham House, Nr Exeter*
Watercolour. 5x7in (13x18cm) courtesy: Devon Record Office

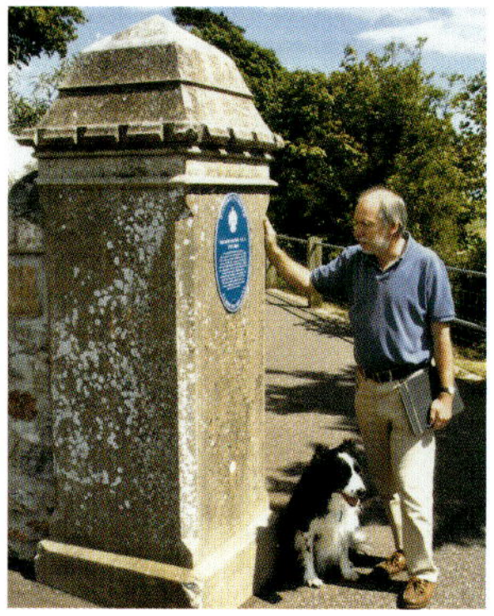

Postscript on Francis Danby ARA

Before ending this chapter on past painters, I would like to indulge in a little self-gratification, if I may. The Exmouth Society's Millennium Project, with the support of Exmouth Town Council and the Exmouth Town Management Partnership, was to create a 'Blue Plaque Heritage Trail' around the town. This excellent scheme was to commemorate the town's famous former residents, their homes and other historic features. During my research on Danby for this chapter, however, I was somewhat surprised to find there was no plaque for this famous Exmouth resident. There is of course, a road and house named after him, but I felt this was an important omission. So early in 2004 in a letter, I suggested that one could be sited on an existing elegant stone pillar situated in Trefusis Terrace, which overlooks the former site of his home. Months passed and I had forgotten all about it until one evening I came across the plaque by chance whilst out walking our dog, Luke. There was a strange sense of achievement when I saw it and as I turned and looked over this favourite view towards the sea, it became even more poignant. I stood and watched the subtle nuances in colour of the evening sky for a while and wished I could have recorded the moment in paint. However, Luke had other ideas and was getting restless, desperate for his run on the Maer before it got dark. As we walked off, I wondered if Francis Danby had ever experienced the same problem?

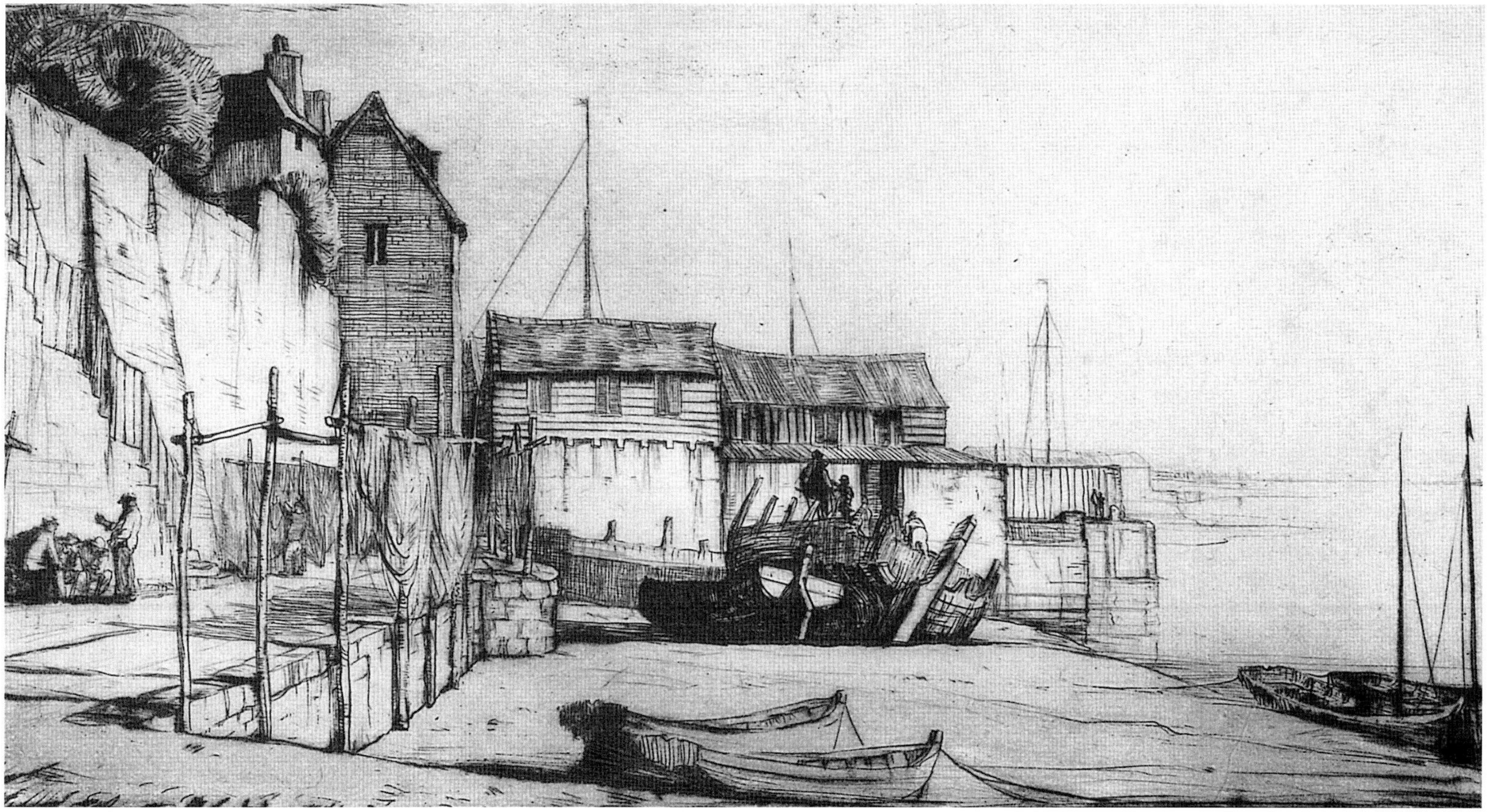

Hester Frood. *Under the Church Wall, Topsham*
Etching 5x9in (13x23cm) courtesy: Alan Frood

LOCATION MAP

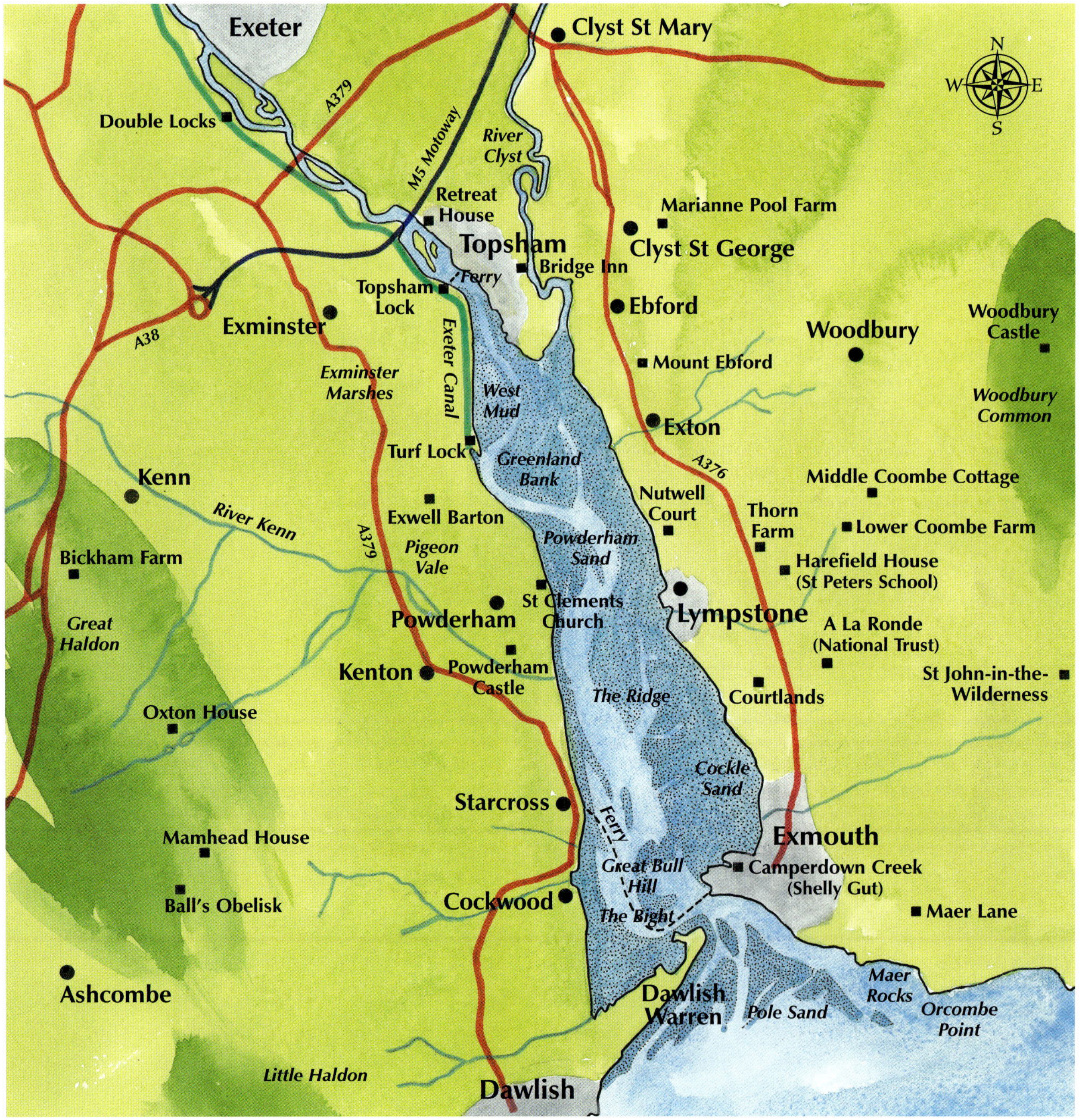

The Paintings

Now join me on my personal journey up the Exe estuary. We will start at the mouth at Exmouth, travel to its upper reaches at Topsham and then on to the cathedral city of Exeter. I will take you to some of my favourite painting spots – not just at the water's edge, but also down the deep-cut lanes into the rich red farmland, either side of the river. In the early pages you will find quite different work that was based on a project on the boat-sheds in Camperdown Creek. Accompanying many of the paintings is a brief commentary on my own thoughts, as well as aspects of the history, wildlife and folklore associated with the river. I believe the most important ingredient in painting is that of individual interpretation and that painting is all about what *you* have to say – making *your* picture and expressing your own vision. It should be a journey of discovery for the artist as well as the viewer. Every time I paint this magical place, a feeling of sheer delight – if not a little awe – steals over me and my fascination never wanes. Being faced with a sheet of white paper, or blank canvas is always a daunting prospect and people have a romantic idea about painting – thinking it takes little effort and that it is a relaxing pursuit. I remember an envious friend once told me how lucky I was being an artist. *'After all,'* he said, *'painting is easy – it's just a matter of mixing the right colour and putting it in the right place!'* If only it was that simple, for in reality it is a roller-coaster ride of high and low emotions. There are days when it is a real struggle, but then there are those times when it flows – just like the river itself, as if the brush is being led by a guiding hand! I suppose that is the reason *why* I paint, for there is no more wonderful feeling in the world than those days! You will find in these pages a wide range of drawing and painting mediums, which include quick sketches, location studies, paintings done in-situ, as well as in the studio. I hope that through this diversity, I have come some way to depicting the true *'spirit'* of the river so near to my heart, together with its surrounding landscape. I also hope that you will enjoy the journey as much as I have.

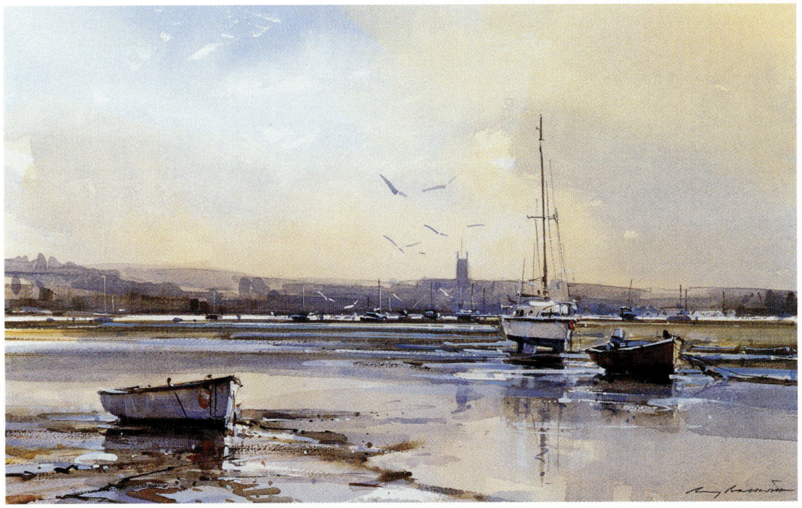

Still Waters, Exmouth
Watercolour 14x21in (35x53cm)

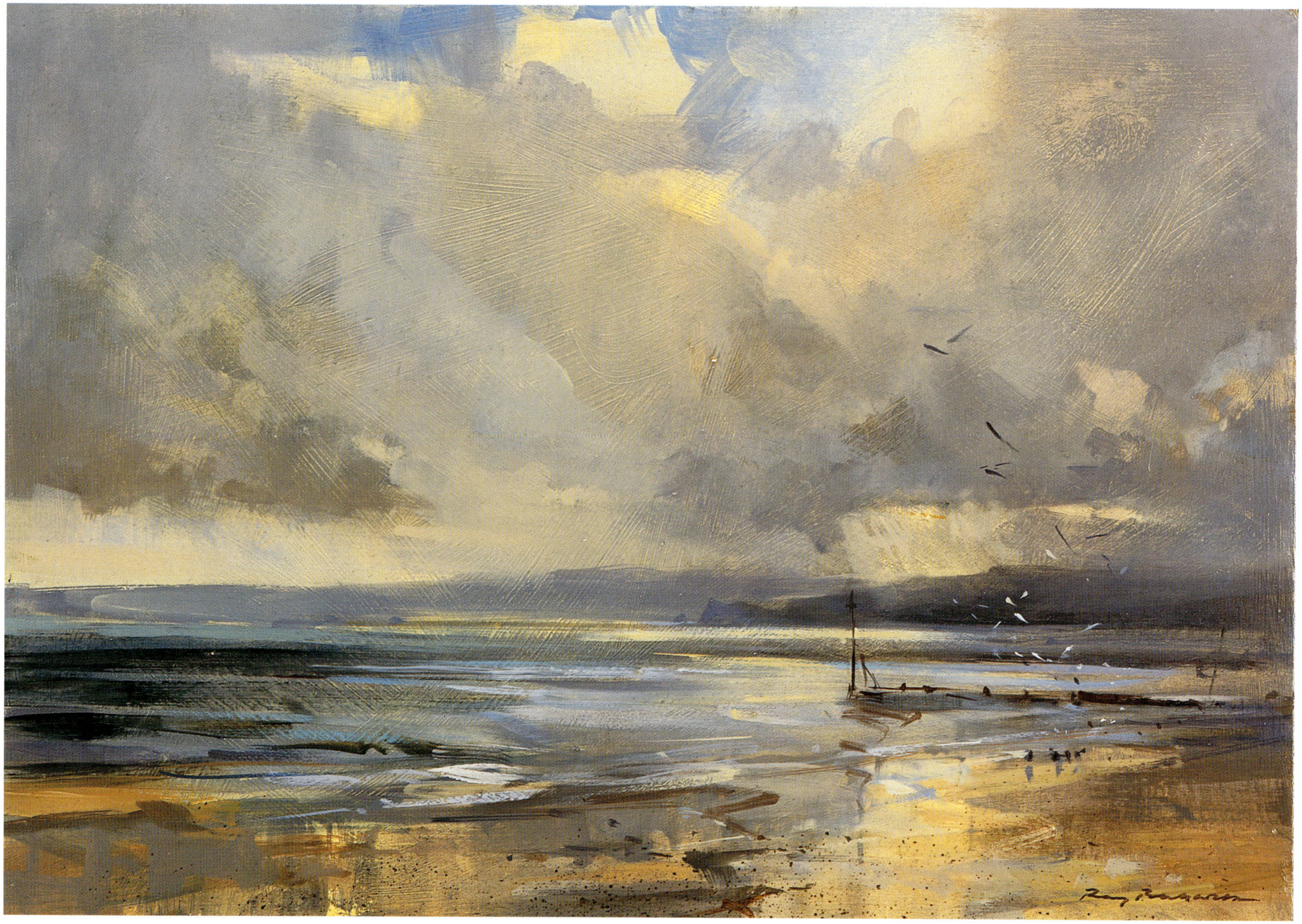

Where Seagulls Fly, Exmouth
Oil 10x14in (25x36cm)

There is something spiritual about the elemental forces in nature and the wide open spaces of sea and sky. What excites me is that it is constantly changing and offers endless variations on a theme. All you have to do is charge the mind's eye.

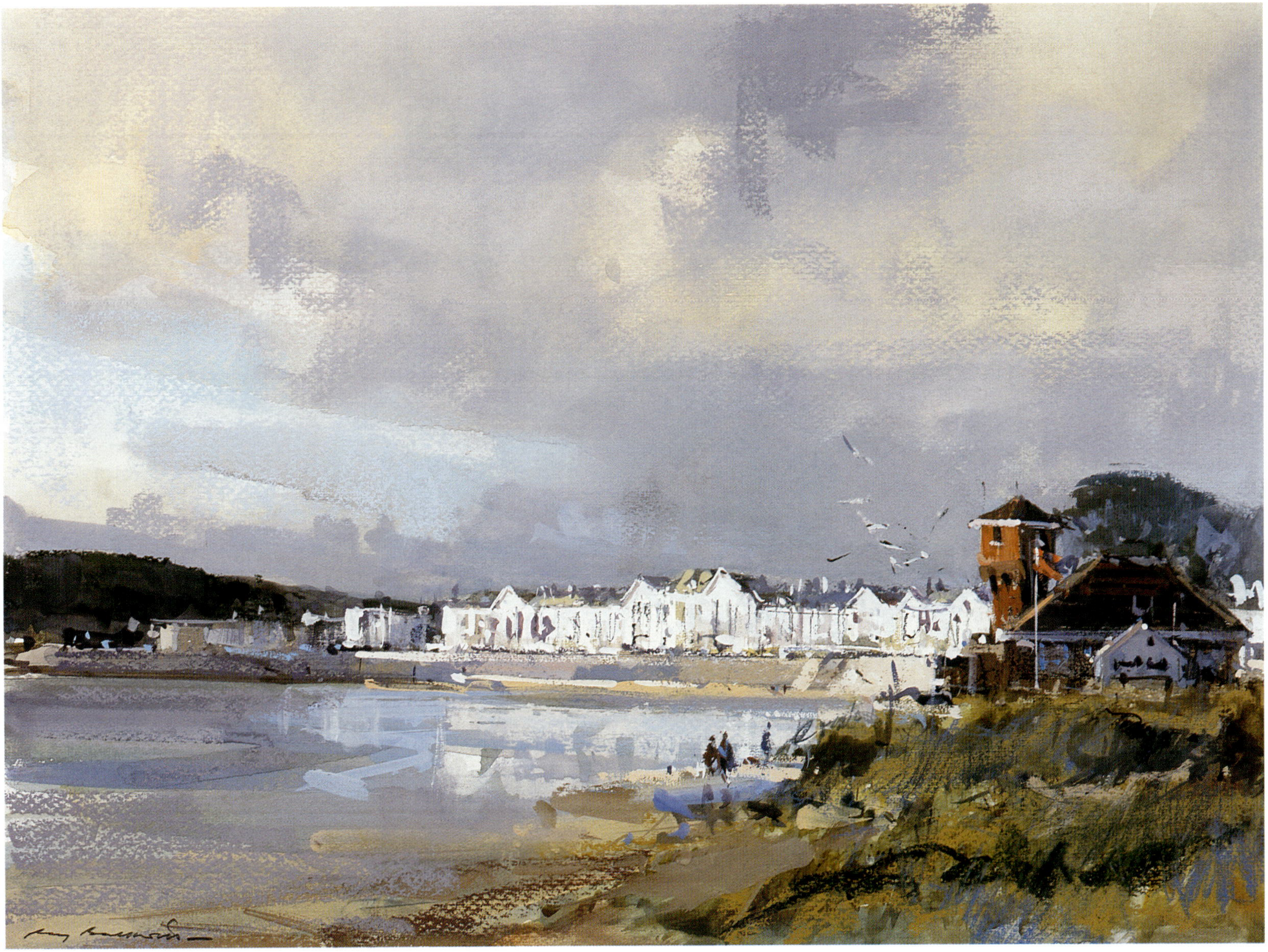

Sun and Shade, Exmouth
Mixed Media 12x16in (30x40cm)

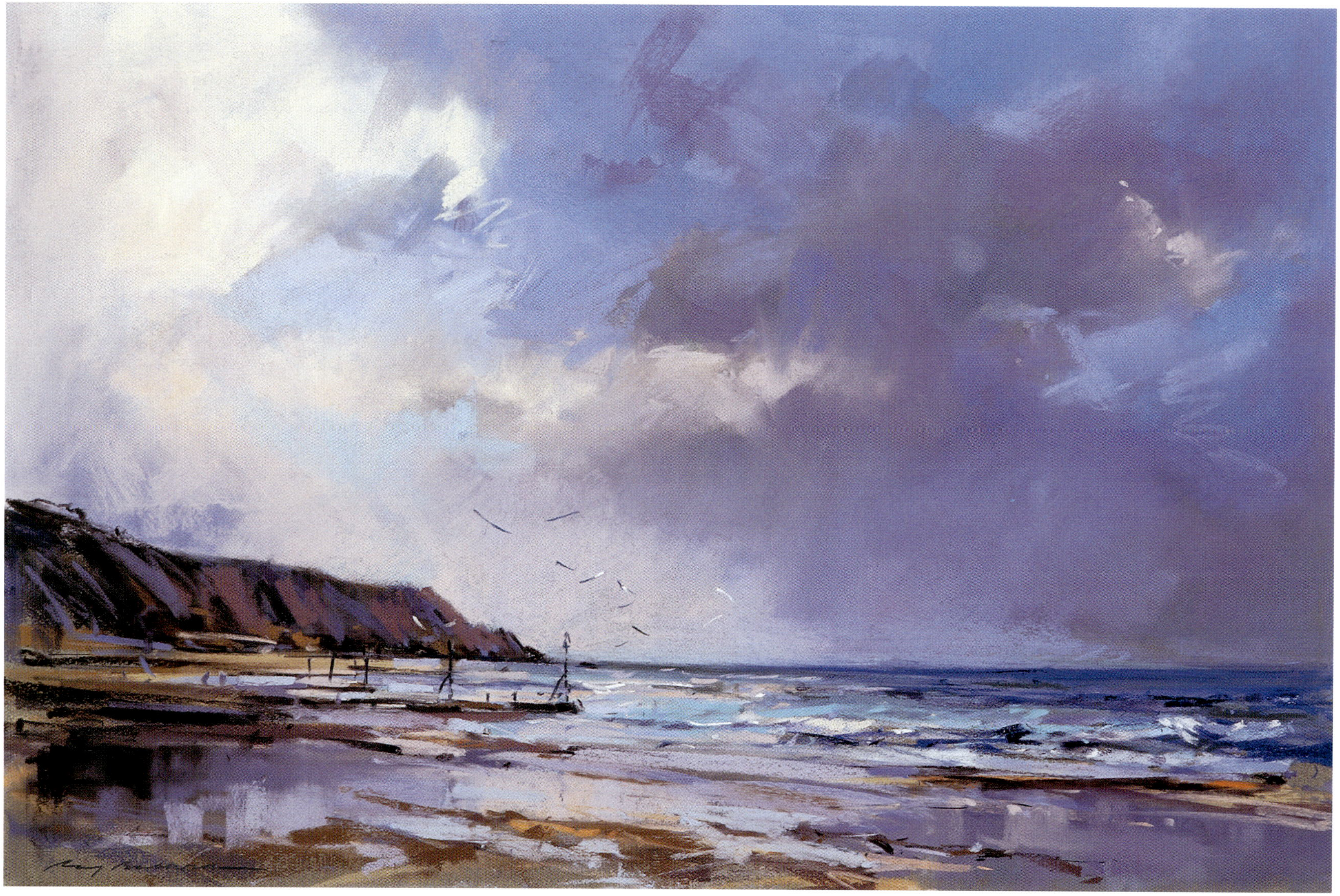

Evening Sky, Orcombe Point, Exmouth
Pastel 14.5x21.5in (37x55cm)

Orcombe Point, at the eastern end of Exmouth's two-mile stretch of sandy beach is the start of the 'Jurassic Coast', England's first natural World Heritage Site, which stretches on into Dorset.

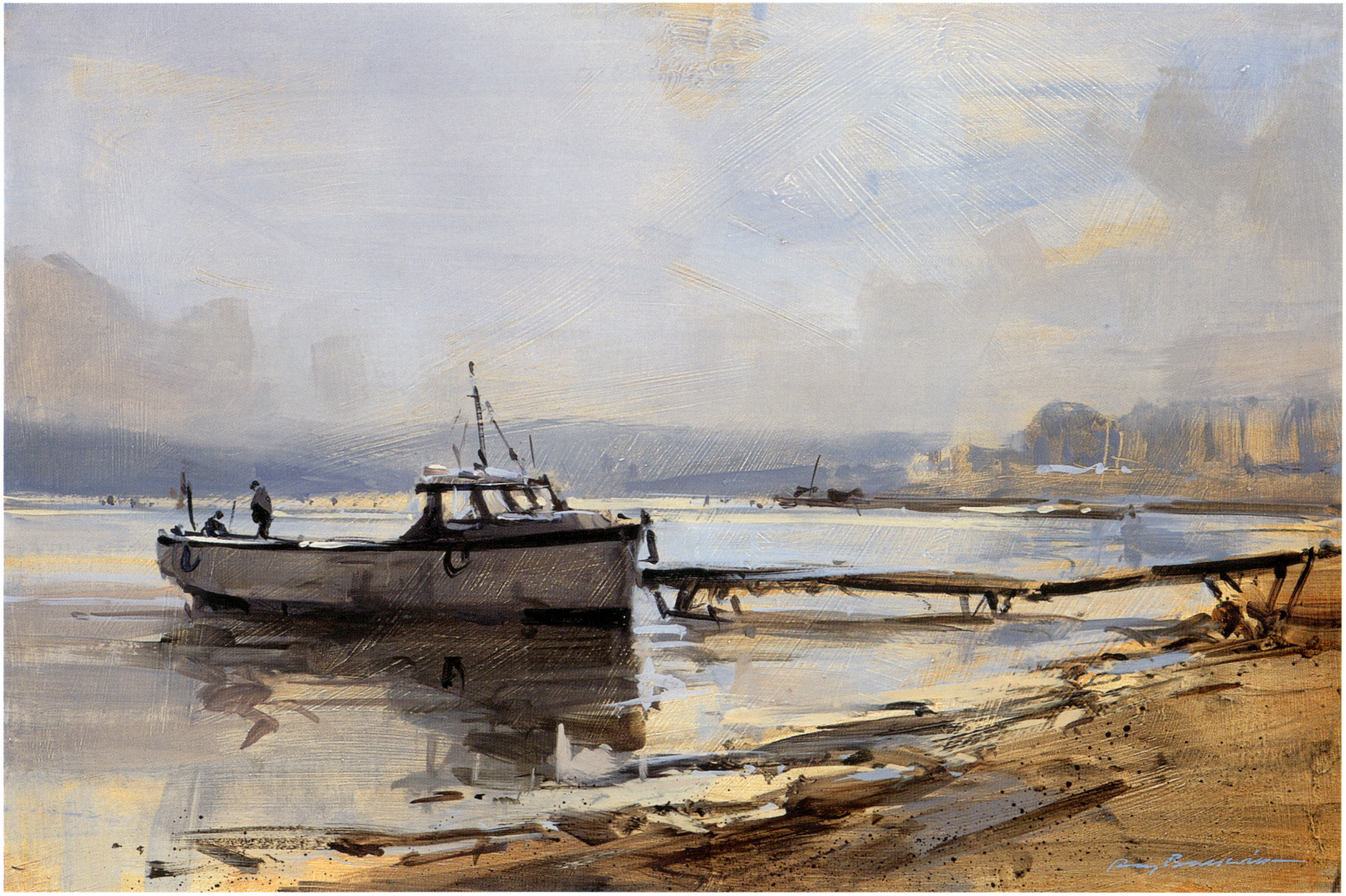

End of the Day, Exmouth Seafront
Oil 10x14in (25x36cm)

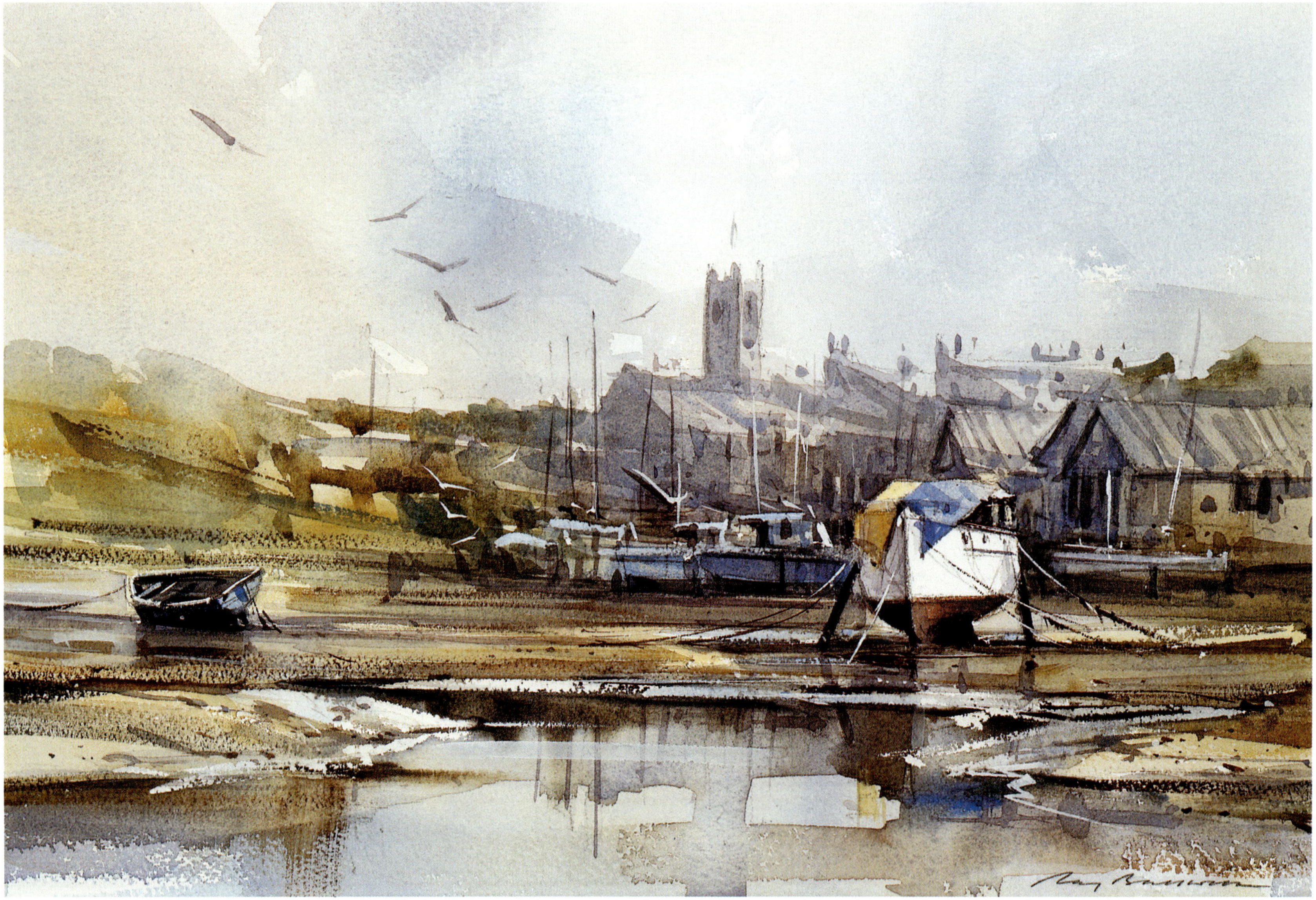

Shelly Gut, Exmouth
Watercolour 10x14in (25x36cm)

The creek at Exmouth still has an overpowering sense of character, history and belonging, and this is perhaps why it is still one of my favourite places to paint. The boat-sheds are visible reminders of the boat-building families whose skills have been passed down from one generation to another.

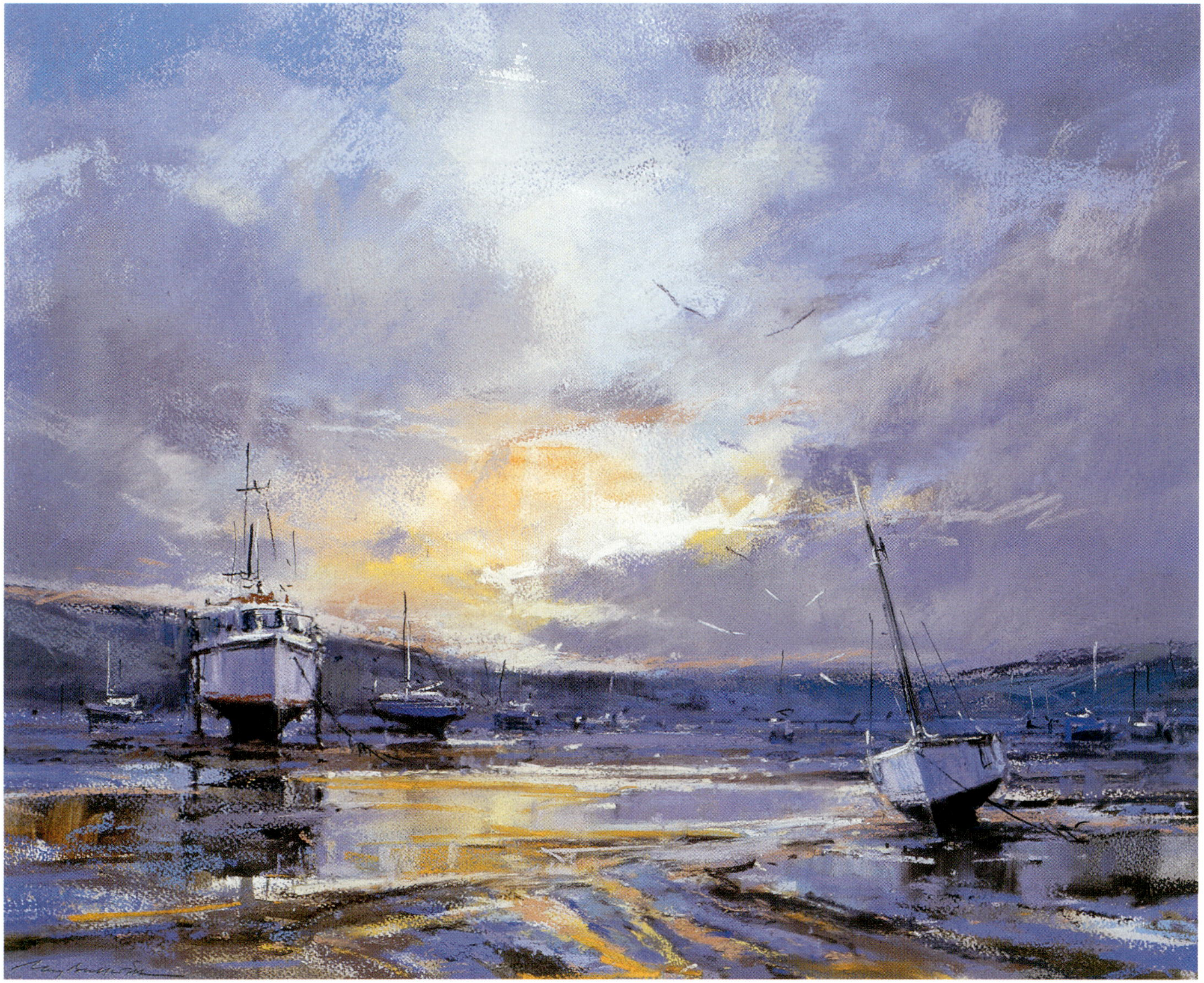

Estuary Sunset
Mixed Media 21x24in (54x61cm)

Looking across the estuary from Exmouth at high tide, the sheet of water can be ablaze with the sunset's reflections, the dying rays making the scene more reminiscent of an Italian lake than an estuary. Whereas at low tide it is a great expanse of mudflats with the navigable channel almost indiscernible.

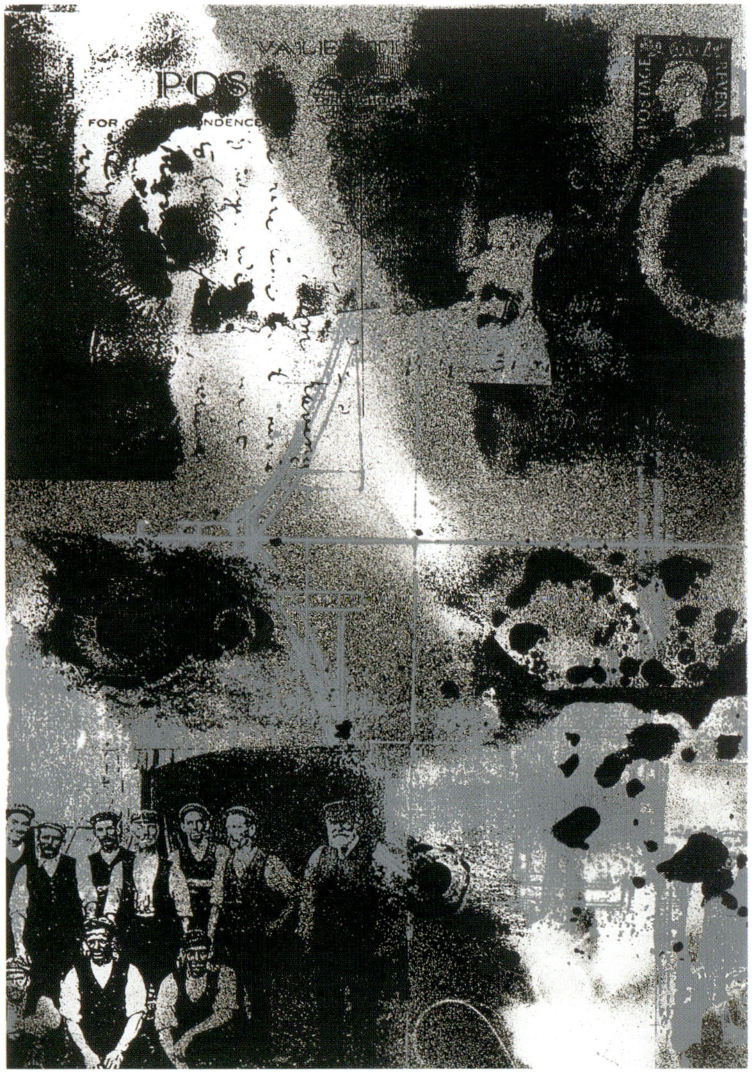

The Boat-sheds I
Silkscreen Print 15.5x10.5in (39x27cm)

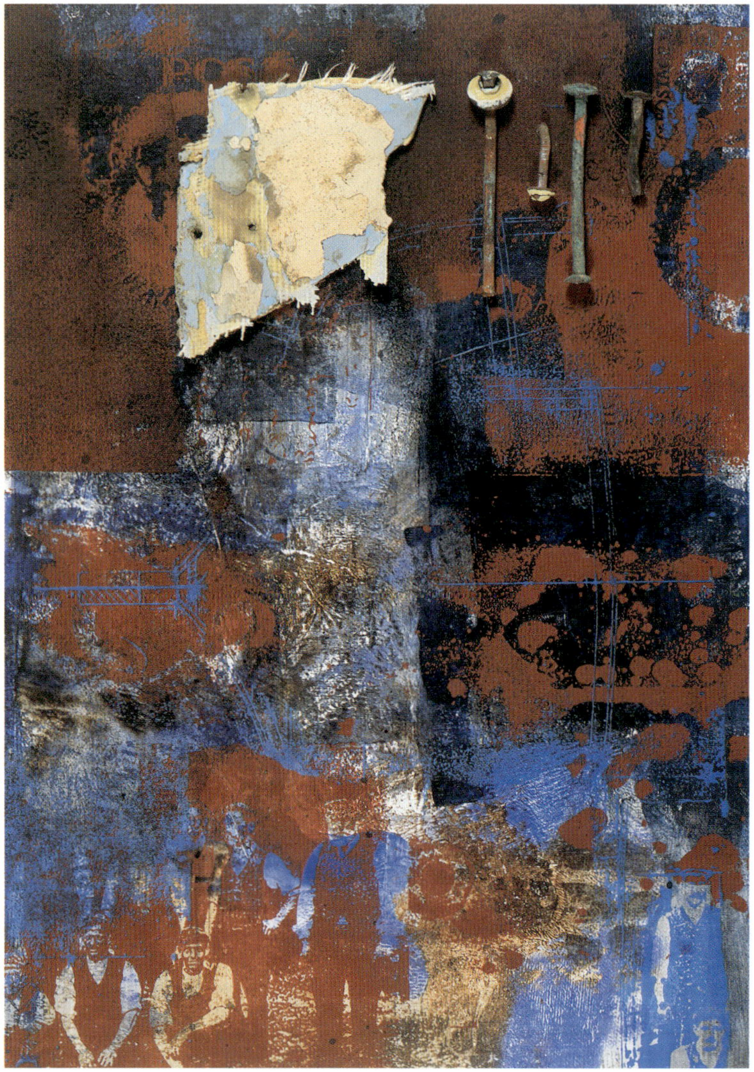

The Boat-sheds II
Mixed Media Assemblage 10.5x15in (27x38cm)

In this print I tried to evoke a 'spiritual layering' of time, as well as Camperdown Creek's maritime past. I also set out to recapture my first impressions, the illuminating sunlight from a small window that streamed through the dark interior falling on cobwebbed corners to 're-awaken' the past.

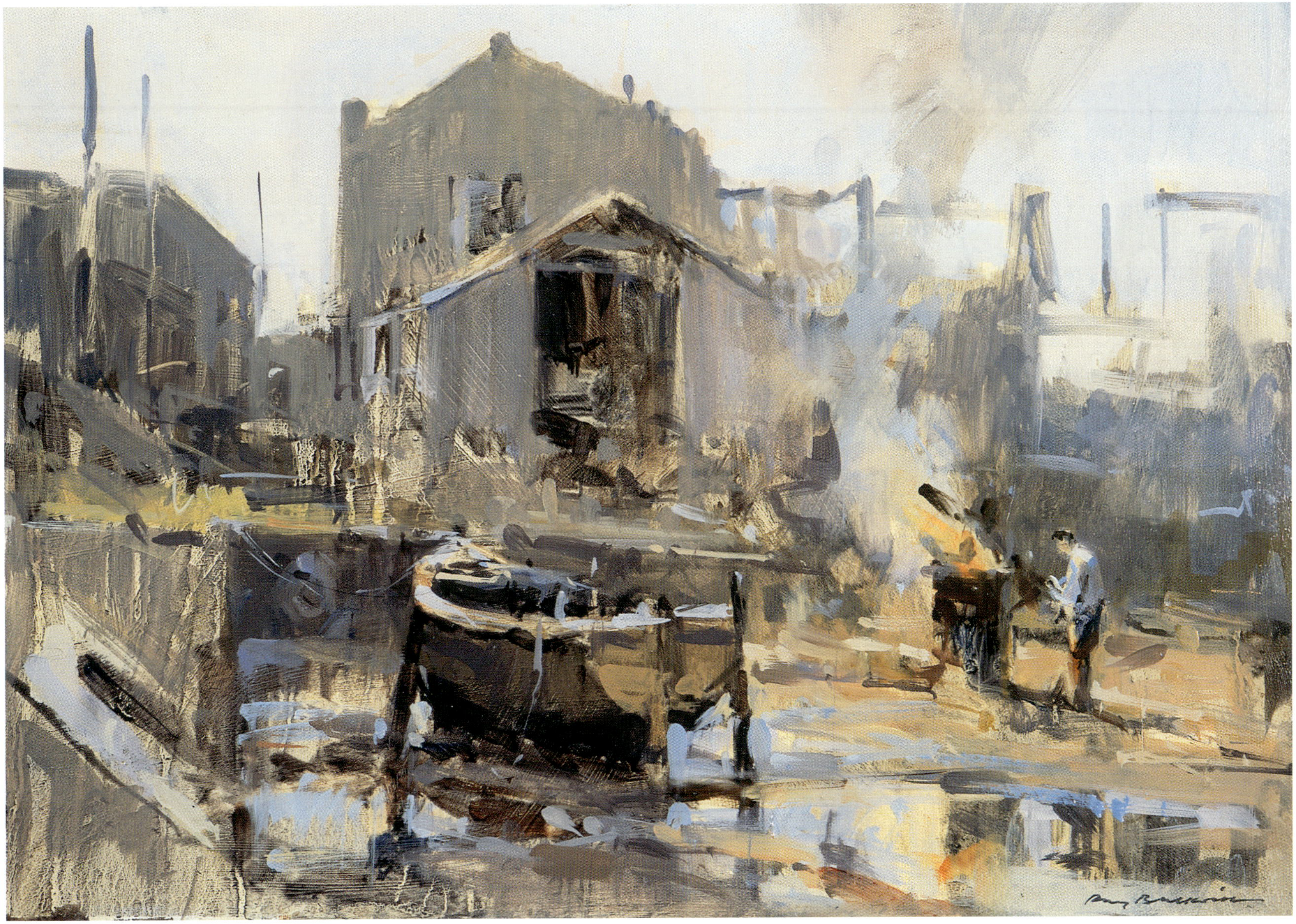

Bonfire on the Beach, Camperdown Creek
Oil 10x14in (25x36cm)

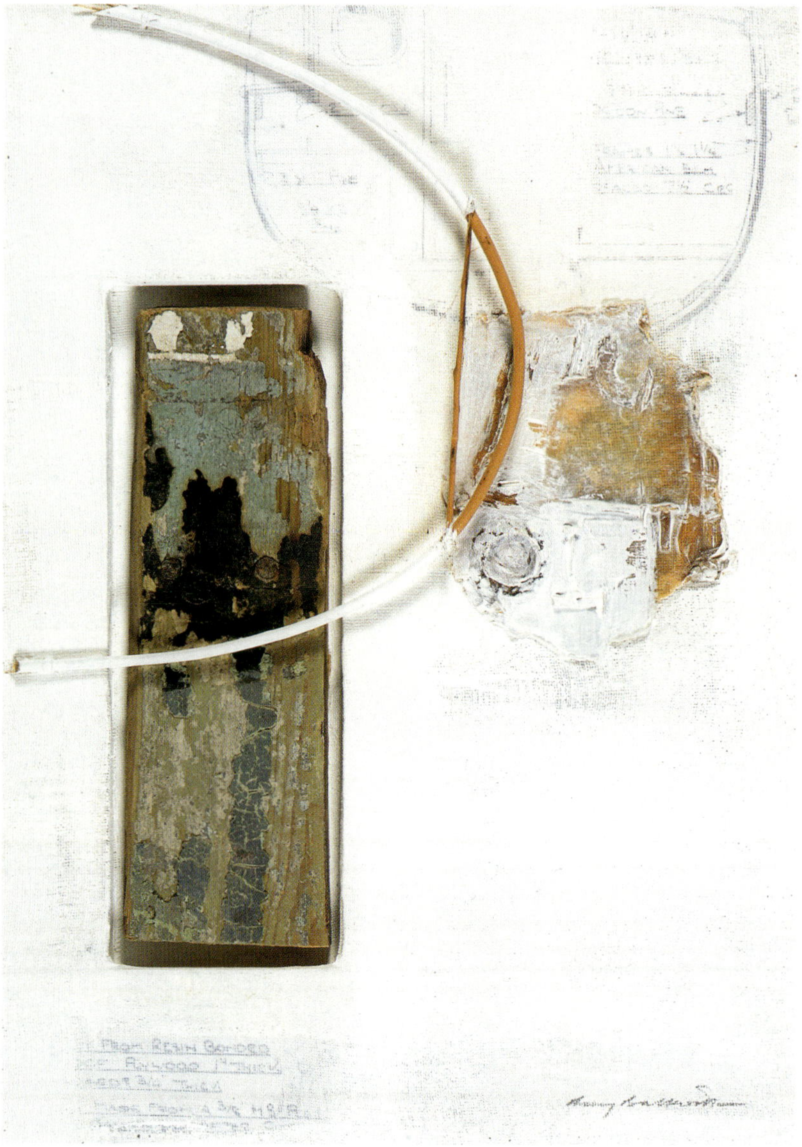

Shelly Gut I
Mixed Media Assemblage 10x14in (25x36cm)

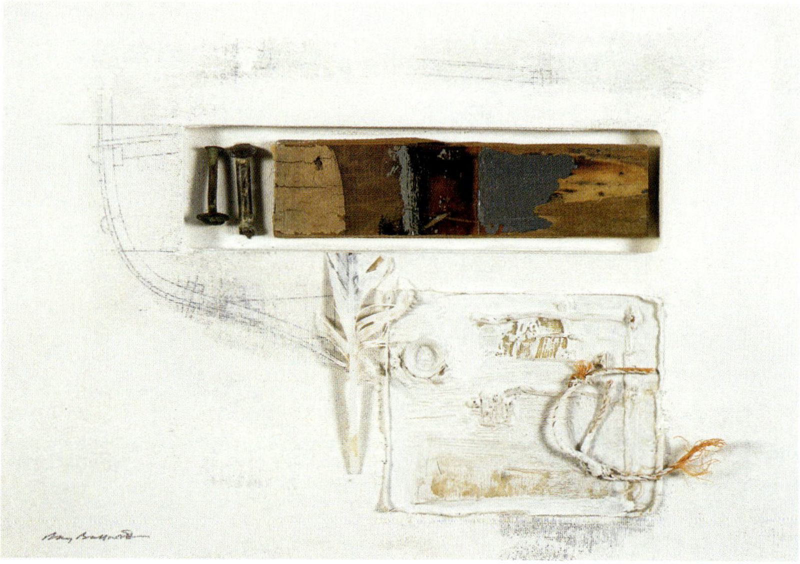

Shelly Gut II
Mixed Media Assemblage 10x14in (25x36cm)

These boxed constructions have been an occasional and experimental diversion from my work in two dimensions. They contain 'found' objects from the creek, as well as boat plans and a latex-rubber cast. I find there is a real beauty in neglect and decay and the 'found' object is often more powerful than the made.

Geoff Holman's boats and his boat-sheds have featured in many of my paintings over the years. One of the first boats built here was *The Dawn* in 1937 by his father and during the Second World War he built many of the lifeboats. Geoff carried on the family tradition and still restores and repairs boats today.

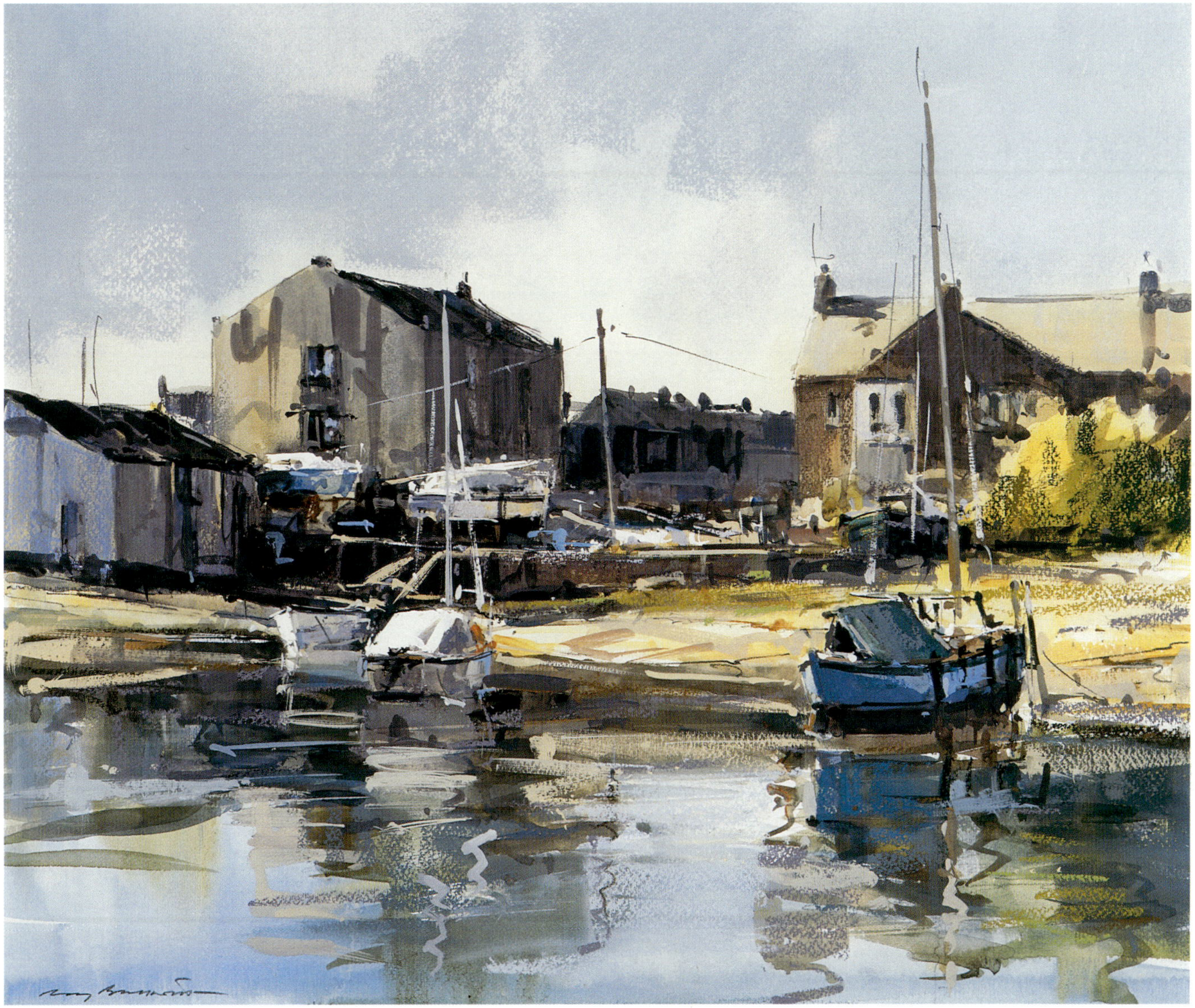

Lavis' Boatyard
Mixed Media 16.5x18.5in (42x47cm)

Lavis' boatyard was established in 1875 and built among other vessels many of the ferryboats used between Starcross and Exmouth over the years, including the present *Orcombe*. Ron Lavis still repairs and restores traditional vessels today. Behind the boatyard is Horn's three-storey sail loft, which was built in 1810.

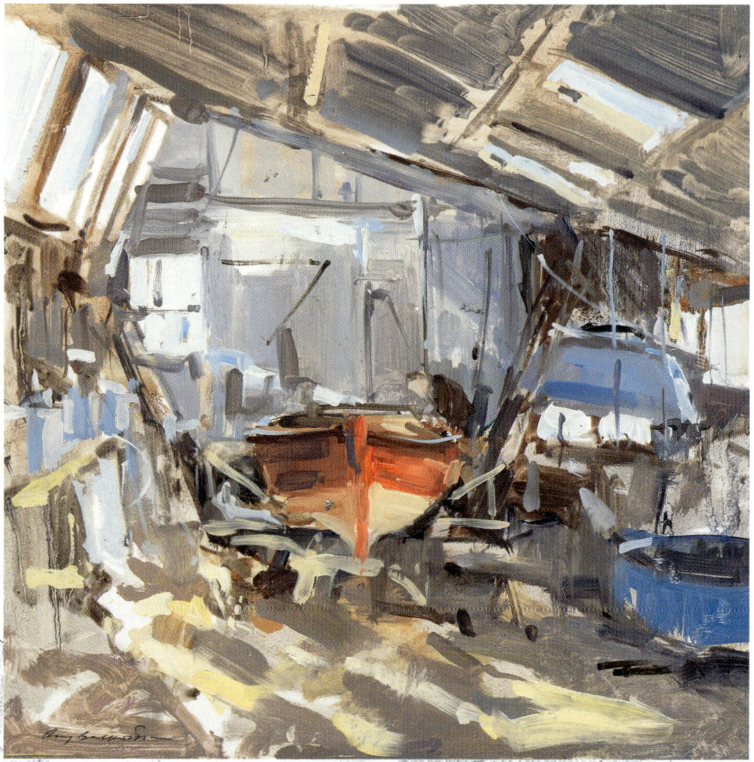

Geoff's Boat-shed
Oil Location Study 14x14in (36x36cm)

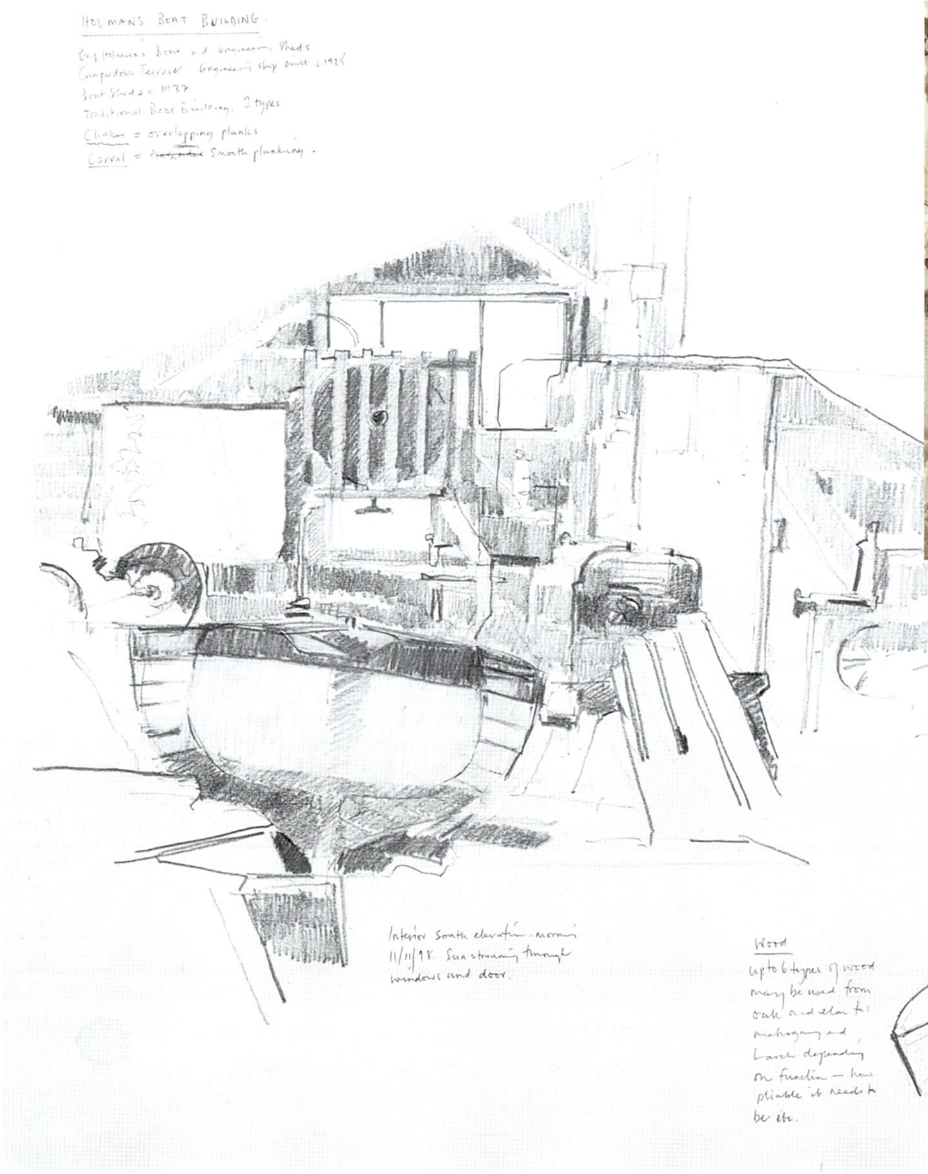
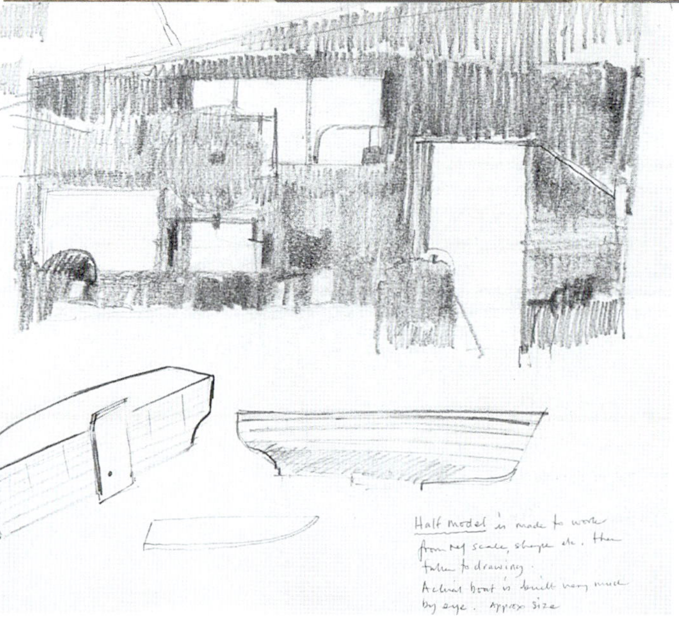

Interior, Geoff's Boat-shed
Pencil Sketch 18x26in (46x66cm)

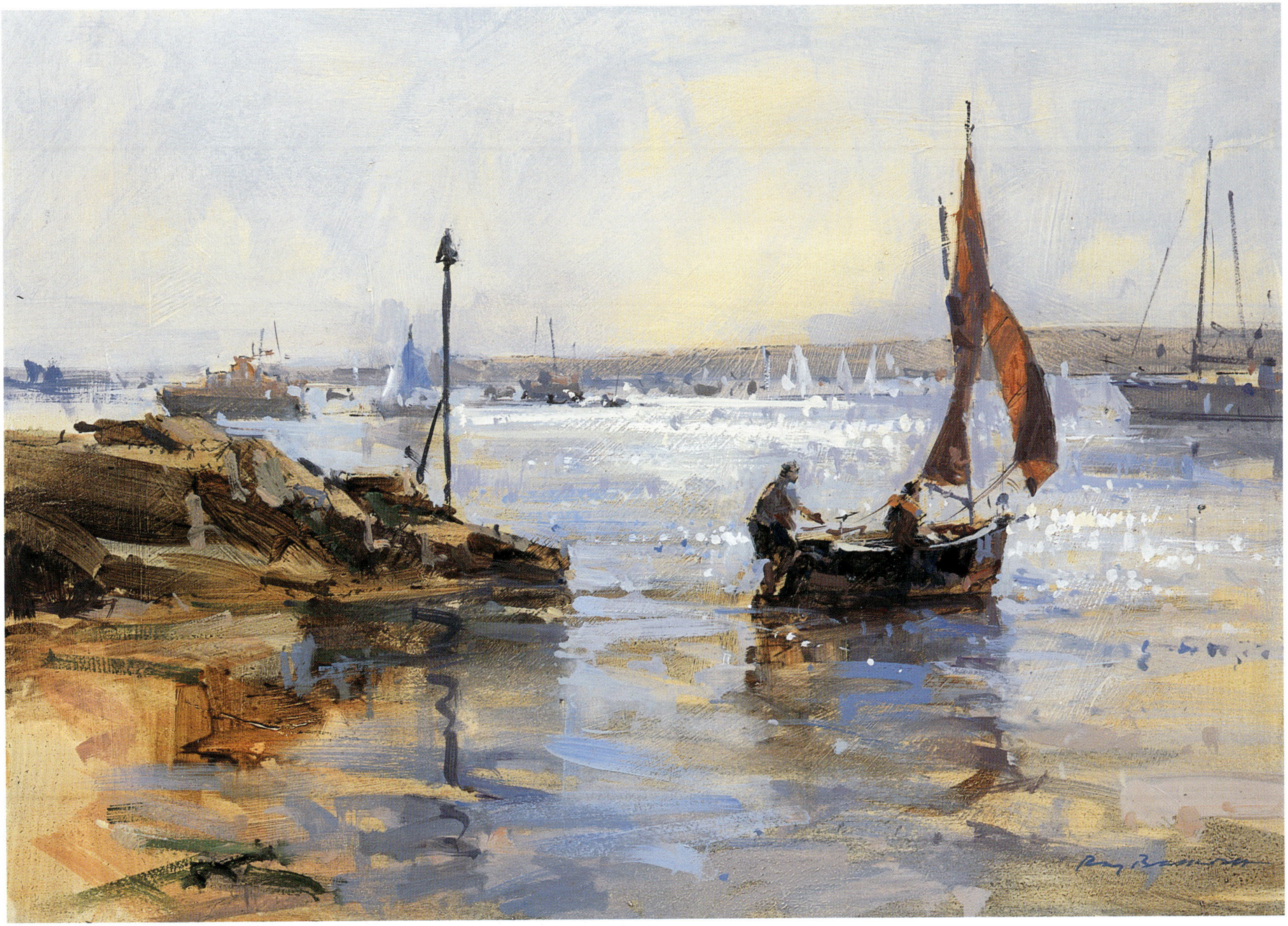

Setting Sail, Exmouth
Oil 10x14in (25x36cm)

Where else could one find more pleasurable sounds? The cry of the gulls, the 'clinking' of the rigging and the gentle lapping of the tide are just a few of the sounds that accompany such scenes as this.

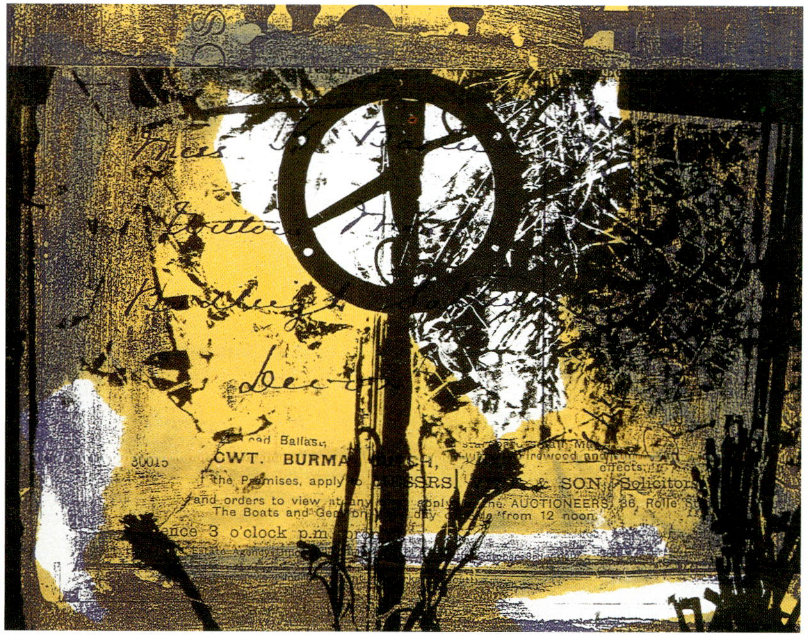

Window I, Geoff's Boat-shed
Silkscreen Print 7.5x9.5in (19x24cm)

Geoff's boat-sheds continue to provide an endless supply of inspiring and often surprising source material. *Window I* is a silkscreen print based on photographs taken in the boat-shed and *Window II* a mixed media painting using gouache and found materials.

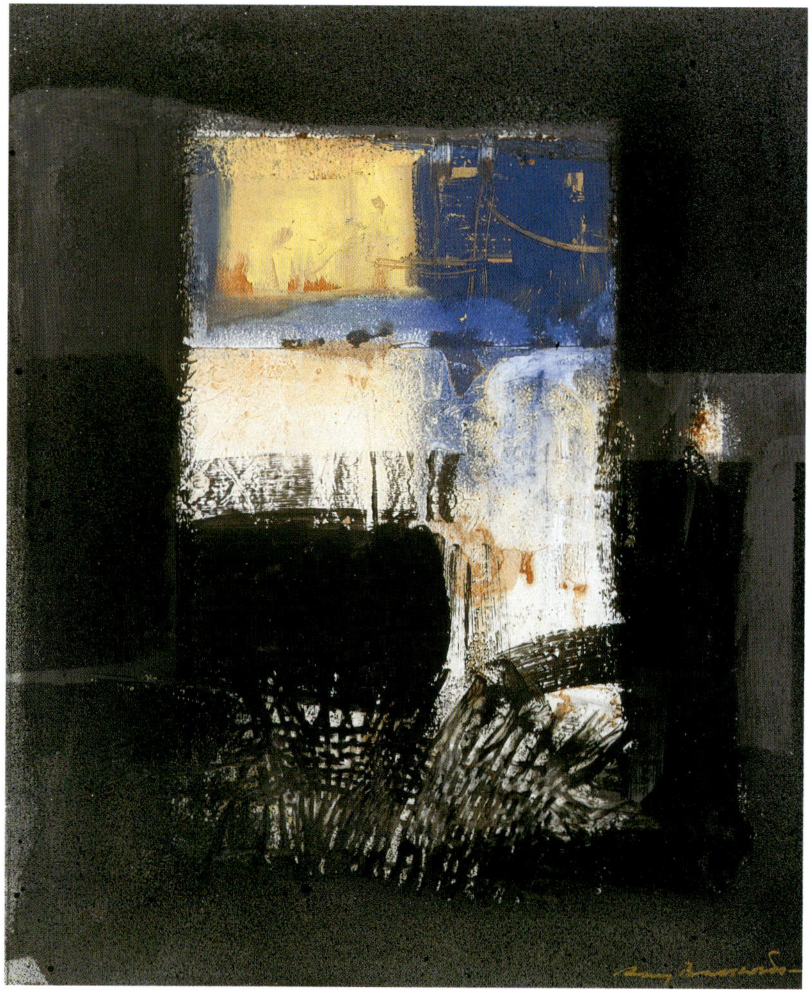

Window II, Geoff's Boat-shed
Mixed Media 11x9.5in (28x24cm)

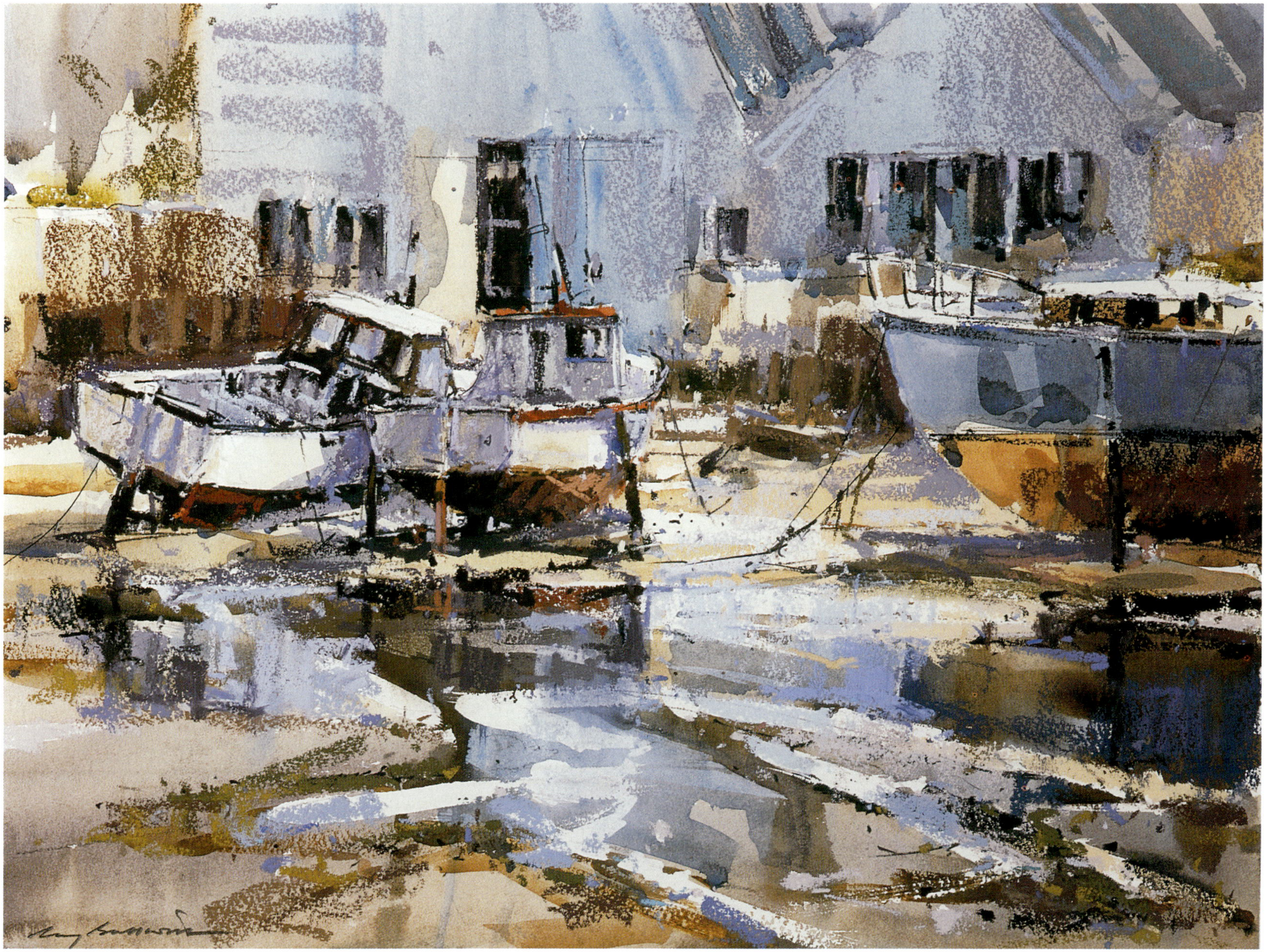

The Boat-sheds, Shelly Gut
Mixed Media 13x17in (33x43cm)

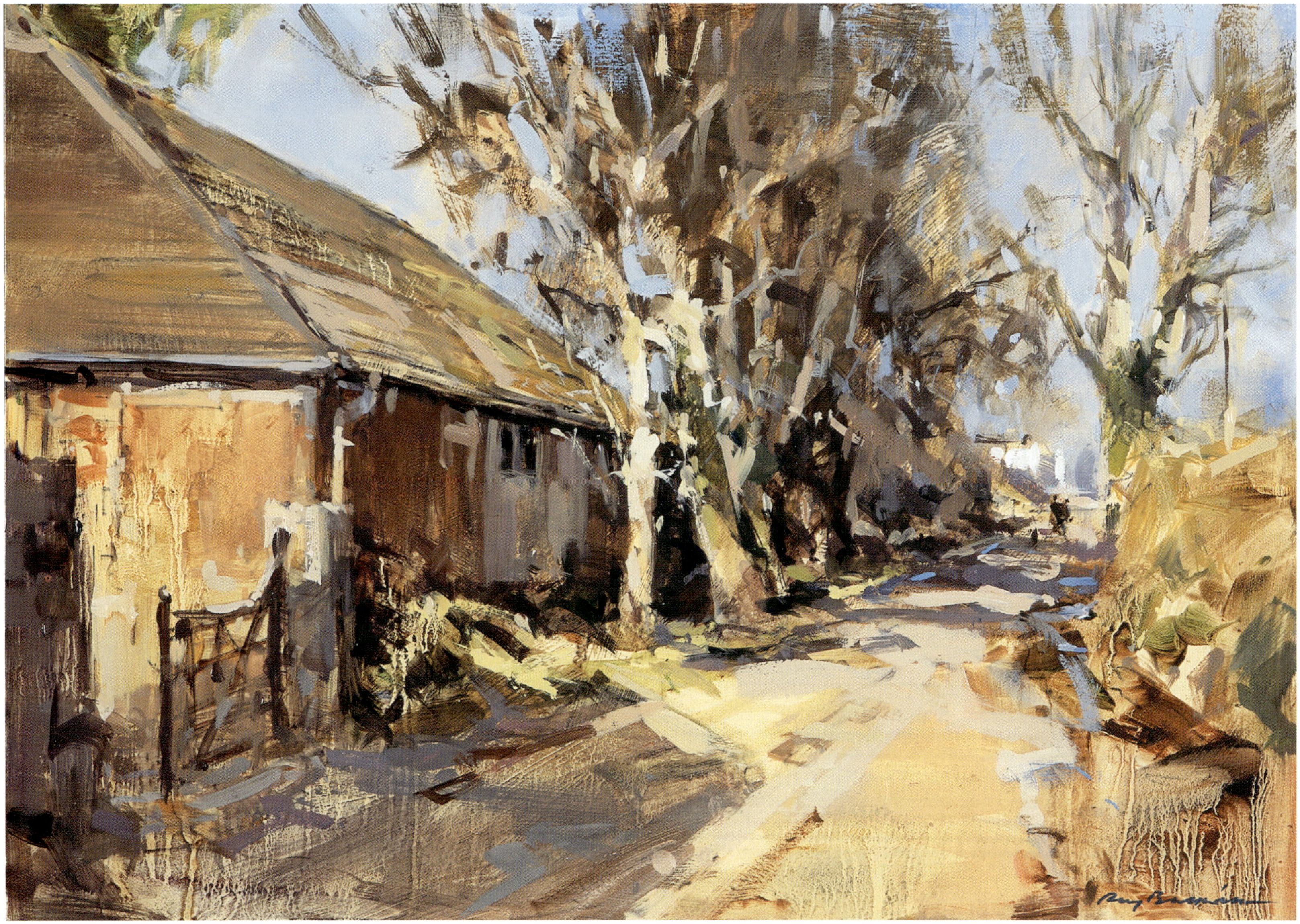

Autumn Sunshine, Maer Lane
Oil 10x14in (25x36cm)

This ancient lane leads from the seafront at Exmouth to Littleham, passing through some unspoilt countryside. *'Maer'* is a Saxon word that means boundary, and on the lane is Spathayes Manor, dating back to the fifteenth century. *'Spat'* comes from an old word meaning a reed or rush, and *'hayes'* means meadows and fields. Here too are some interesting old farms including Maer, Prattshayes and Green Farm.

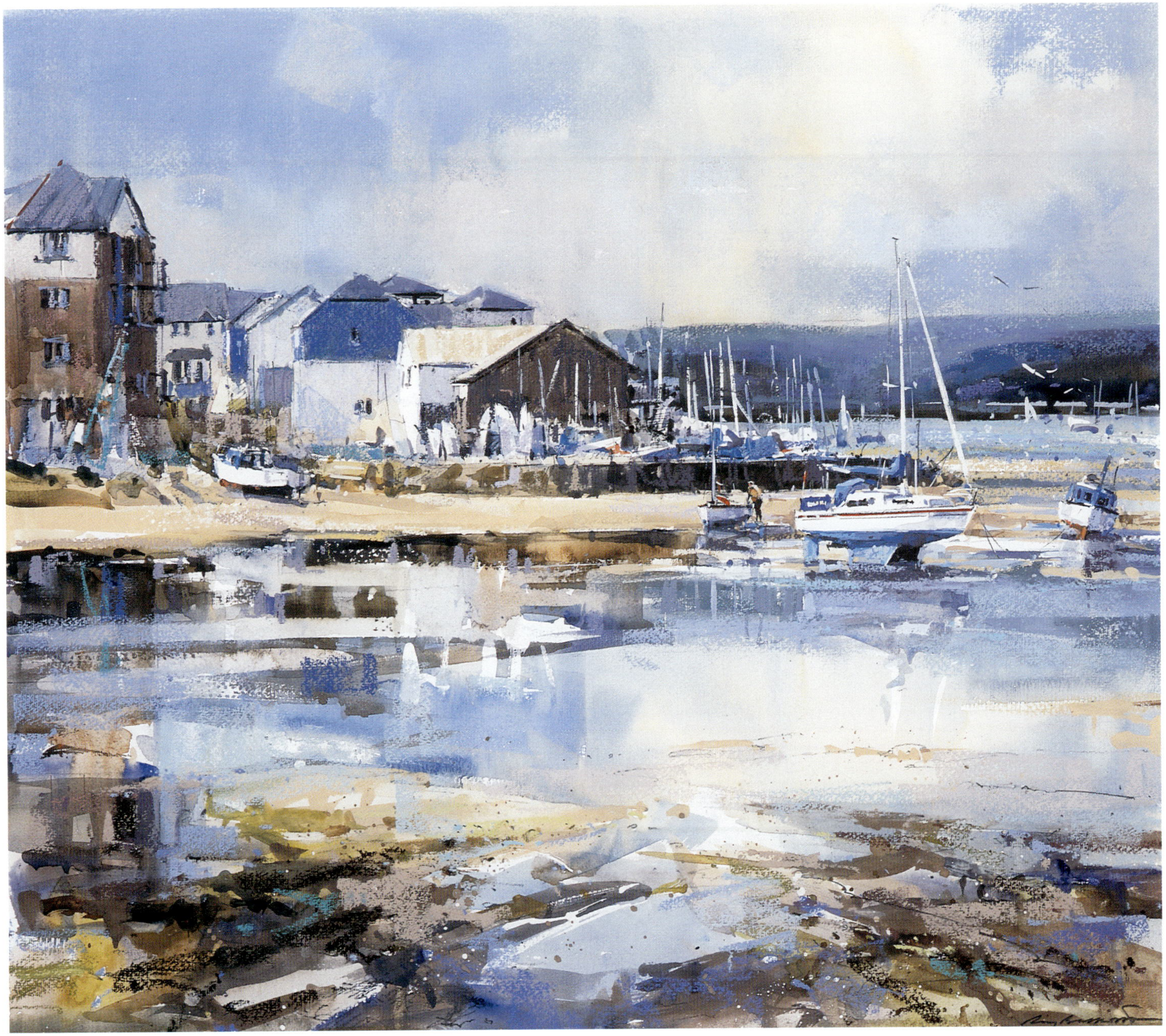

Reflections, Shelly Gut
Mixed Media 16.5x18.5in (42x47cm)

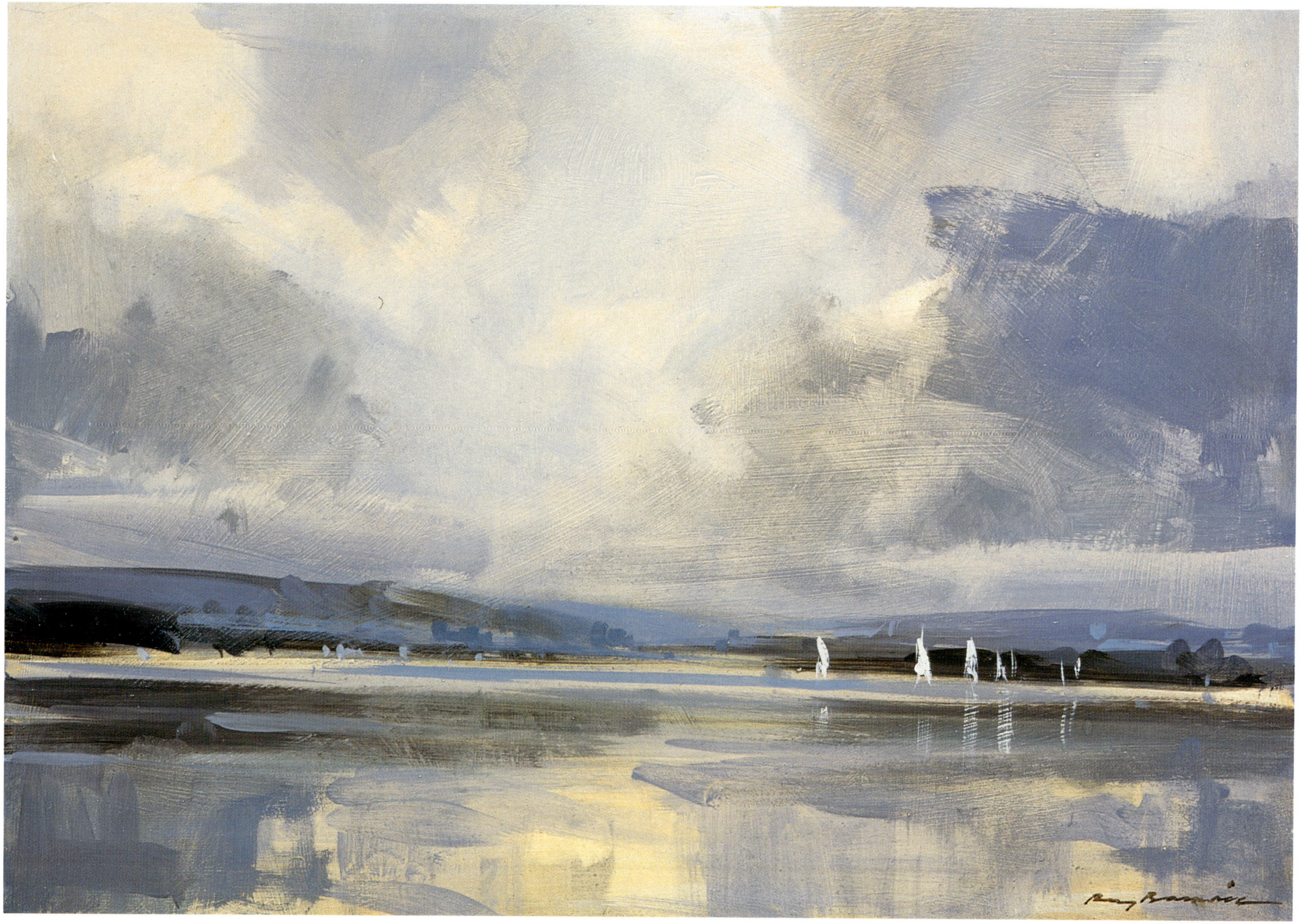

A Good Day for Sailing
Oil 10x14in (25x36cm)

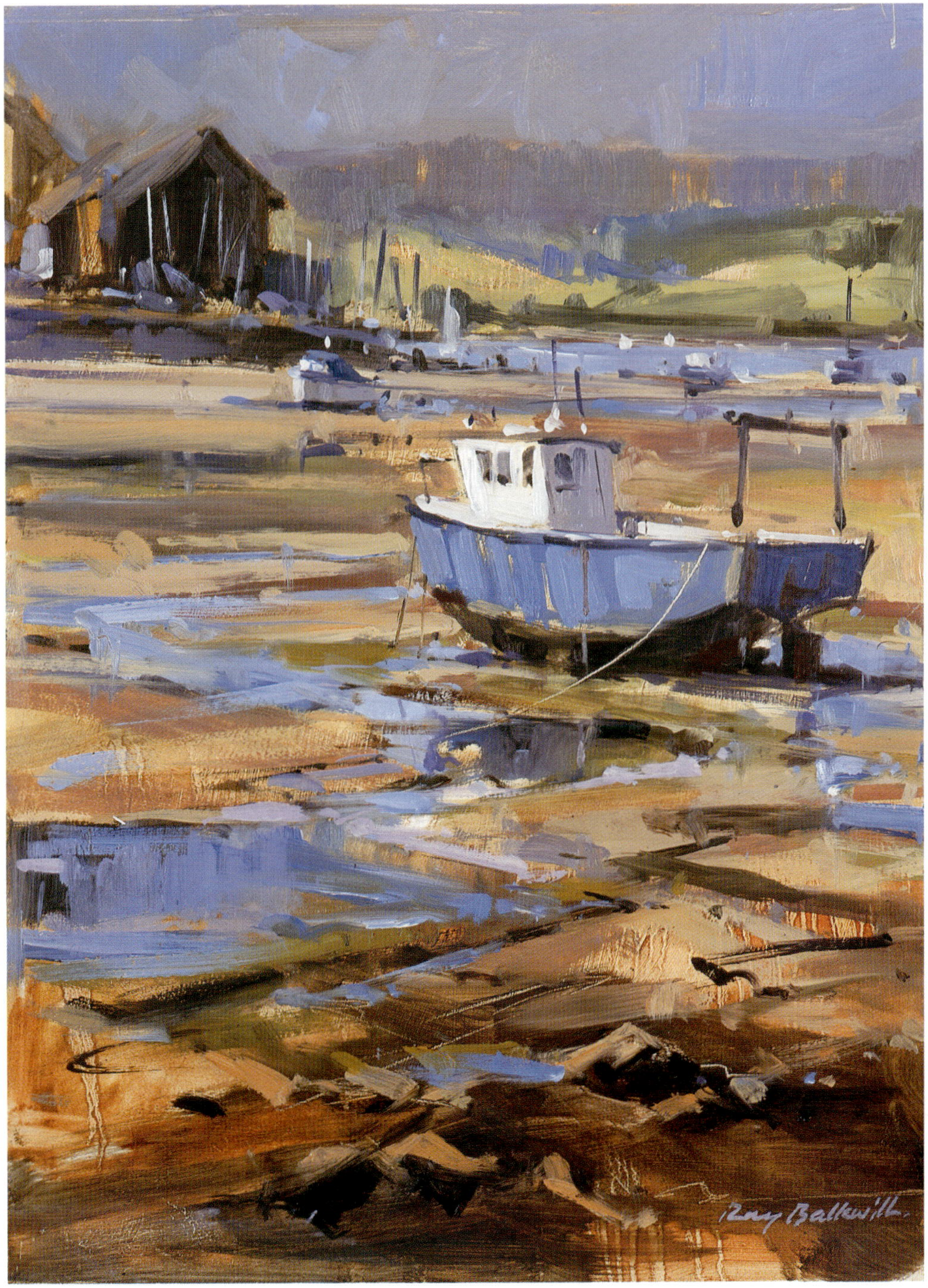

The Blue Boat
Oil 13x10in (33x25cm)

In the 1860s shipbuilding, as well as many other associated trades were carried on here. The Redway brothers employed an army of craftsmen in rope, sail and block- and spar-making, eventually building 200–300 ton sailing ships. The boat-building tradition continued in Exmouth, with family names such as Dixon, Lavis, Holman, Hayman and Rowsell being synonymous with the town. The construction in 1865 of a dock served by the railway made Exmouth an important port well into the twentieth century. The official midnight closure of the commercial port came on 31 December 1989. The departure of the cargo ship *Star Libra* next day marked the end of an era stretching back more than 125 years.

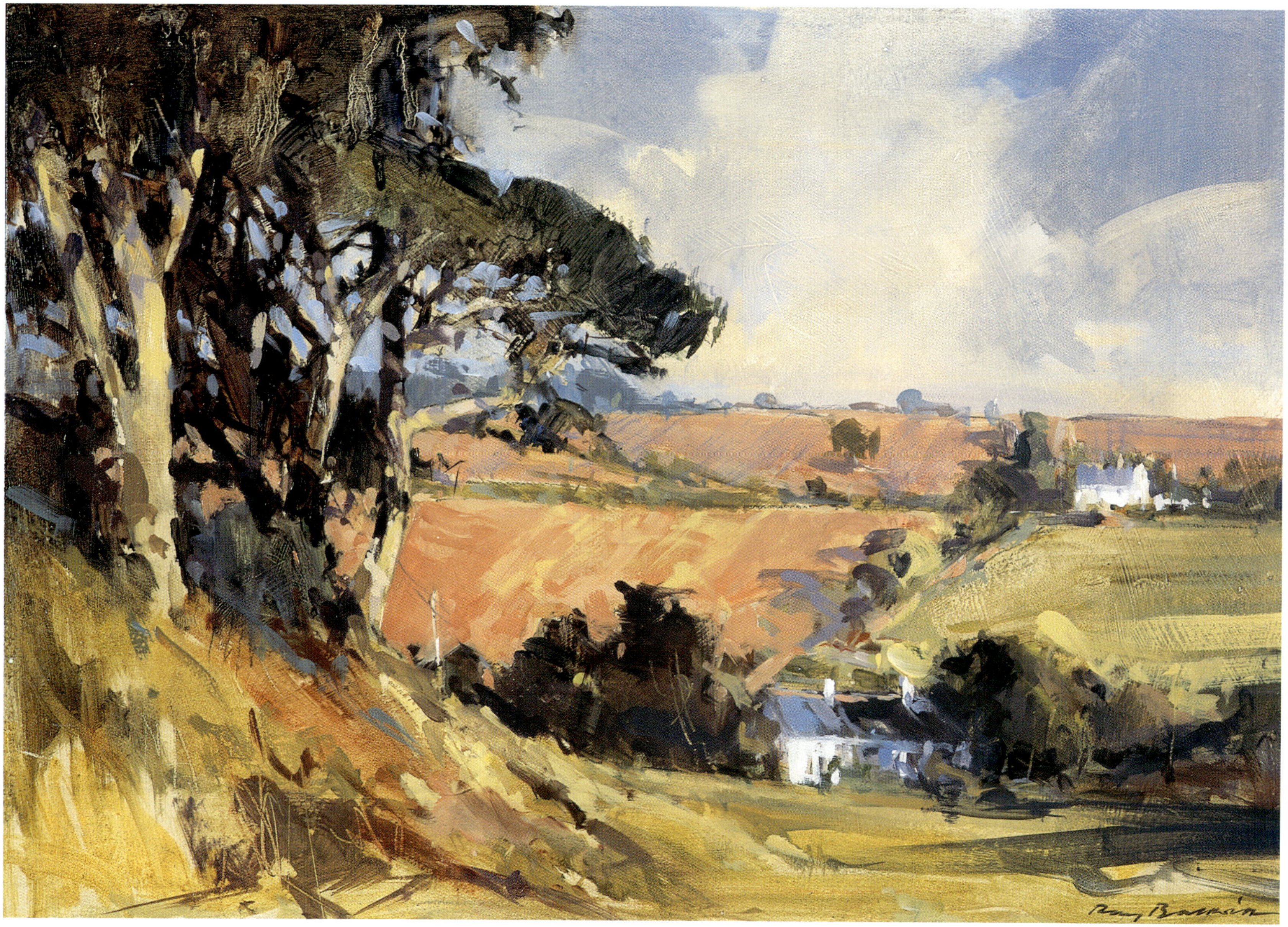

Summer Fields, Ashcombe
Oil 10x14in (25x36cm)

In the upper reaches of the deep lush valley of Dawlish Water lies Ashcombe, with its towering and beautiful church of St Nectan's. Ash trees were fairly common in Devon, so you will find many villages and farms named after them.

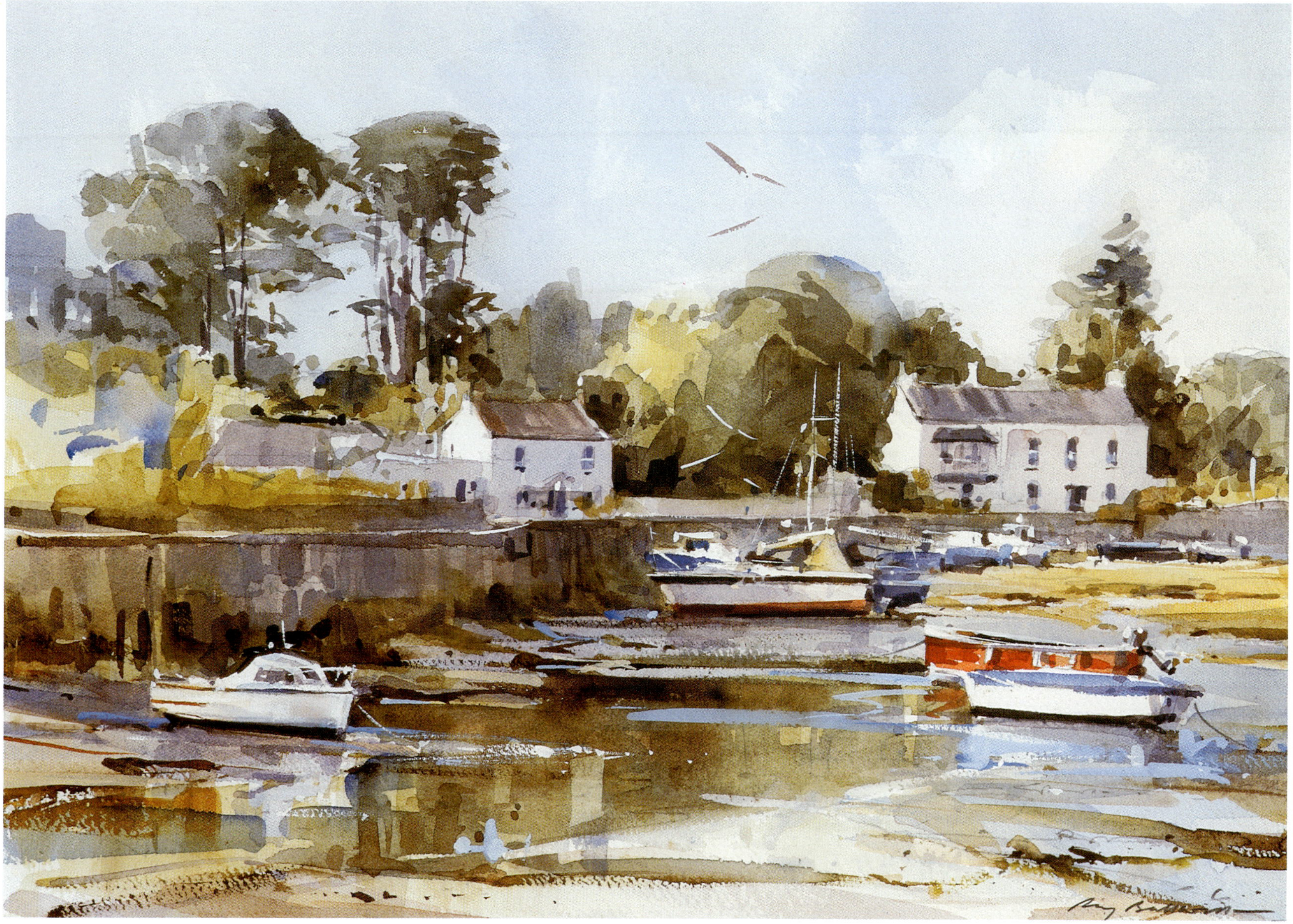

Sheltered Moorings, Cockwood
Watercolour 10x14in (26x36cm)

Across the river from Exmouth is Cockwood, which originated as a fishing village in the thirteenth century. The building of the railway has resulted in the river silting up, but it is not difficult to imagine sea-going vessels being tied up, on what was the quay outside the Ship Inn.

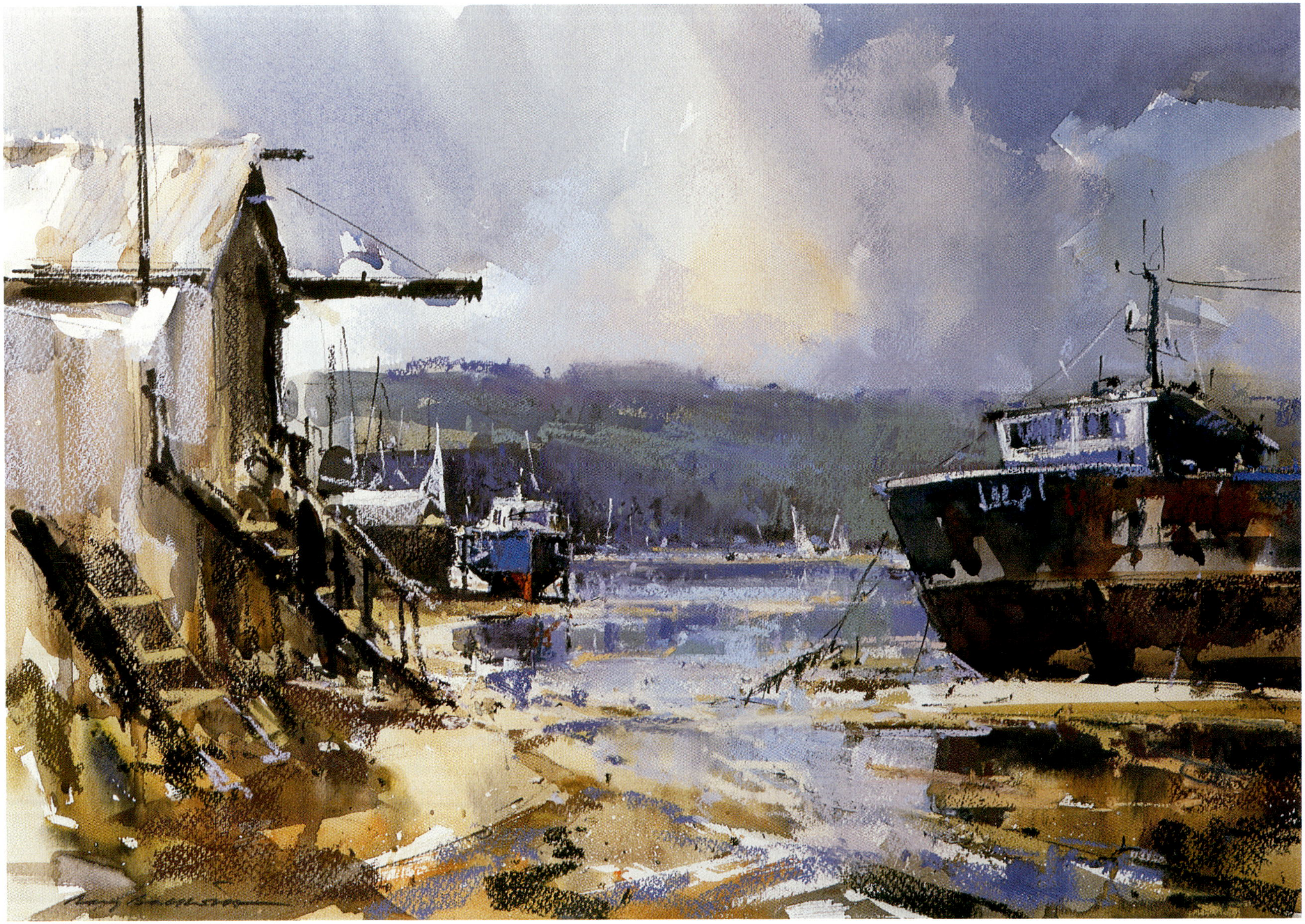

Camperdown Creek
Mixed Media 13.5x19in (34x48cm)

This was done as a demonstration to a group of students on one of my recent painting courses and is an example of how quickly scenes can change. On returning a week later the boat-shed with its characteristic gantry had been demolished. It was originally built by W.F. Holman at the turn of the century.

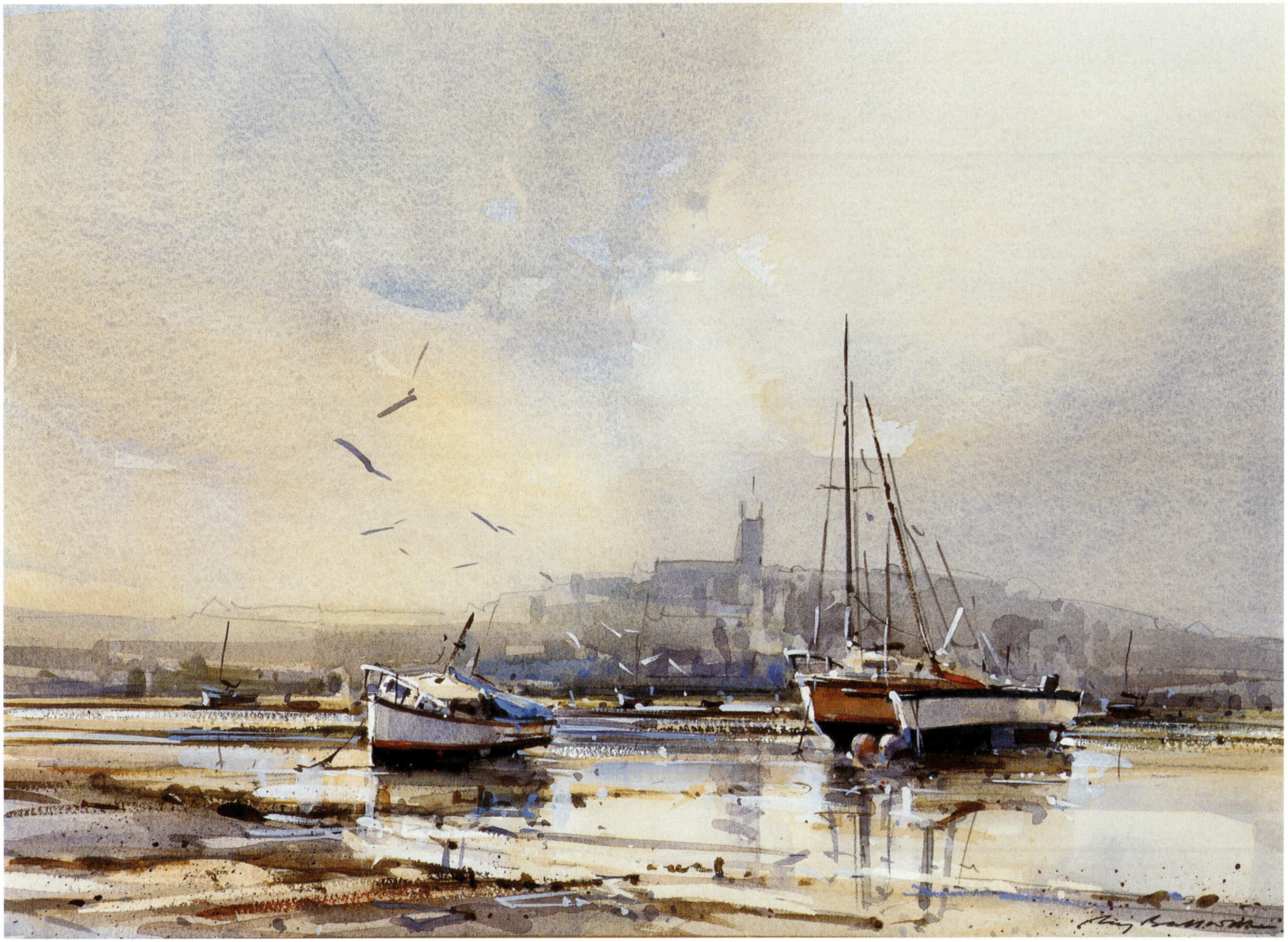

Dawn over Exmouth
Watercolour 14x21in (36x53cm)

Another day dawns as the first breath of sunshine washes over the town and estuary. The tall pinnacled tower of Holy Trinity Church has been a spectacular landmark from both land and sea for over a century. Early morning skies are usually more subtle in colouring than those at the close of the day, so watercolour lends itself beautifully to these soft atmospheric effects.

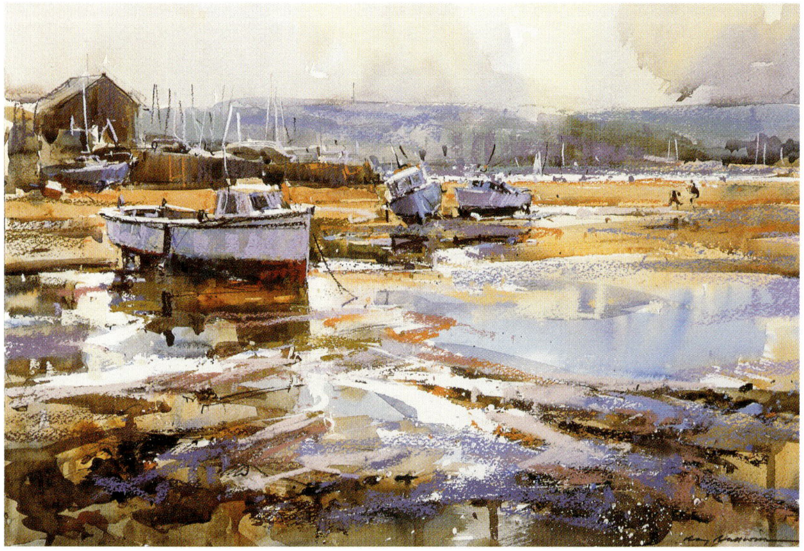

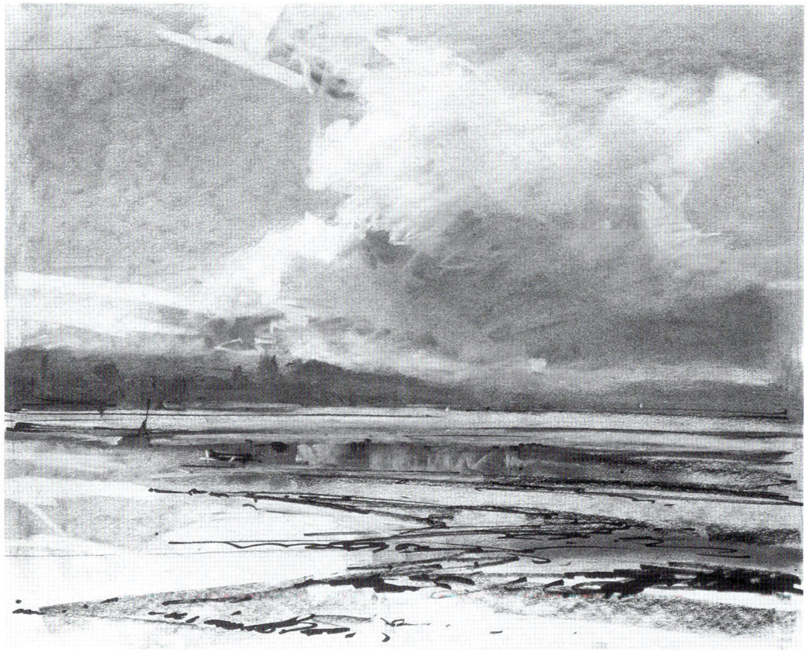

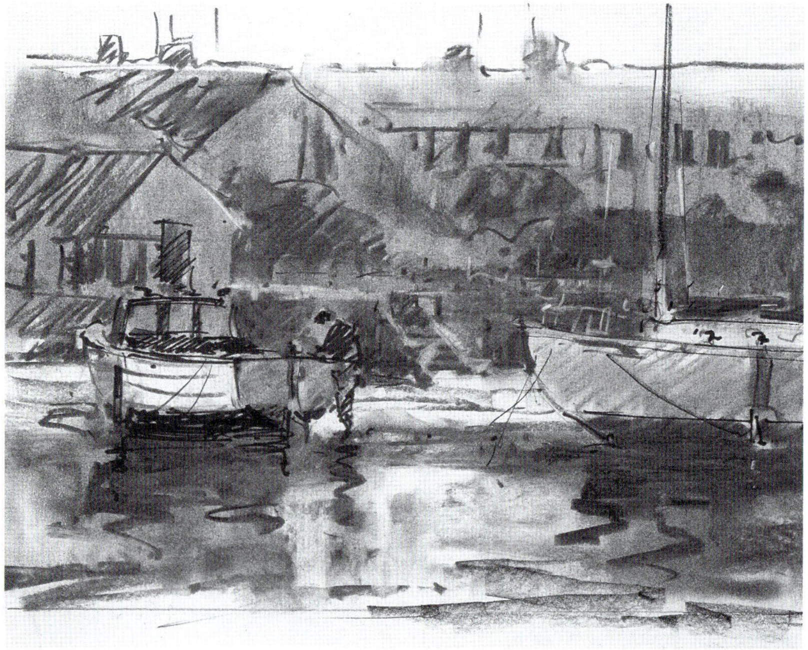

Clockwise, from above:
Across the Exe Estuary
Mixed Media 14x21in (36x53cm)

Exe Estuary Sky
Charcoal Sketch 11x14in (28x36cm)

Boat Repairs
Charcoal Sketch 9.5x13in (24x33cm)

Charcoal is a wonderfully expressive medium, and perfect for working quickly to capture mood and atmosphere. Seeing the scene in black and white is vital in exploring composition and tonal relationships.

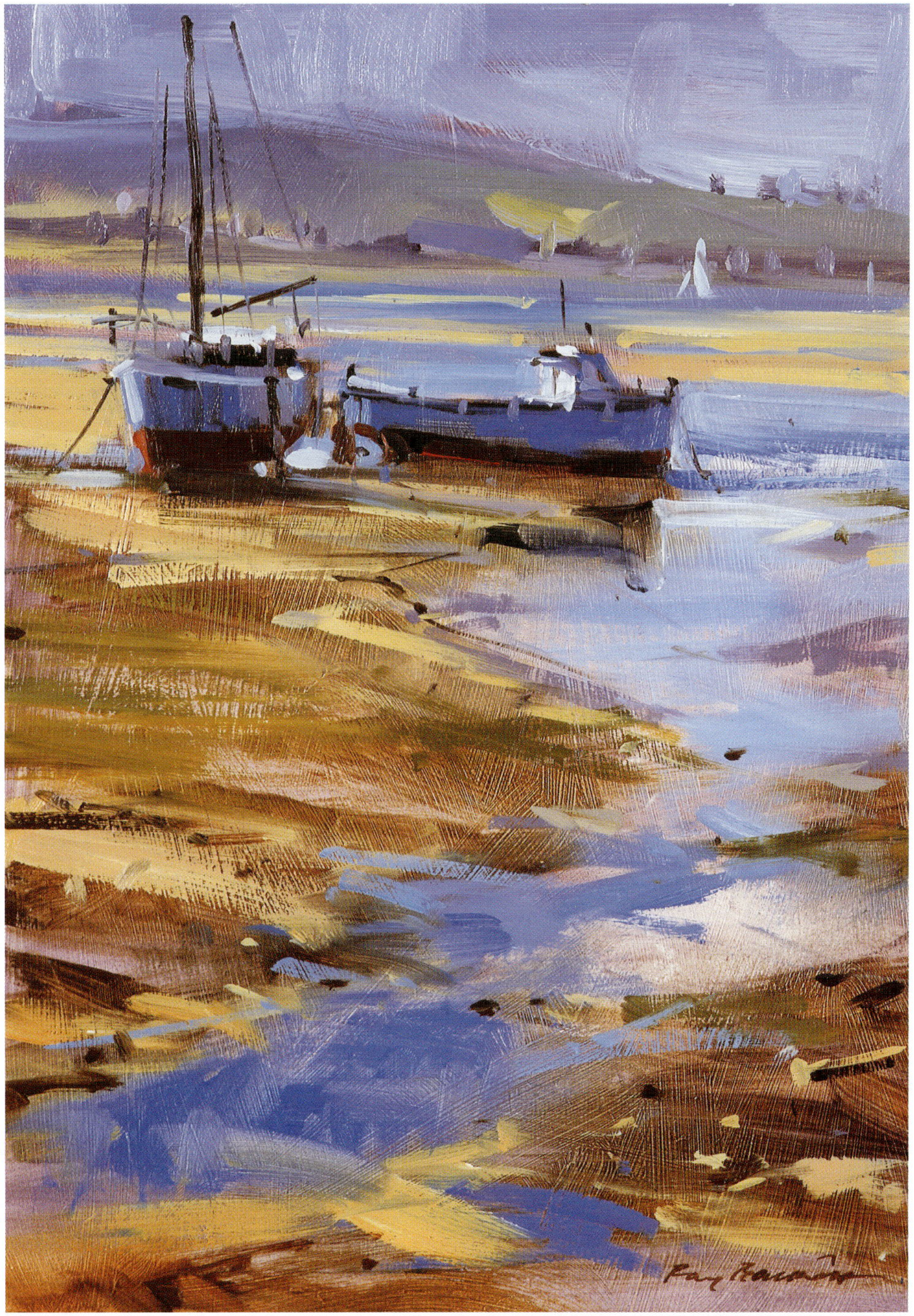

30. *Shelly Gut*
Oil 14x10in (36x25cm)

These two boats have always been favourite subjects of mine. On the left is *Windance* a 1950s launch which Geoff Holman rebuilt from a wreck, and alongside is *Lady Charlotte,* a carvel-built open launch, built by his father in 1935. At the outbreak of the Second World War the Admiralty requisitioned *Lady Charlotte* and she served the war years along the North African coast being used to clear harbours of sunken wreckage. This painting was recently chosen for use on confectionary products by Sherriff's of Kingsbridge in their 'Memories from Devon' range.

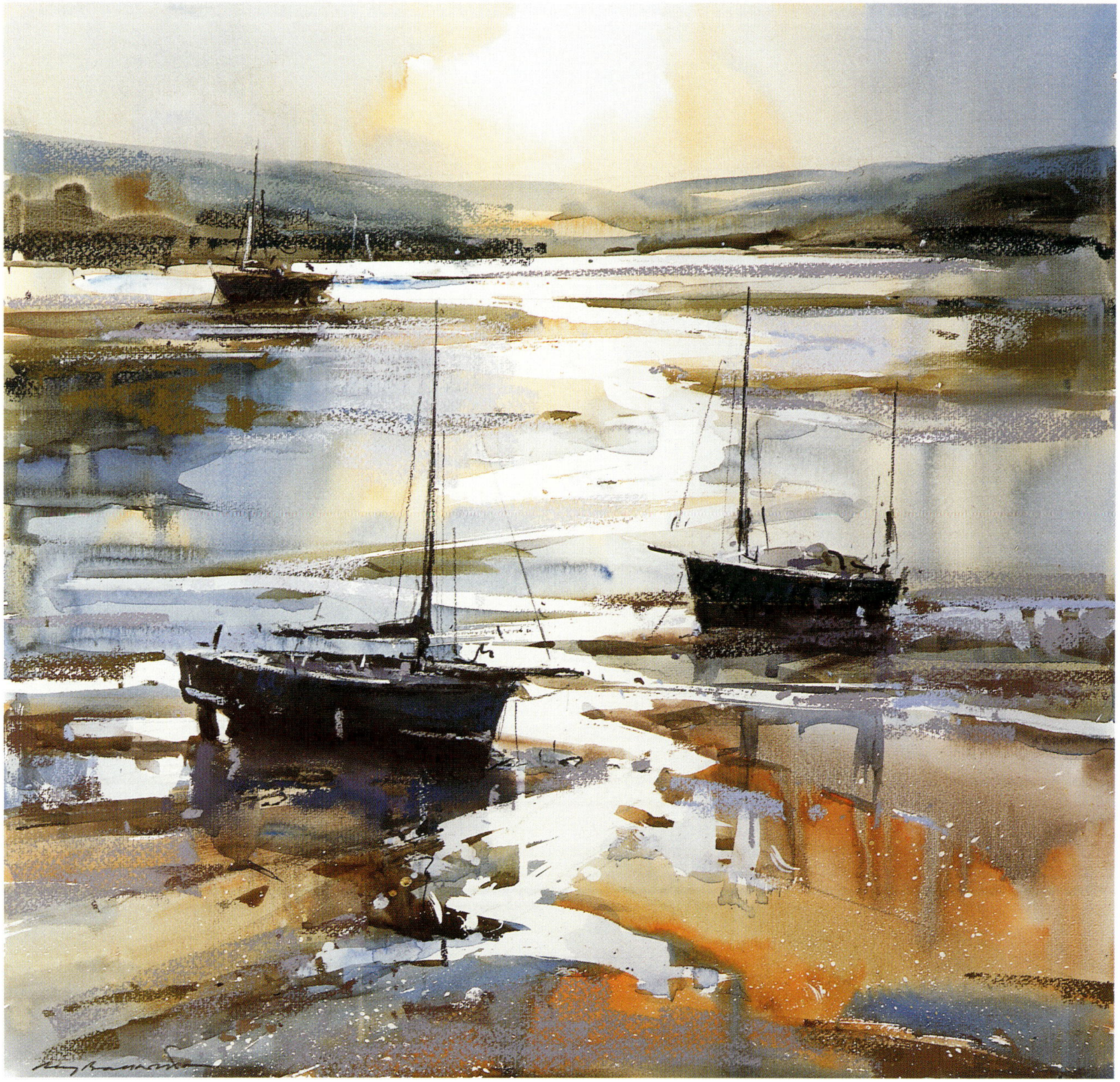

Sunset on the Exe
Mixed Media 17x18in.(43x46cm)
Exhibited at the South West Academy Exhibition 2004.

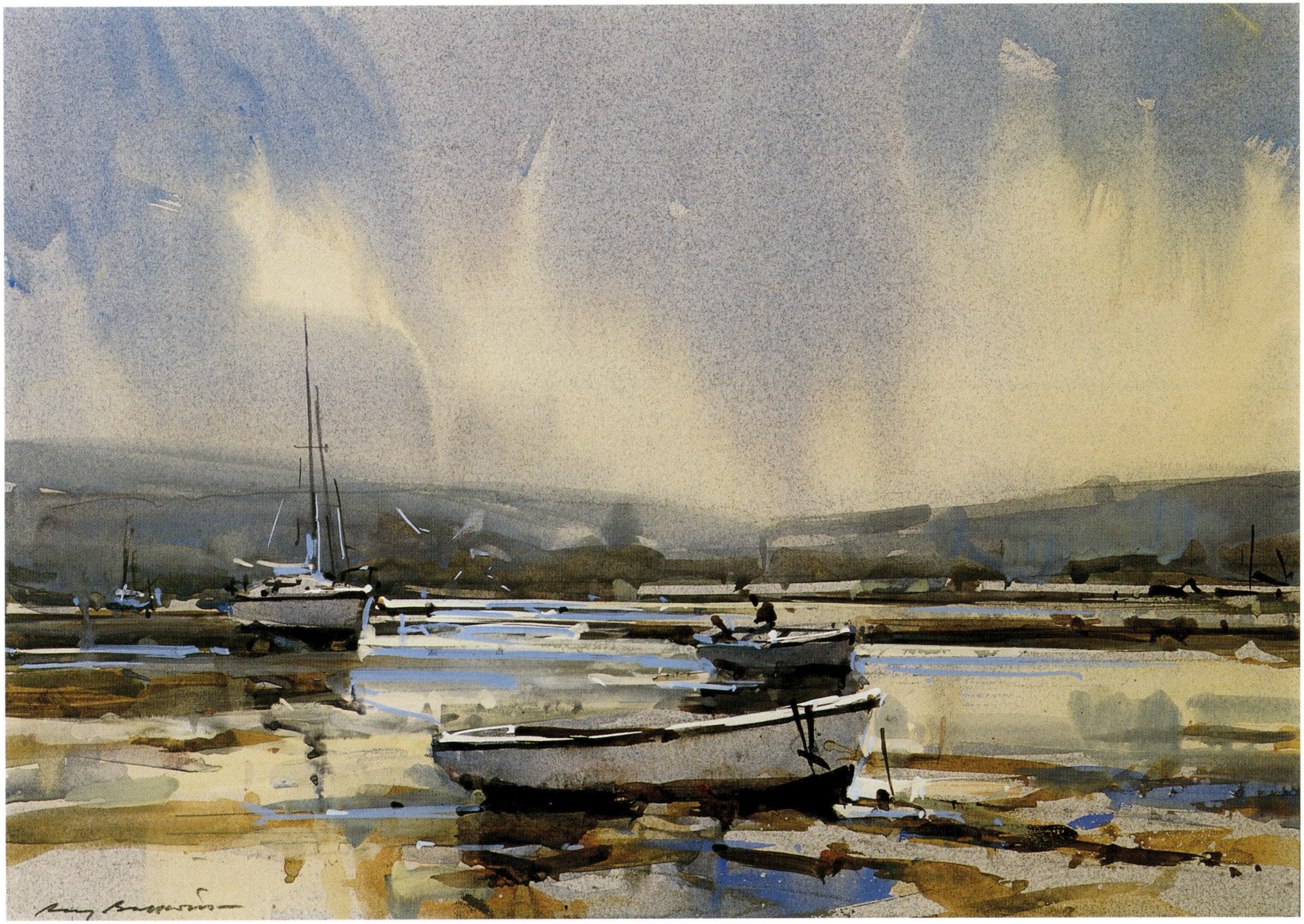

Shower over the Haldon Hills
Watercolour/Gouache Location Study 10x14in (25x36cm)

Across the river from Exmouth stand the Great Haldon and Little Haldon hills. Haldon derives its name from the 'hill of hail' or 'holy hill'. Its highest point is 817feet (249m) above sea level. There is an old Devon saying regarding the weather that goes: *'When Haldon hath a Hatt, Let Kenton beware a Squatt!'*

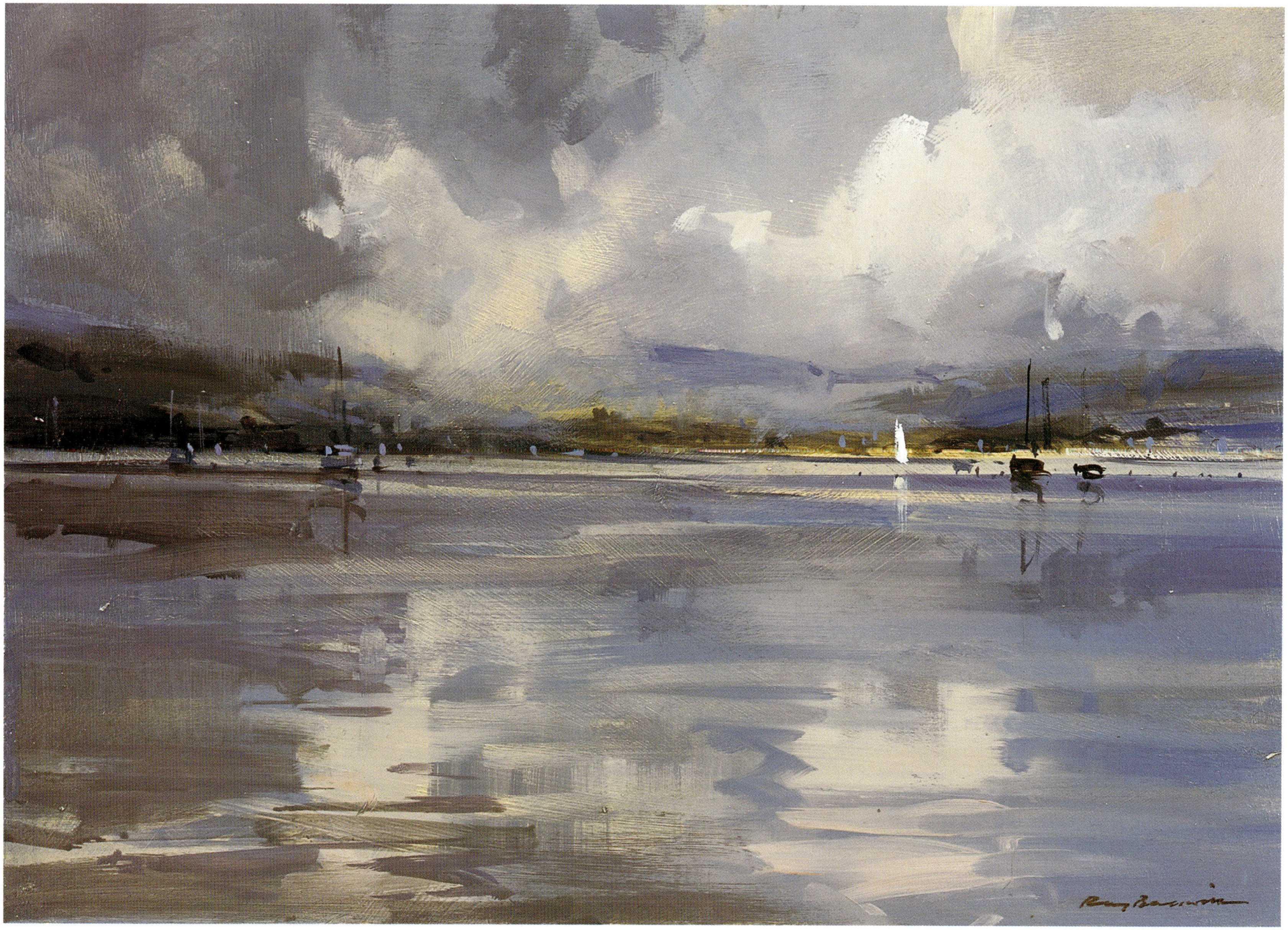

'Tidn't 'arf Looking Black over Bill's Mother's!'
Oil 10x14in (25x36cm)

This shows the view across the estuary from Shelly Gut to Starcross. The title for the painting is from a conversation I had with Geoff Holman. He told me that his mother would often look out and say this. However where exactly 'Bill's mother's' was, he never quite found out!

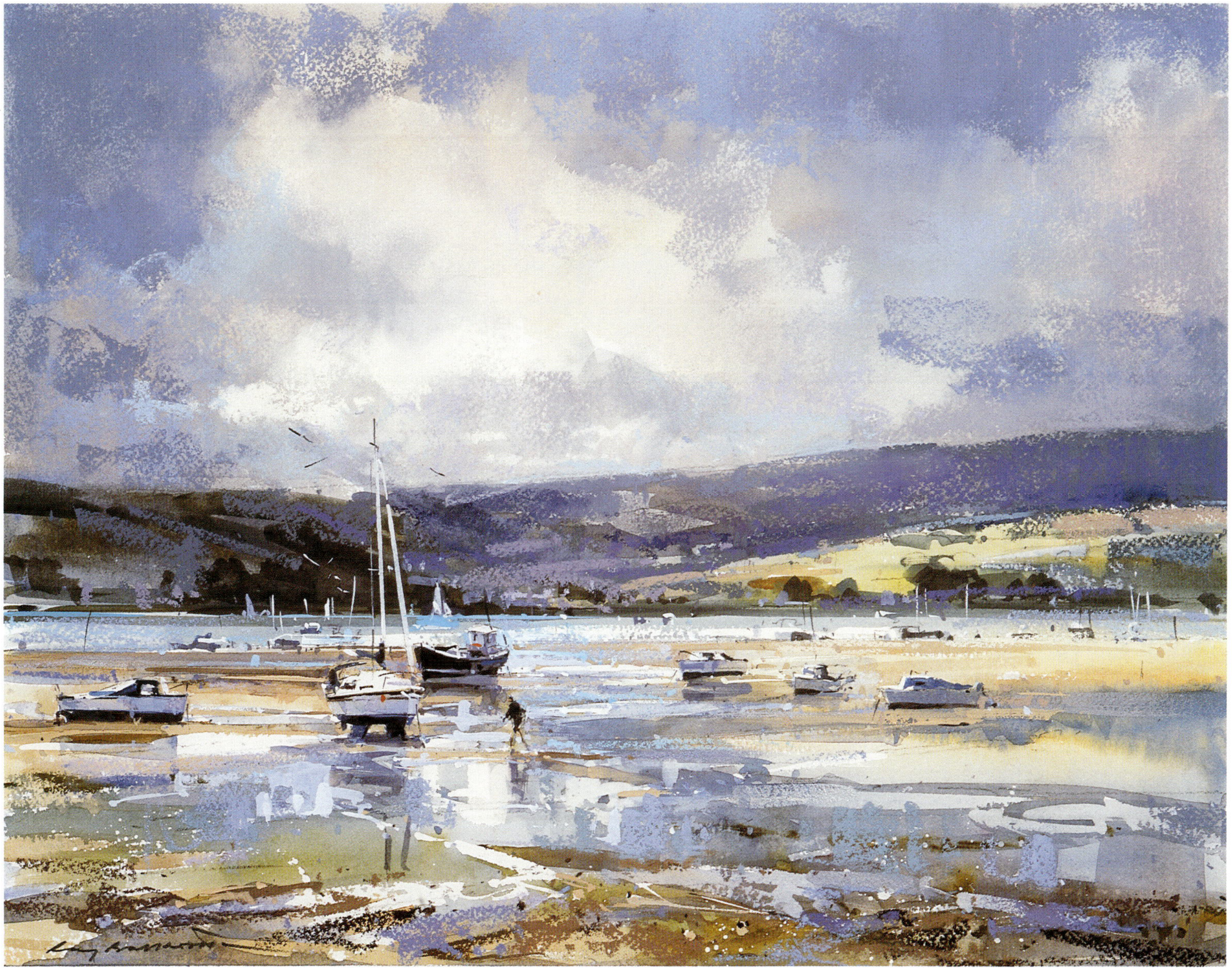

Silver Light on the Exe
Mixed Media 14x20in (36x51cm)

Francis Danby once noted that there were no finer landscapes to be seen anywhere in the British Isles, and said *'The cloud vistas are particularly good and early morning sharpness of atmosphere ideal light for a distant view.'*

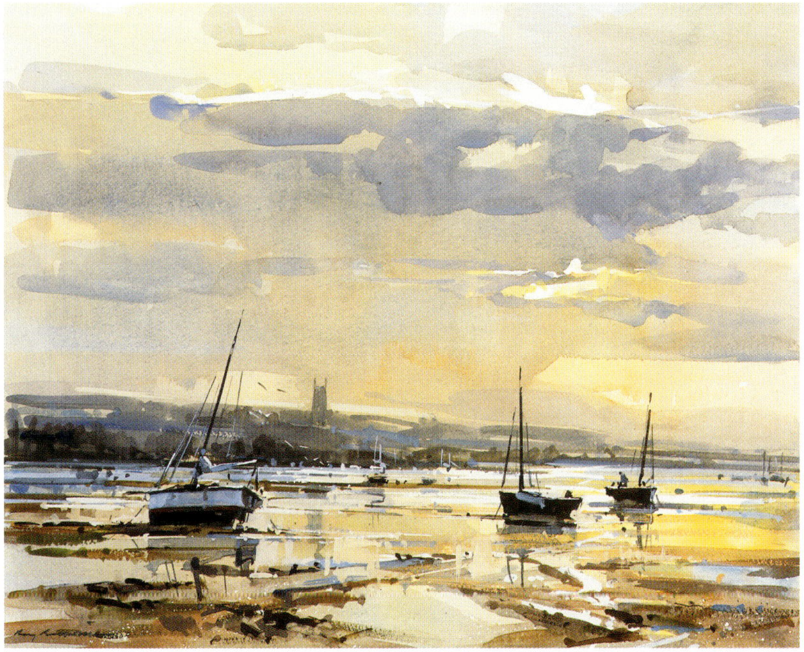

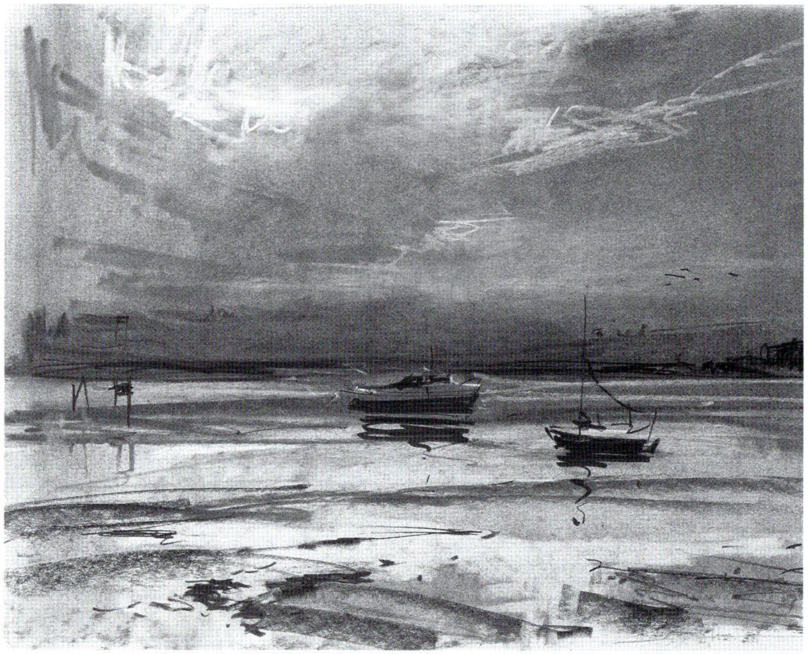

Clockwise, from above:
First Light of Day, Exmouth
Watercolour 13x16in (33x41cm)

Low tide brings together all the elements that I enjoy best in marine subjects; contrasts of wet sand, tide pools and reflections. The shapes of boats too are more interesting, being able to see the hull and keel, particular if they are leaning and creating interesting angles.

Across the Exe
Charcoal Sketch 11x14in (31x36cm)

Tidepools
Charcoal Sketch 10.5x13.5in (27x34cm)

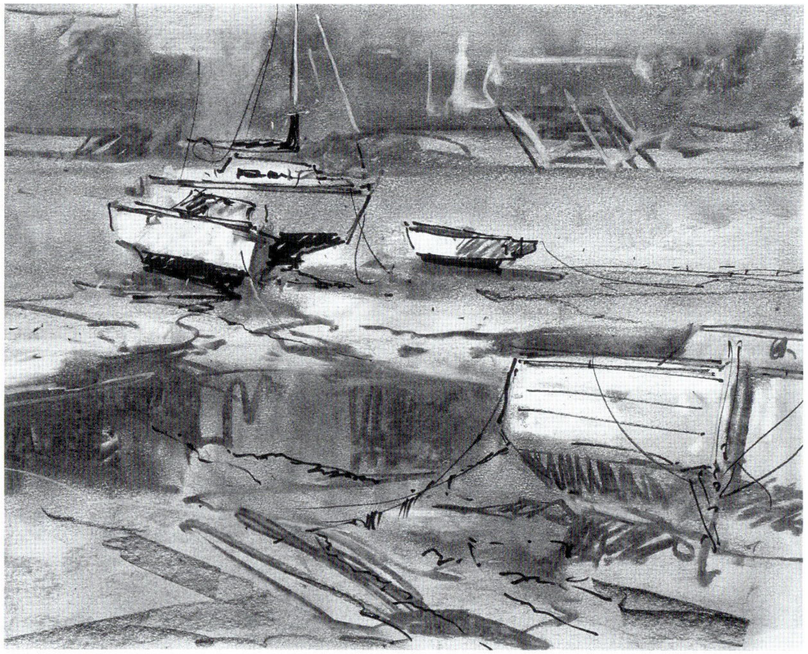

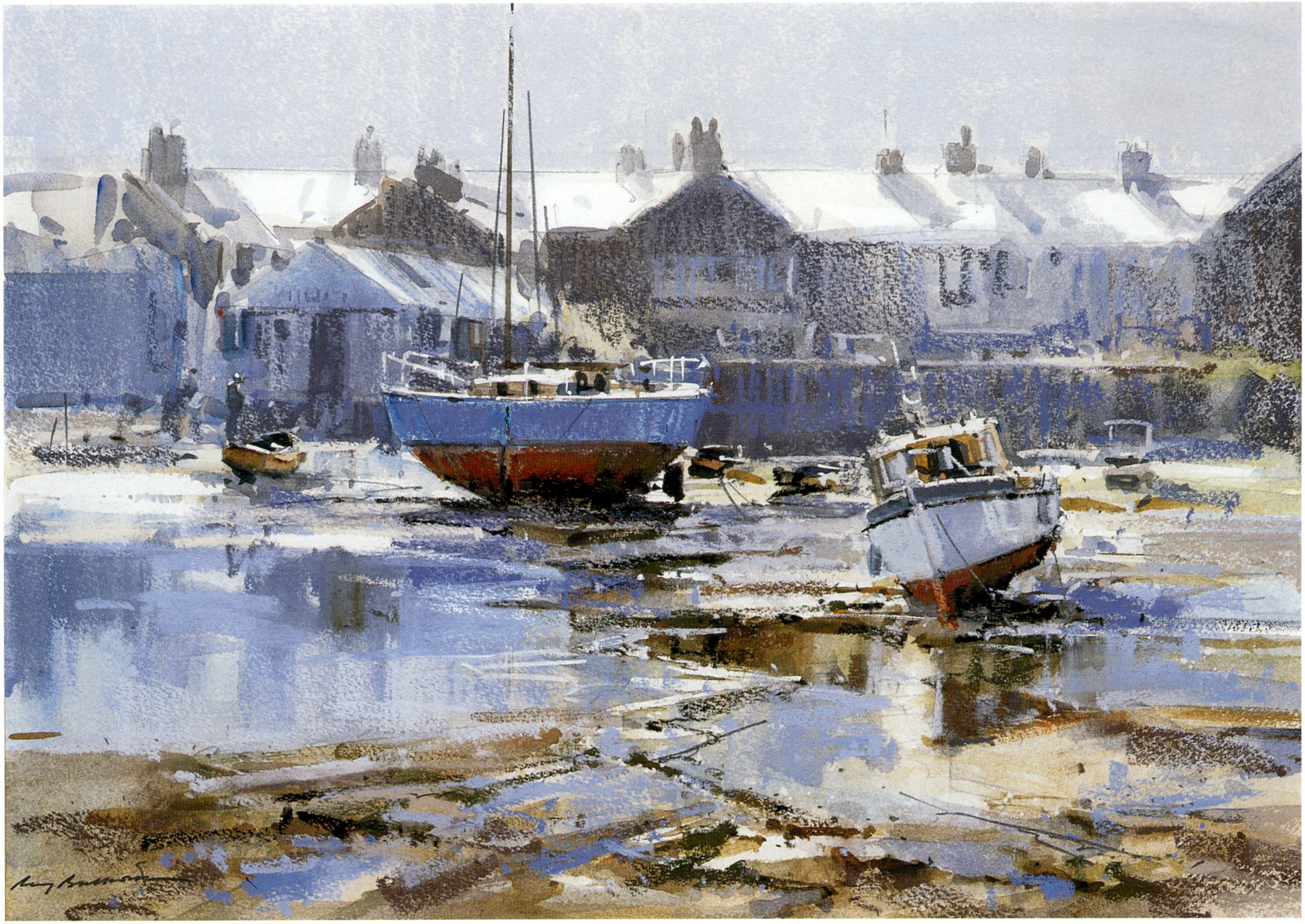

Morning Light, Camperdown Creek
Mixed Media 10.5x14.5in (27x37cm)

Camperdown Terrace runs alongside the creek and takes its name from a disaster that occurred in the Mediterranean when these houses were being built in 1893. Whilst on manoeuvres HMS *Camperdown* collided with HMS *Victoria* which resulted in the loss of the *Victoria* and the death of 321 sailors.

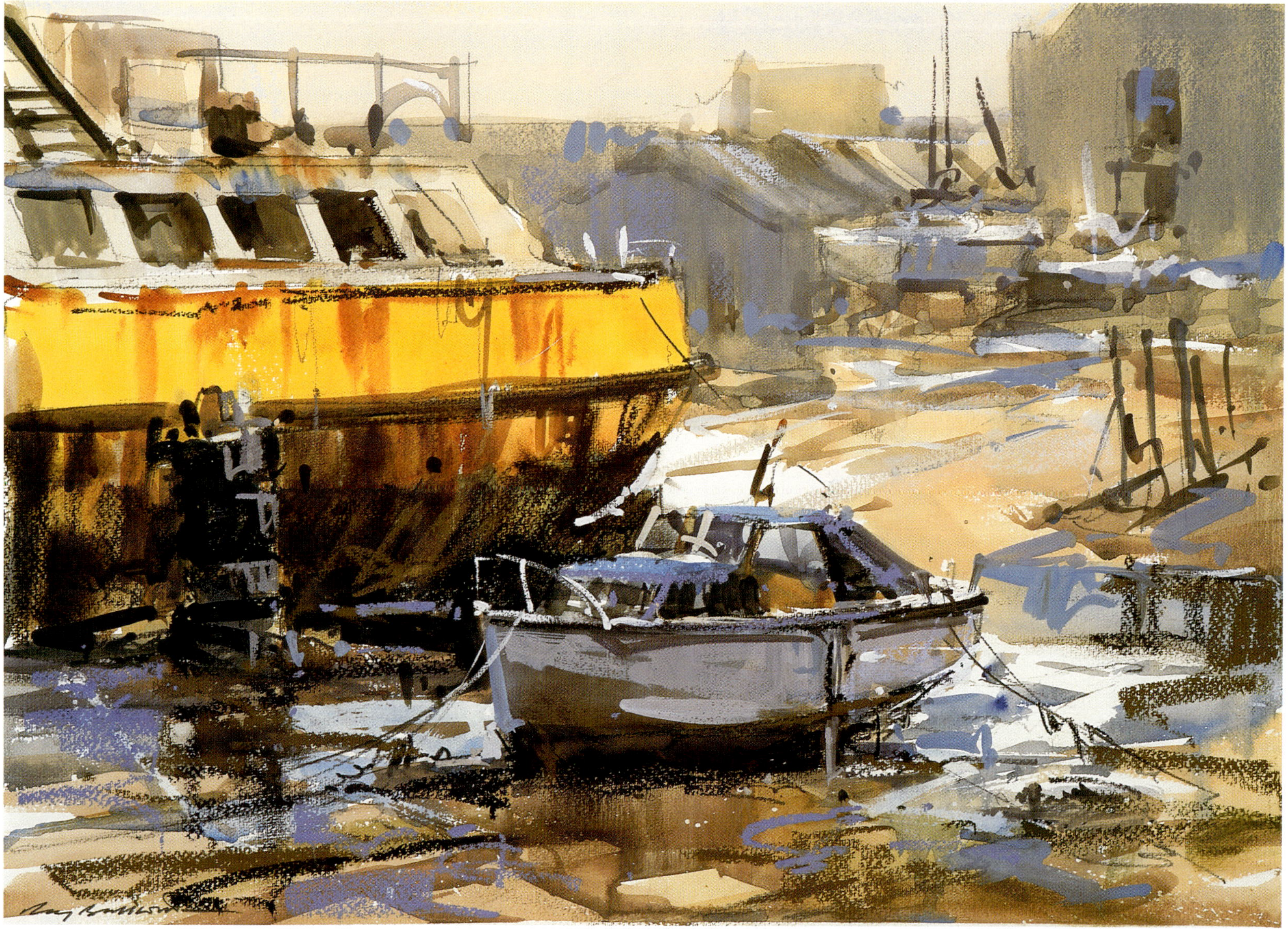

The Flamborian
Mixed Media 13x18.5in (33x47cm)

The *Flamborian* arrived in Exmouth in January 2004 to be restored and join the Stuart Line, a family-run business that has been running river trips and sea cruises from Exmouth for over thirty years. First registered as *Boys Own* in 1938, the *Flamborian* saw service in the Second World War on the Tees, Tyne and Humber and reputably was the first boat to shoot at a German plane.

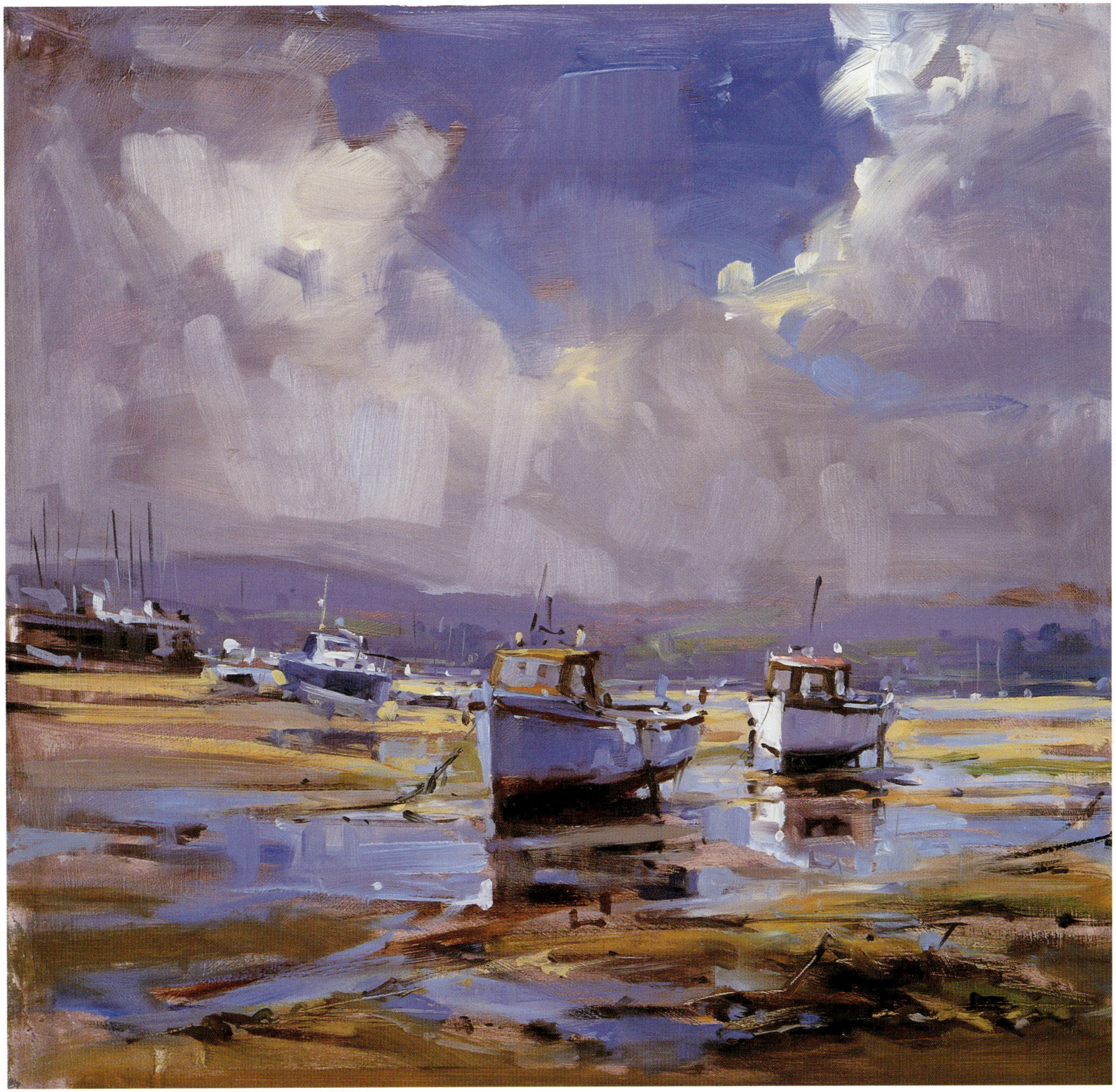

Summer Sky, Exmouth
Oil 14x14in (36x36cm)

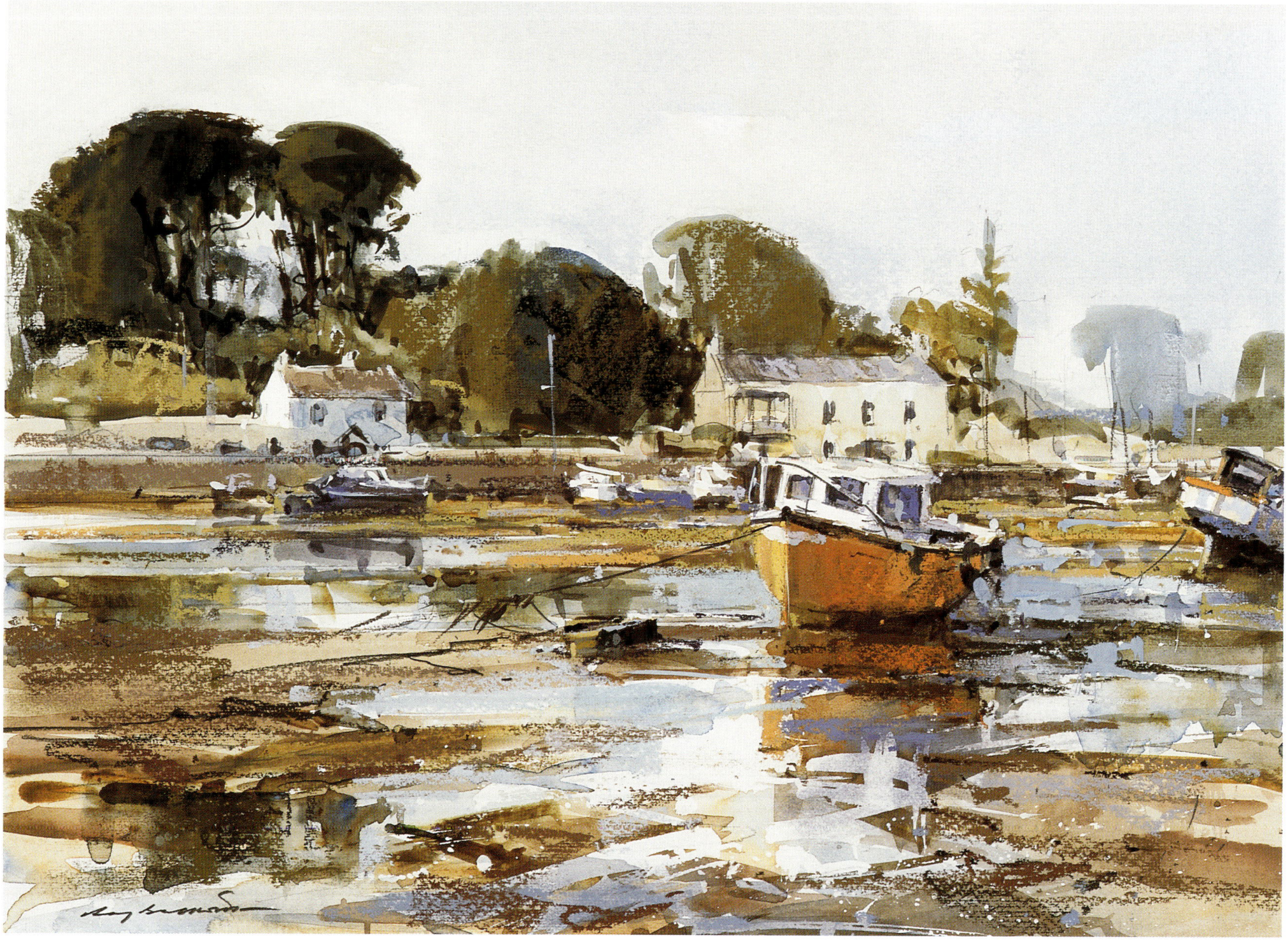

Across the Harbour, Cockwood
Mixed Media 12x15in (30x38cm)

The name of Cockwood or 'Cock-ood' as it is correctly pronounced, is associated with the nearby Red Brook, a stream whose waters take on the colour of the local soil. For centuries cockle-raking was undertaken here, exclusively by women.

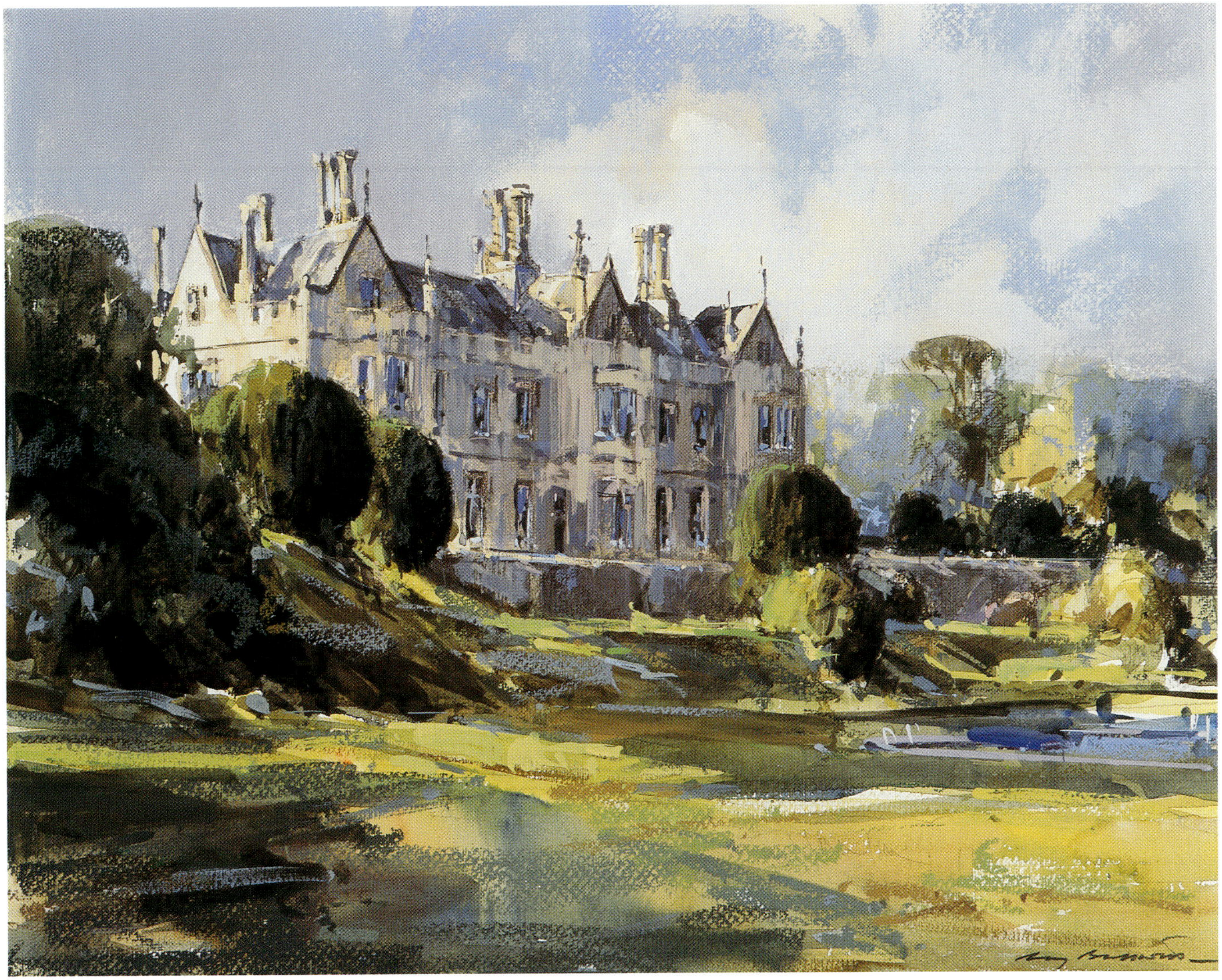

Sun and Shade, Mamhead House
Mixed Media 13x16in (33x41cm)

This private house is magnificently set below Haldon and overlooking the Exe estuary and coast to Sidmouth. This old estate has a history that dates back to Domesday, the first record of a mansion being in 1646. In 1779 Capability Brown landscaped the park at a cost of £105, and the estate is said to have the widest-spreading oak tree in the world, along with an English yew over a thousand years old.

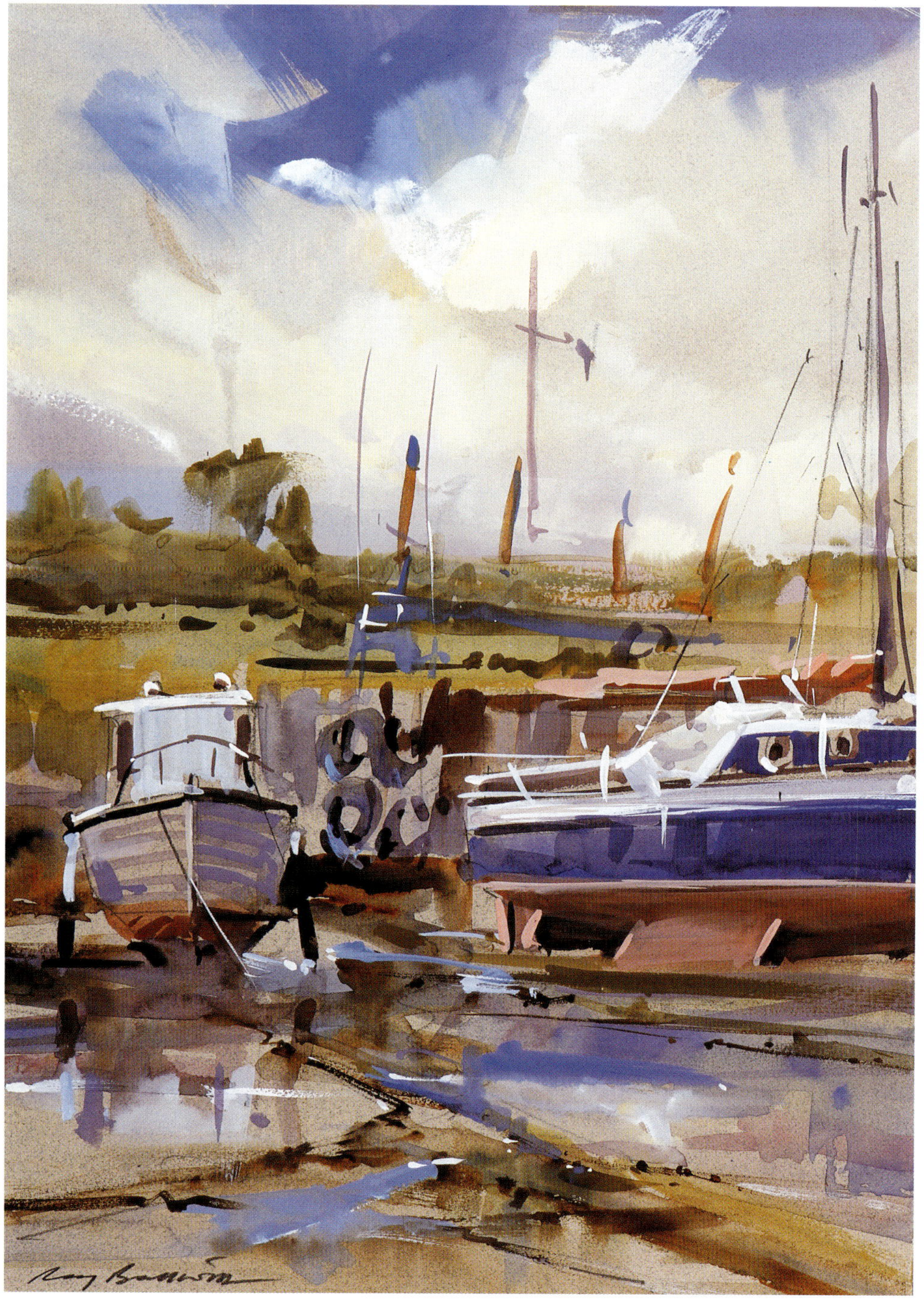

Shelly Gut
Watercolour/Gouache Location Study
14x10in (36x25cm)

This quick sketch was done at the head of the gut opposite the Lavis boatyard. Ron told me that there is a saying among boat builders: *'Never launch on a Friday, or something will surely go wrong'*. Only once did he break with tradition, due to the insistence of the owner of the vessel – with some disastrous results. So the axiom still holds good! Geoff told me of two further stories associated with superstition. It was deemed unlucky if a crow should fly over whilst salmon fishermen were 'shooting the net' to the totter buoy in the middle of the river. If one did the exercise had to be repeated. It was also unlucky to mention rabbits by name around boats, instead they are referred to as 'four-leggers,' or 'underground mutton'. Breeding 'four-leggers' on Dawlish Warren has now long since disappeared, but I came across this interesting entry in *Memorials of Exmouth* compiled in 1885. *'20th January 1817 – A heavy storm occurred, by the violence of which five acres of the Warren were washed away, and a great number of rabbits drowned.'*

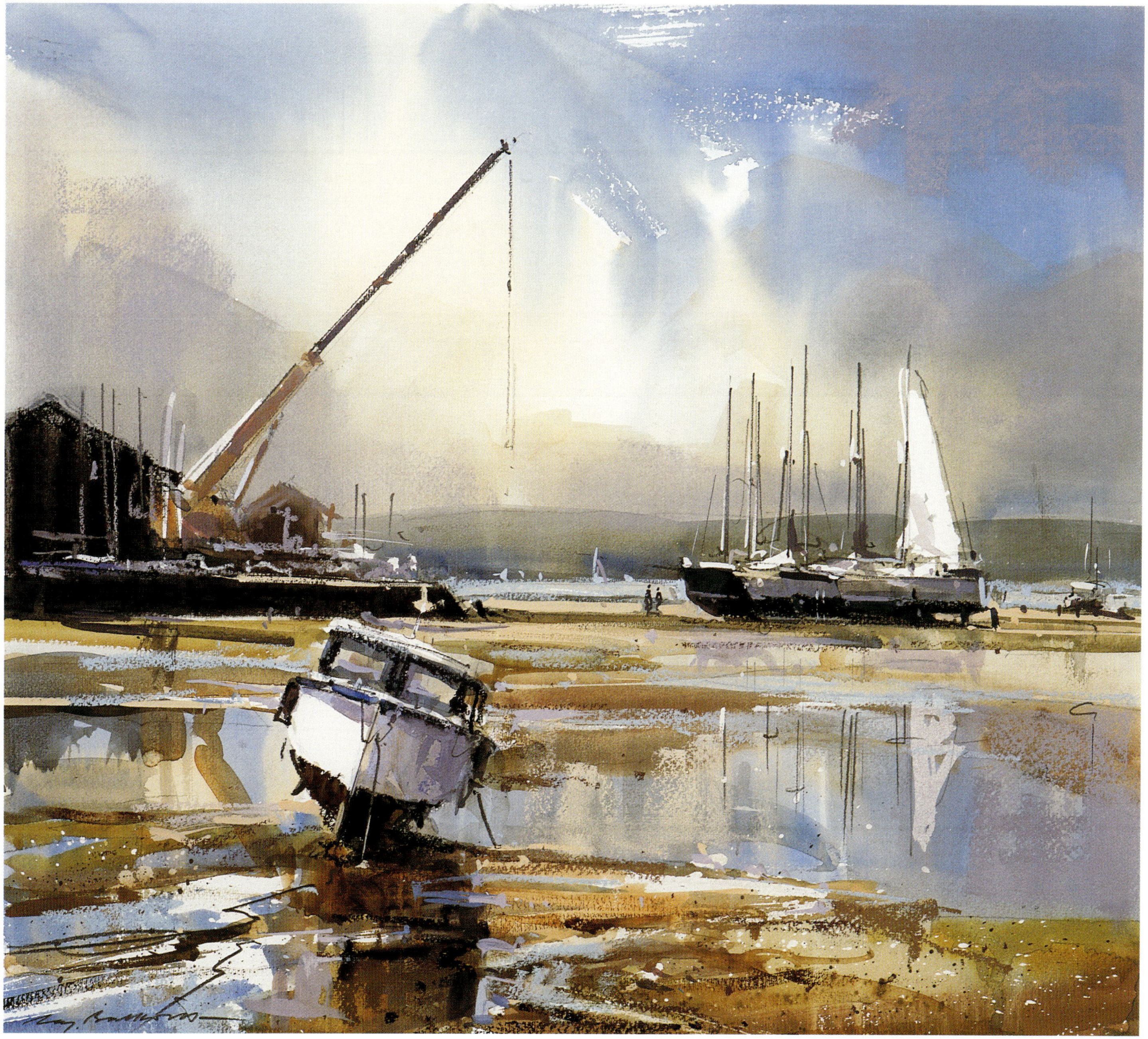

Craning-in and Stepping the Masts, Exmouth
Mixed Media 16x18in (41x46cm)

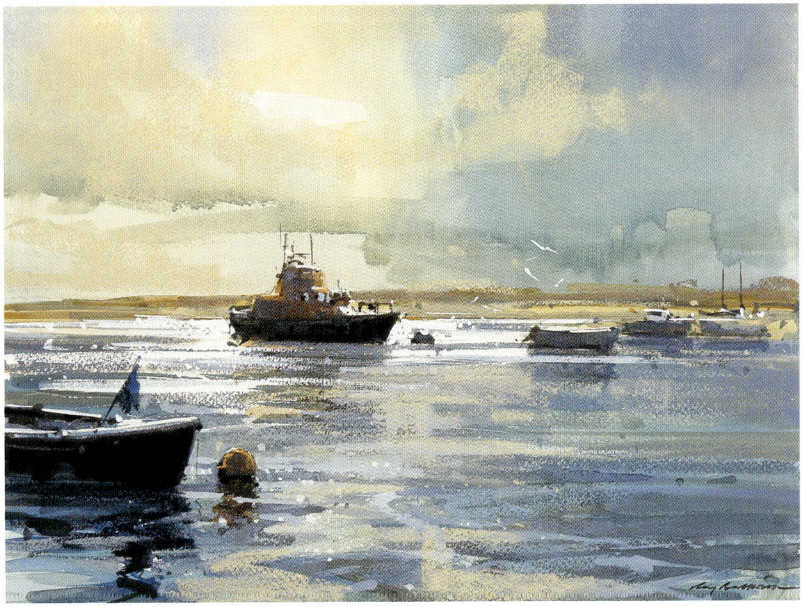

Sun Breaking Through over the Warren
Mixed Media 13x15.5in (33x39cm)

A shaft of sun falls on the Exmouth lifeboat *Forward Birmingham,* moored at the mouth of the estuary. There has been a lifeboat stationed in Exmouth since 1803. The present lifeboat, commissioned in 1996, is so called because of its links with the people of Birmingham who played a large part in raising the money for it.

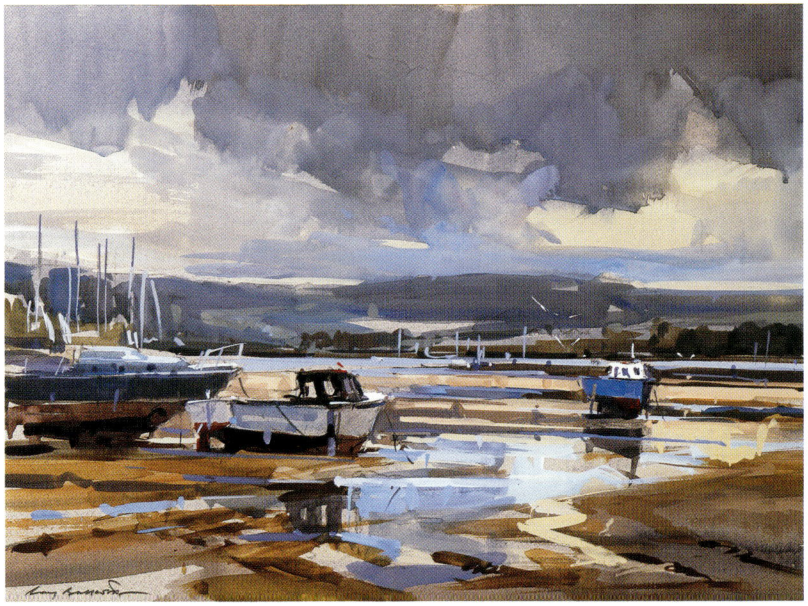

Towards the Haldon Hills from Exmouth
Watercolour/Gouache Location Study 10x14in (25x36cm)

Glinting high on the skyline of the Haldon hills stands Ball's Obelisk built of Portland Stone by merchant Sir Thomas Ball, who lived in Mamhead House. Built in 1742 as a daymark for shipping, the views of the estuary and coast from here are stunning.

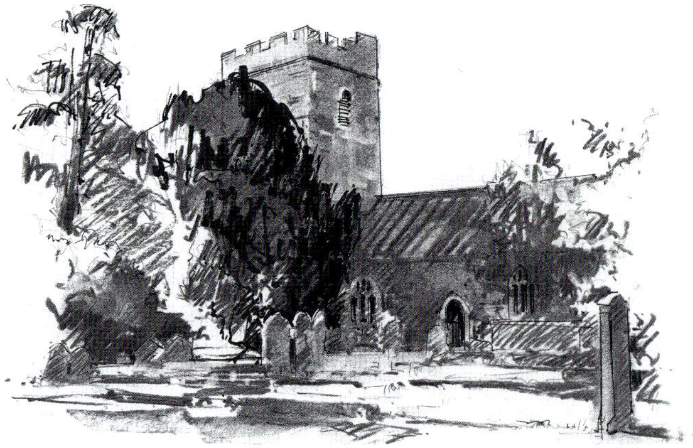

This sketch shows the church of St John-in-the-Wilderness, with Francis Danby's grave to the right.

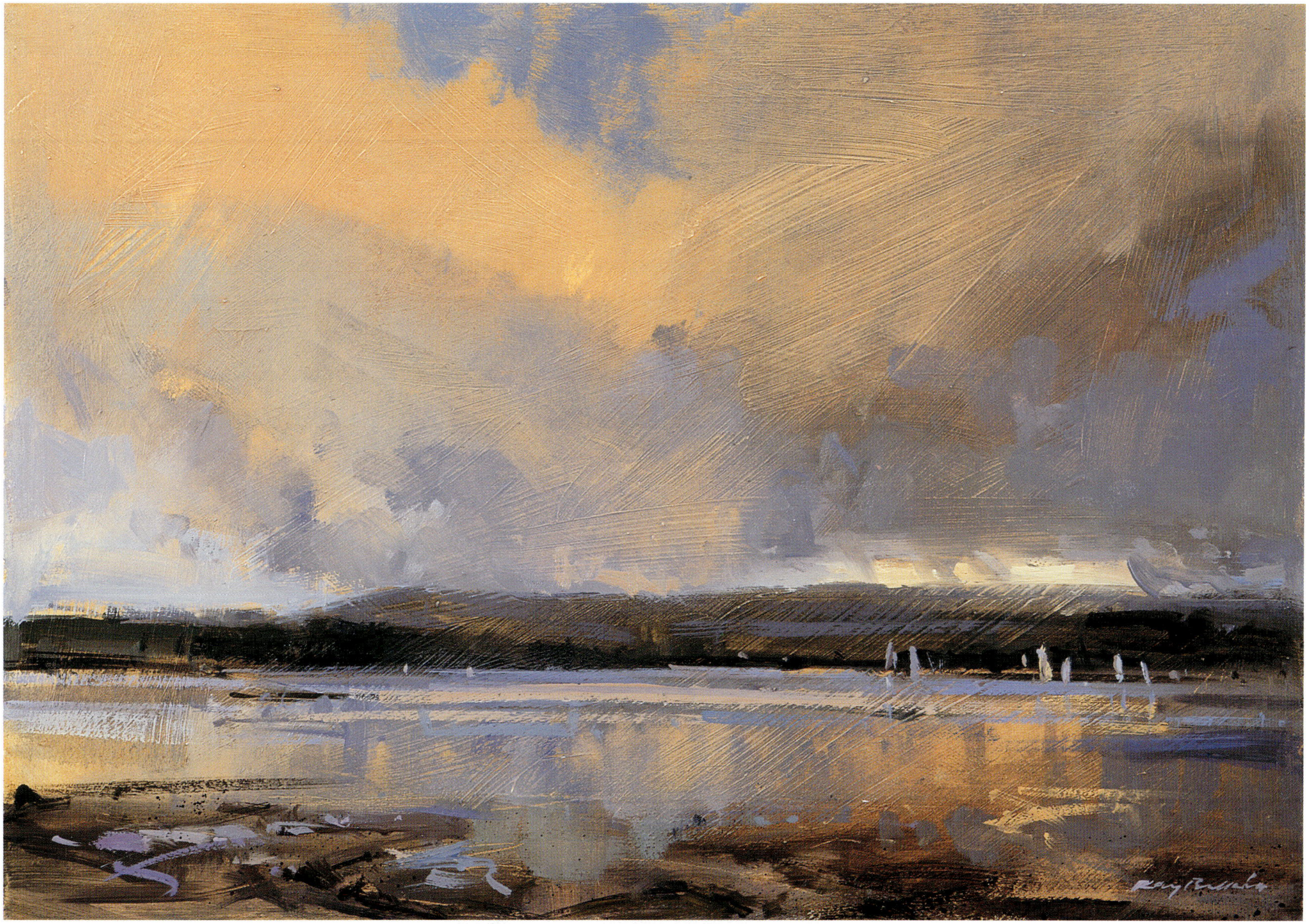

Sailing On Winter Sun
Oil 10x14in (25x36cm)

One of the most amazing sights of the estuary at this time of year is watching the movements of vast flock of Knots as they swirl above the waters at dusk. The movement is accentuated by the pale undersides and darker backs of the birds as they twist and turn, creating a spectacular moving sculpture of beauty and precision.

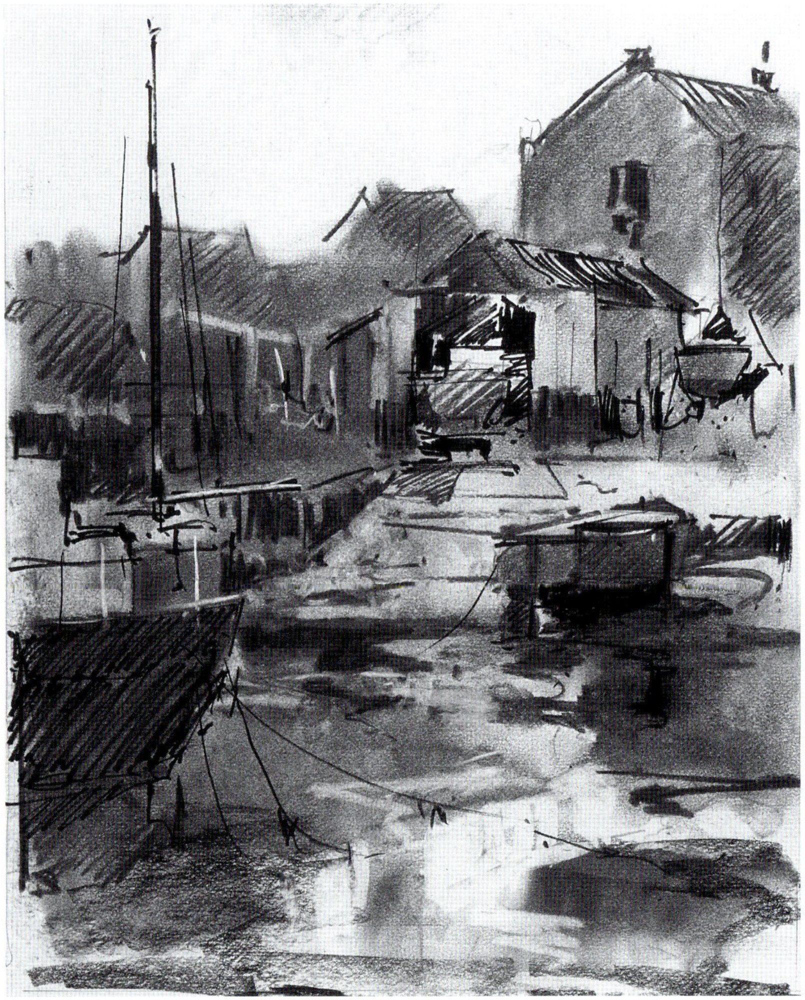

Lavis' Boatyard
Charcoal Sketch 13.5x10.5in (34x27cm)

(Right) *Summer Haze, Exmouth*
Watercolour 10x14.5 (25x37cm)

'*Summer Haze*' shows the new face of Exmouth with its luxury apartments around the new marina, as well as the trawler *My Three Girls*. The diffused light on hazy days like this makes the scene a much simpler subject to paint, and an ideal watercolour subject.

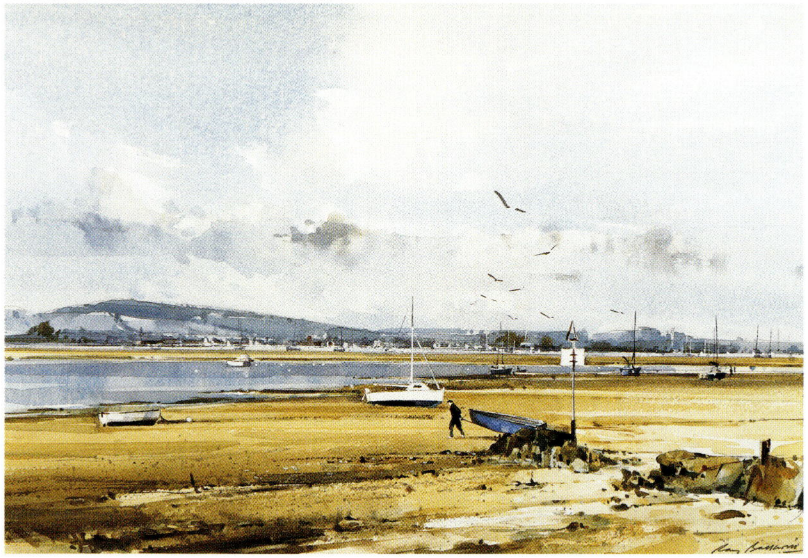

Low Tide at Exmouth
Watercolour 10x14in (25x36cm)

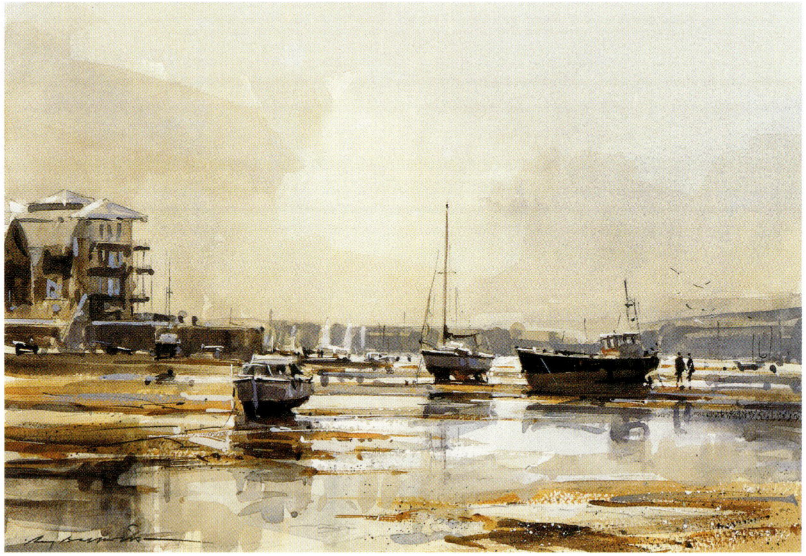

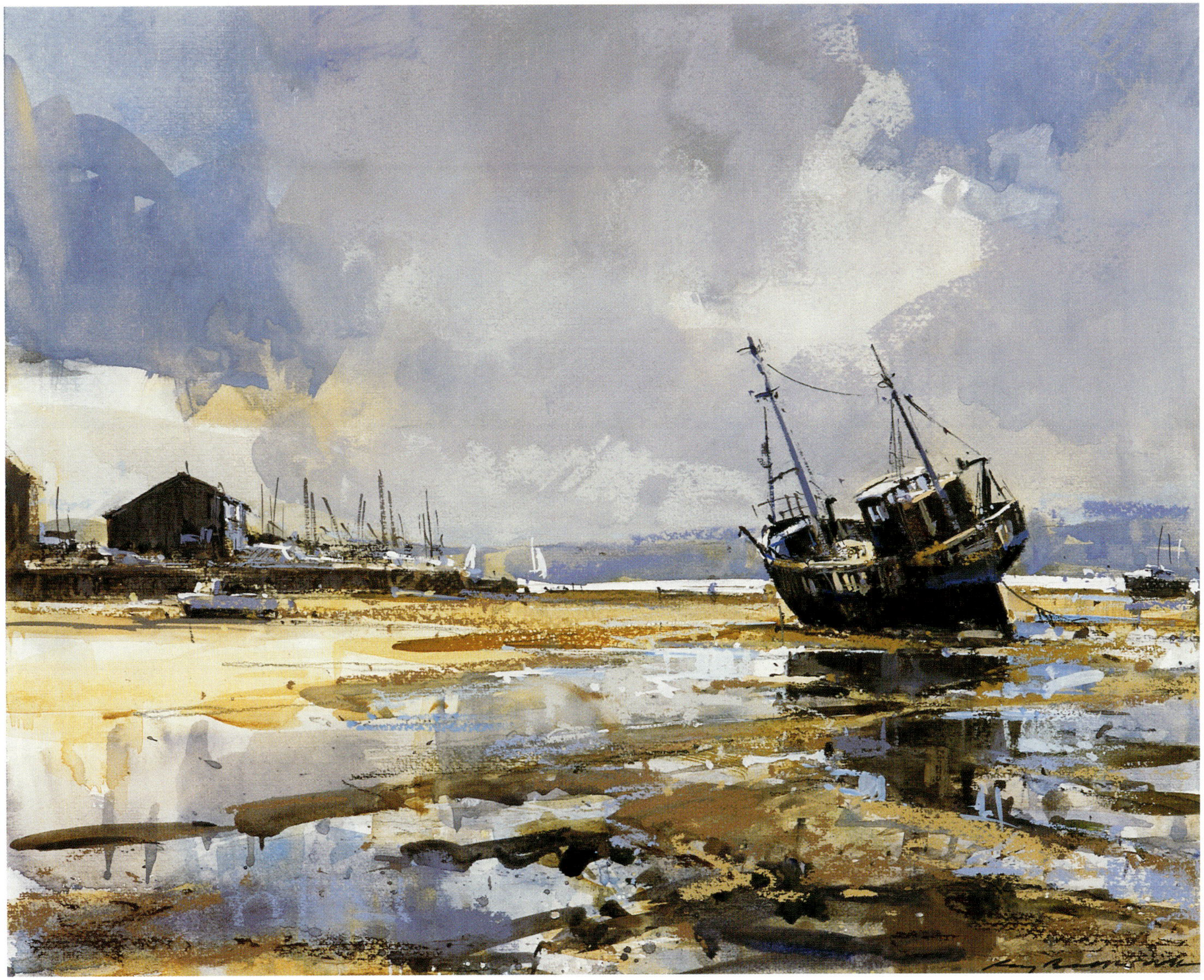

Fair and Bright, Exmouth
Mixed Media 12x14in (30x36cm)

This scene has changed considerably with the redevelopment around the docks. The Exmouth Sailing Club is still there of course, but the old trawler *Aline*, or E70 as it was also known, has long gone. It was always a great favourite with artists and also featured in many of my early watercolours of Shelly.

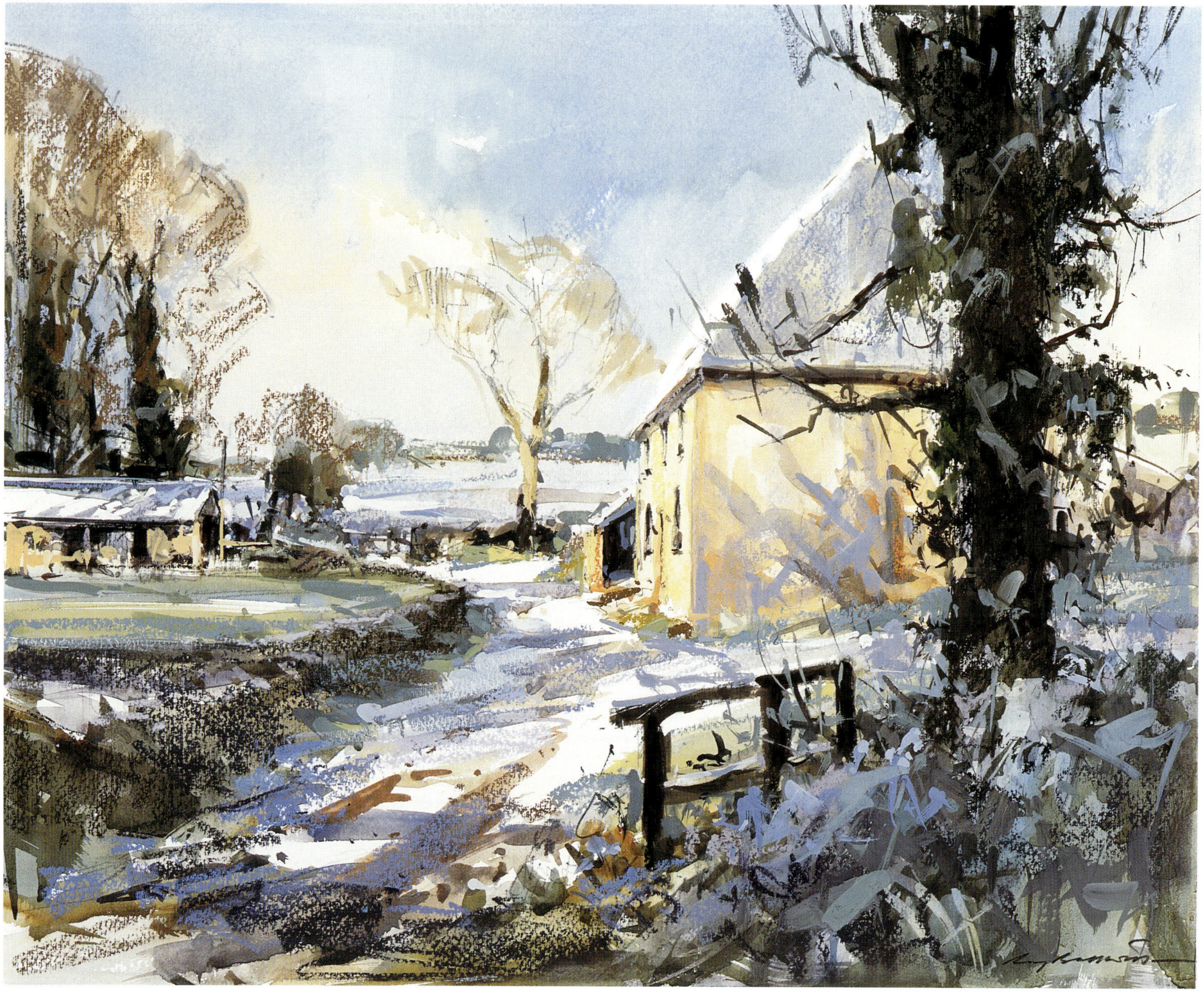

Last Snow of Winter, Middle Coombe Cottage
Mixed Media 14.5x17.5in (37x44cm)

Set in a deep valley next to Wootton Brook, this traditionally built cob and thatch cottage dates to about 1700 and was once used by the gamekeeper for the Harefield estate.

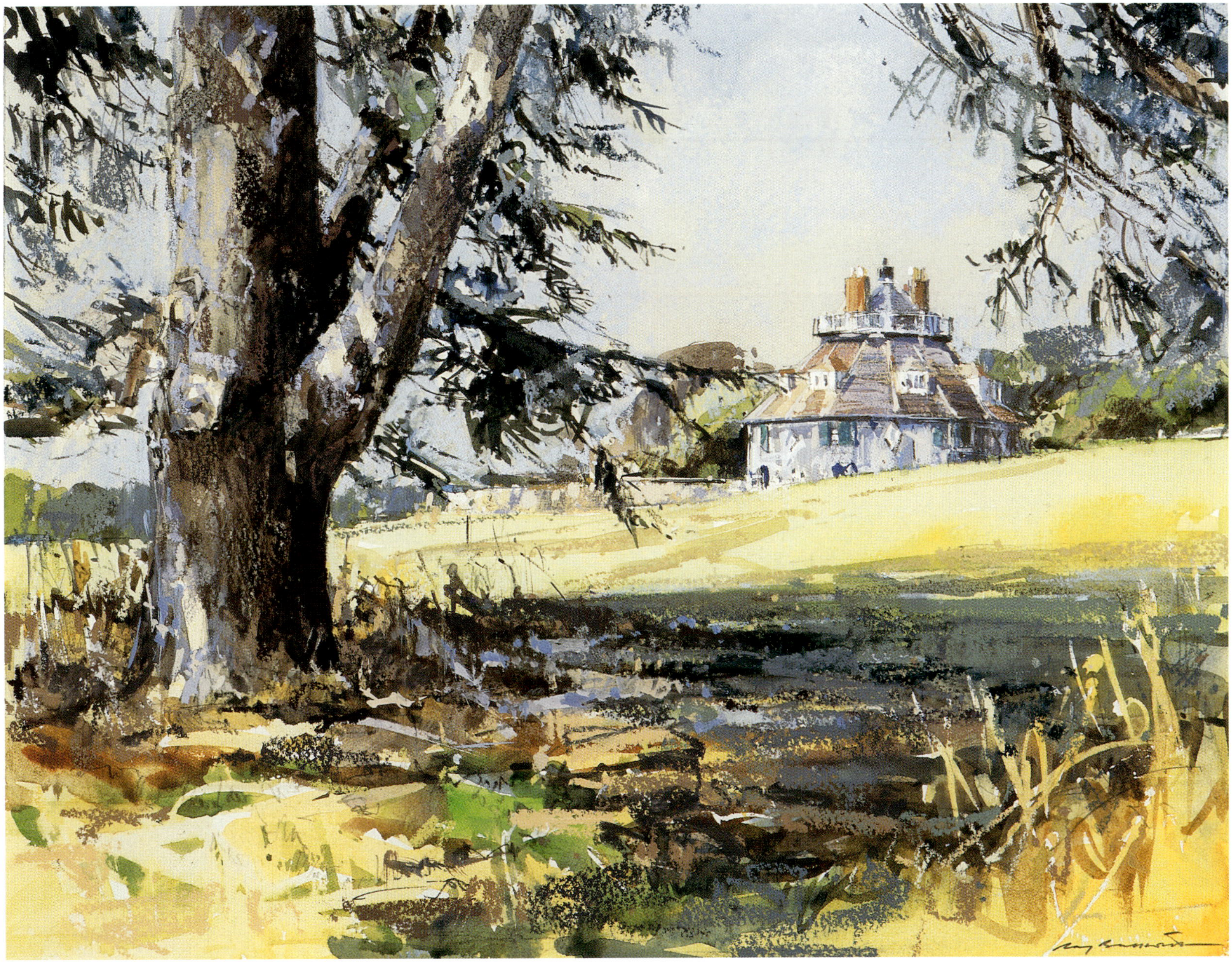

High Summer, A La Ronde
Mixed Media 12.5x16in (32x41cm)

This incredible eighteenth century sixteen-sided house was recently restored by the National Trust and is now open to the public. It was inspired by a church in Ravenna and built by Jane and Mary Parminter.

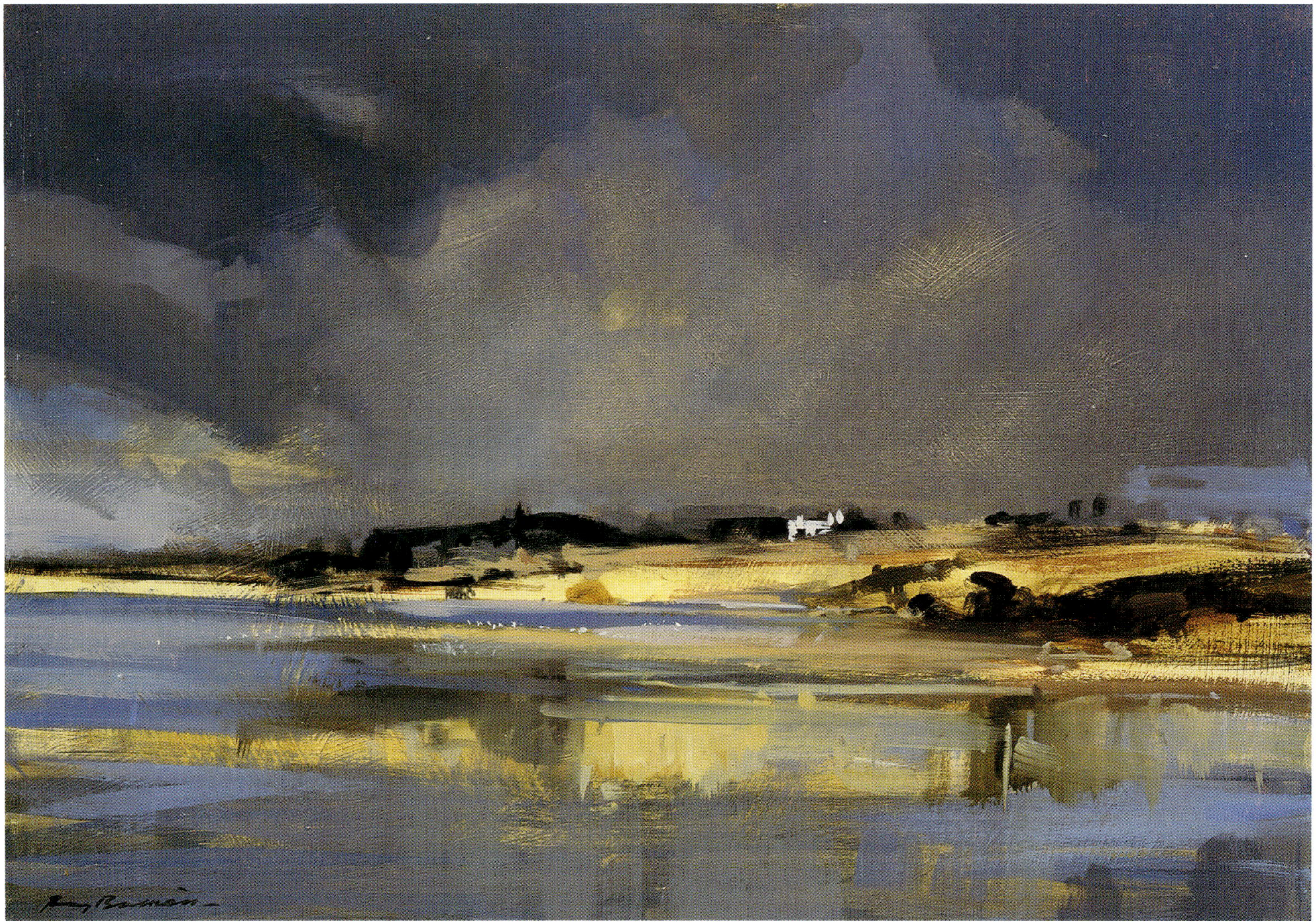

Rain-washed Sky over Courtlands
Oil 10x14in (25x36cm)

Set in vivid relief by the sun against a threatening sky stands Courtlands, named from the fields in which it this elegant mansion stands. This painting is dedicated to the memory of farmer Stanley Long who gave 44.5 hectares of farmland at Lower Halsdon, set below Courtlands, to the National Trust in 1995. In resisting pressures to sell the land for development, his generosity means that the land will be held by the National Trust to preserve the open views across the Exe estuary in perpetuity.

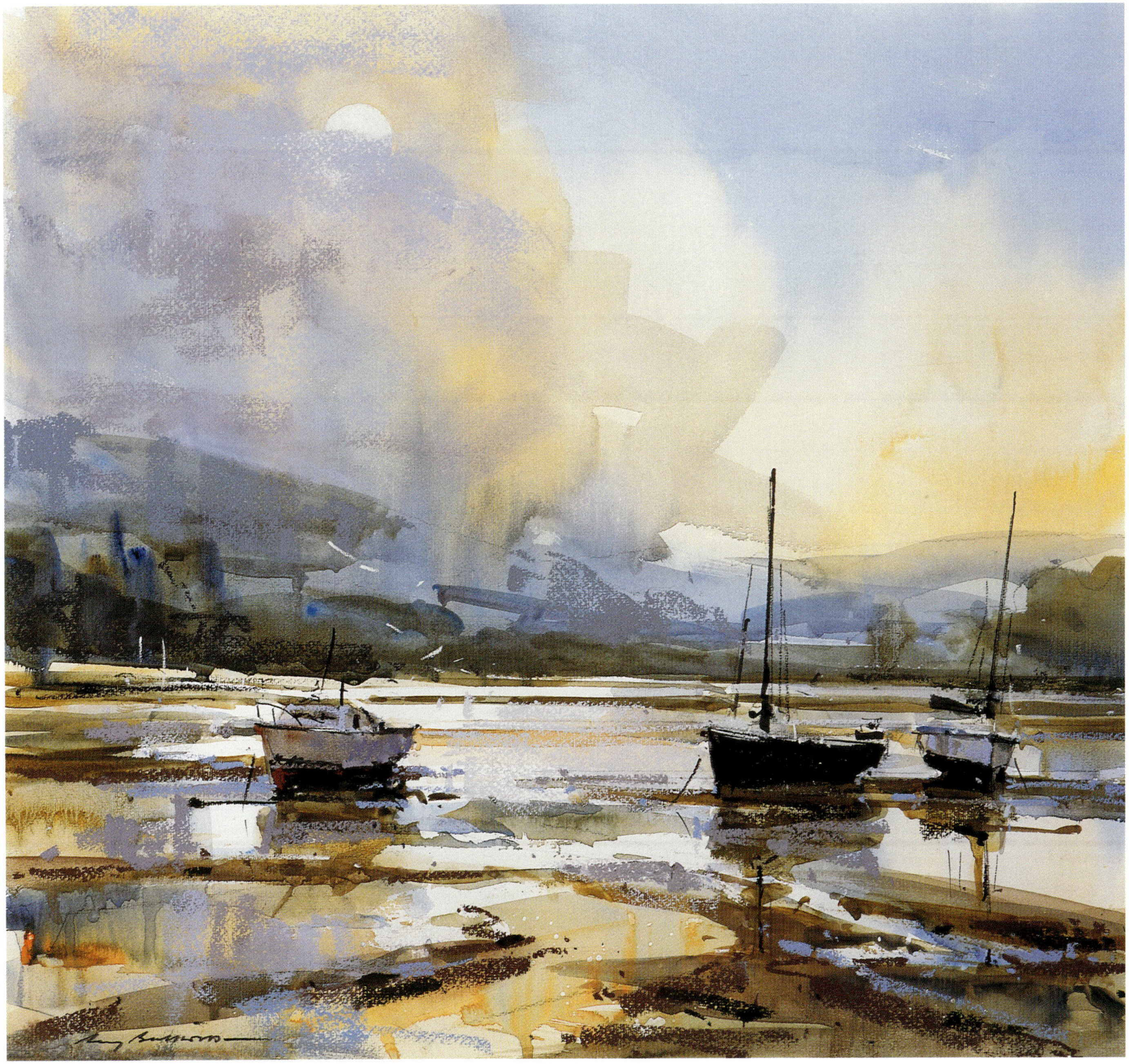

Setting Sun
Mixed Media 17x18in (43x46cm)

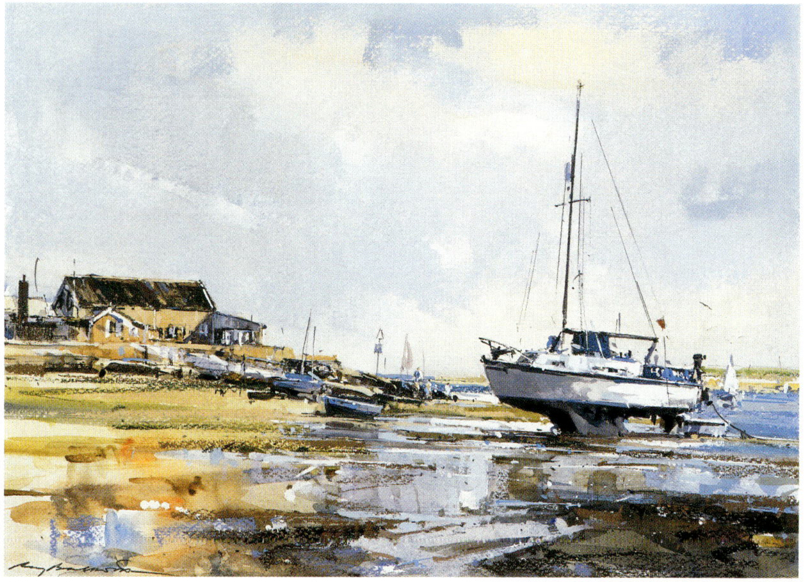

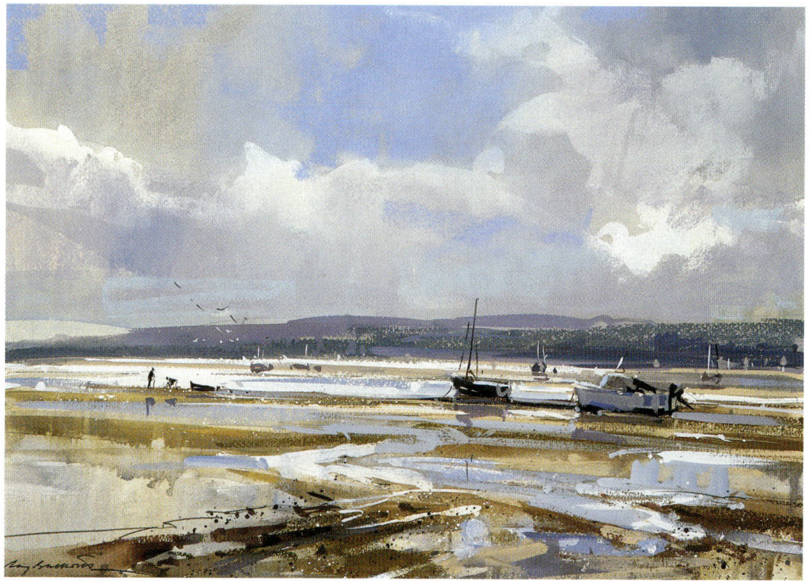

Clockwise, from above:
Incoming Tide, The Point
Mixed Media 12x16in (30x41cm)

Originally the chalets on Shelly beach were boat-sheds used for storing nets and fishing equipment. With the decline in fishing however, these then became holiday chalets and, in some cases, permanent homes. With the redevelopment of the dock area they are now just fond memories.

Bright and Blustery
Mixed Media 15.5x18.5in (39x47cm)

Rise Upon the Morning Tide, Exmouth
Mixed Media 12.5x17.5in (32x44cm)

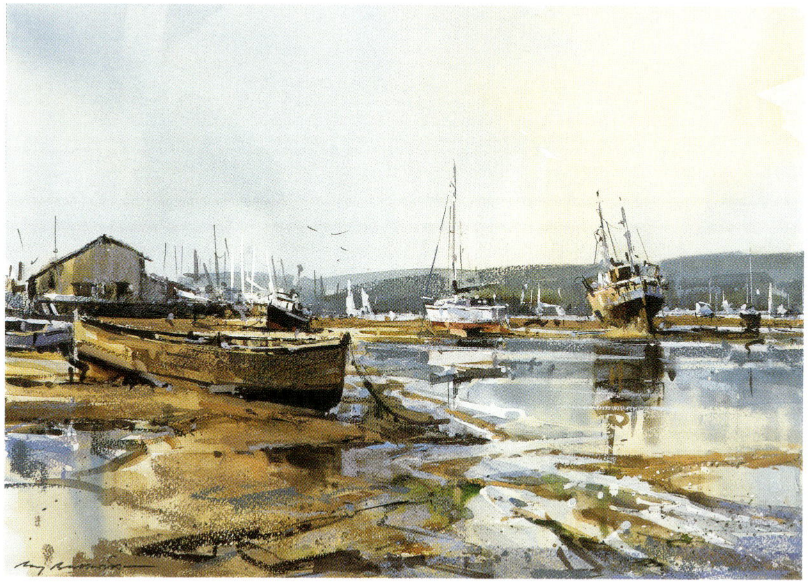

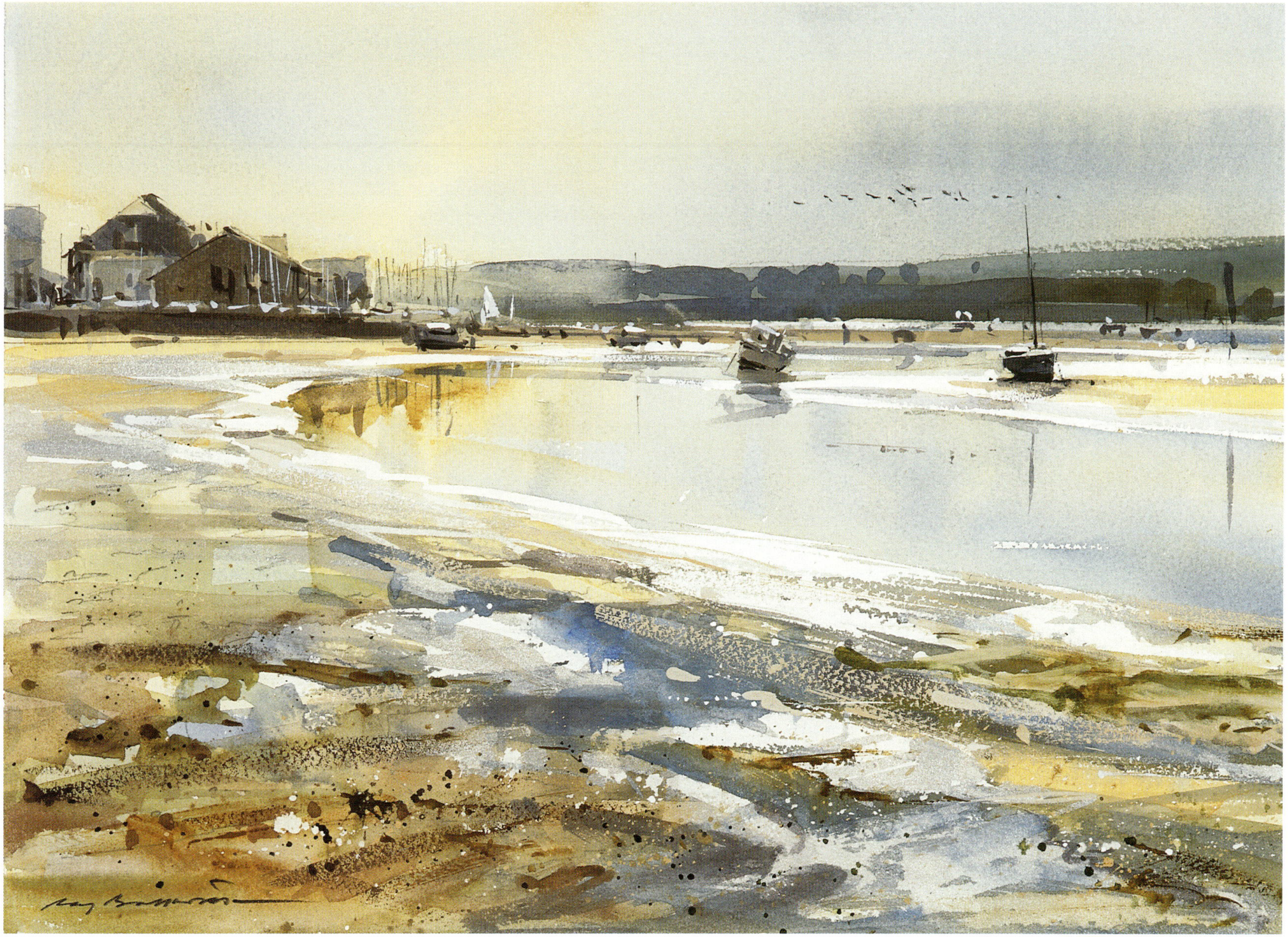

Morning Flight over the Exe
Watercolour 10x14in (25x36cm)

There is always a new delight awaiting the senses with this subject, whether it is the sharp piping calls of an Oystercatcher, or the 'bubbling' call of a Curlew. On this occasion it is the beating wings of a flock of Canada Geese as they pass over the estuary.

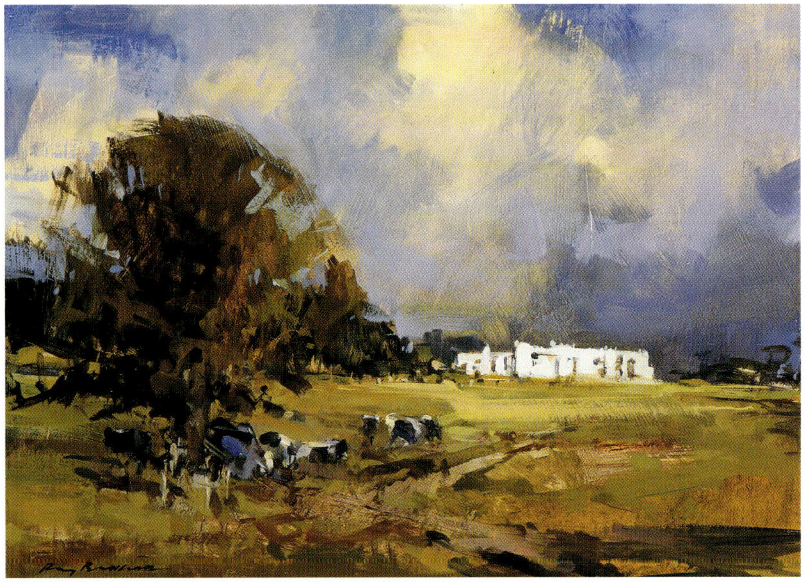

Between Showers, Harefield House (St Peter's School)
Oil 10x14in (25x36cm)

Set in its prominent position this grand house commands superb views of the estuary. The house has gone through many chapters in its history, including being a nursery school and country club. It is now a flourishing private school named after General Peters for whom the house was built in 1830.

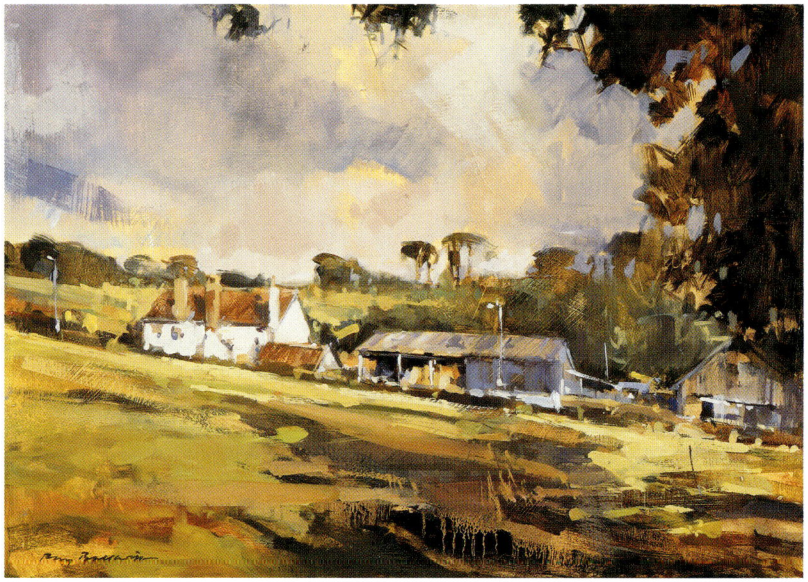

Across the Fields to Thorn Farm, Lympstone
Oil 10x14in (25x36cm)

Farming is an integral part of the estuary landscape and set beside the busy Exeter to Exmouth main road is Thorn Farm which dates back to the fourteenth century. It is now farmed by the third generation of the Bailey family, producing milk and beef.

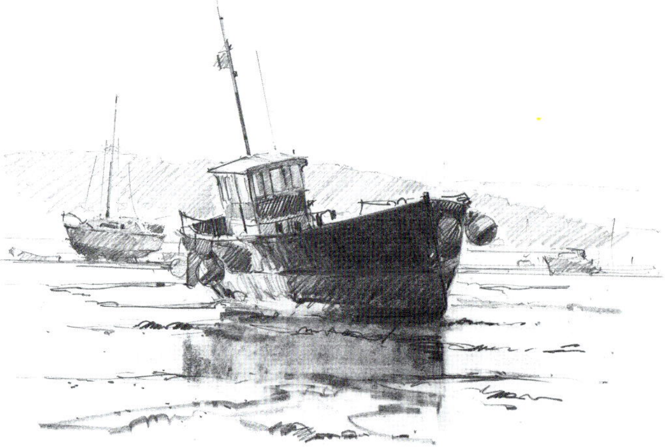

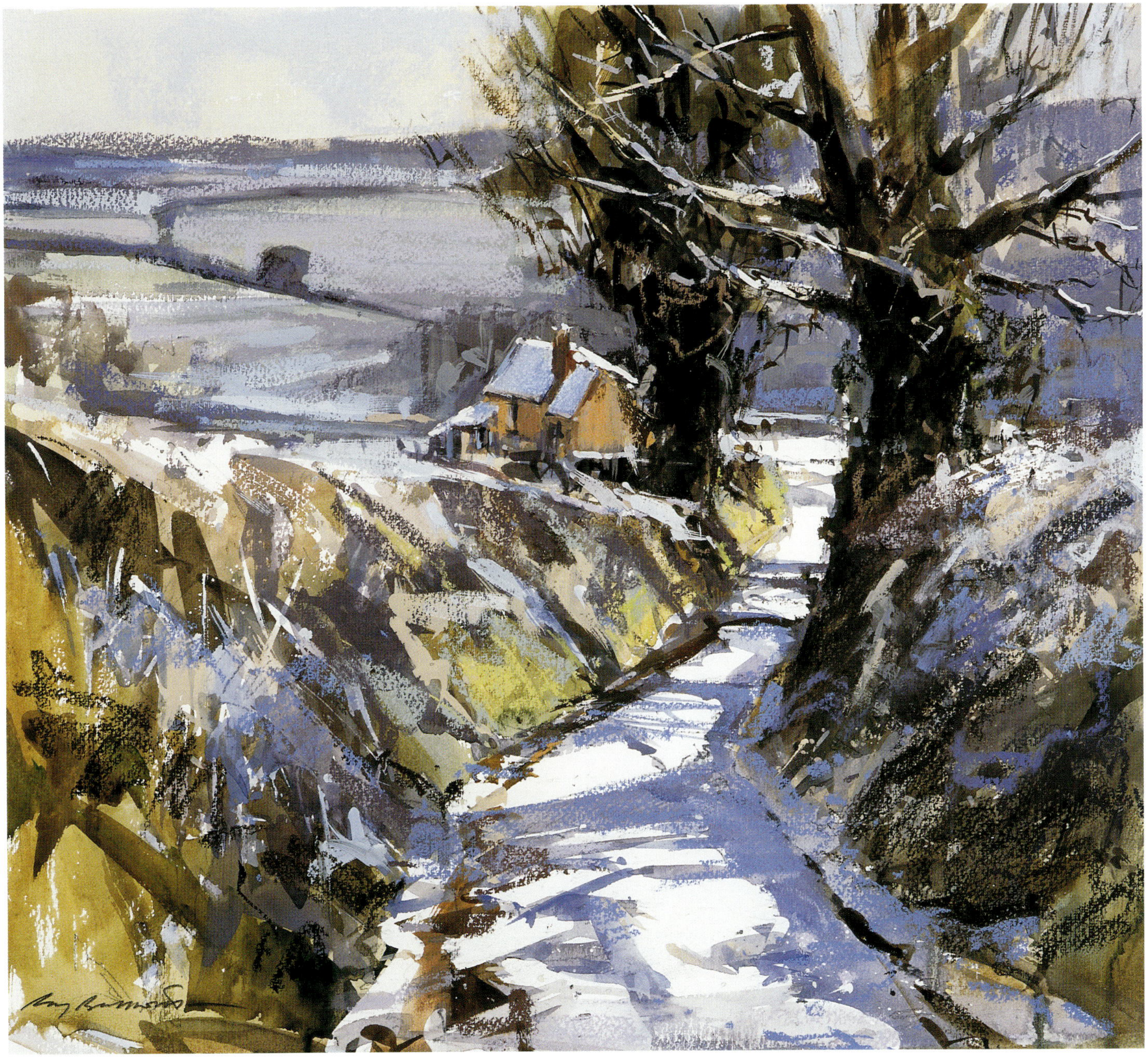

Down the Deep Lane to Middle Coombe Cottage
Mixed Media 15.5x17in (39x43cm)

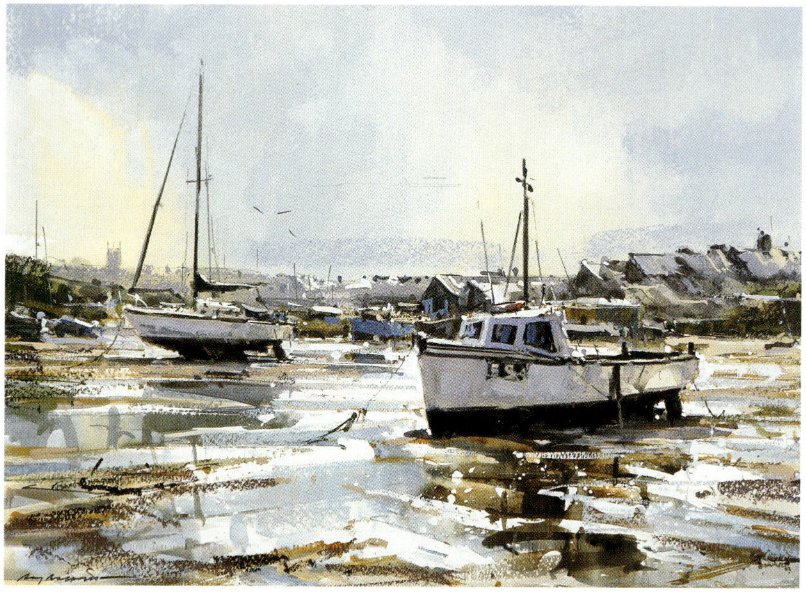

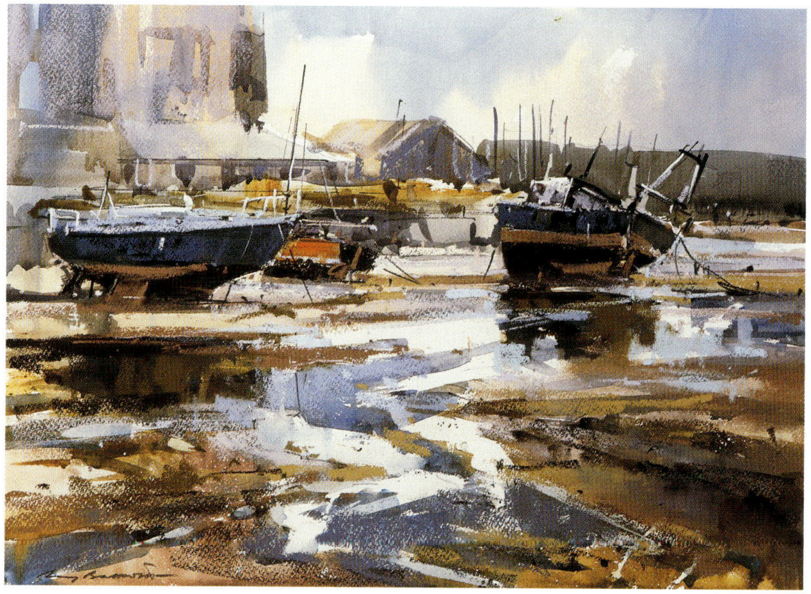

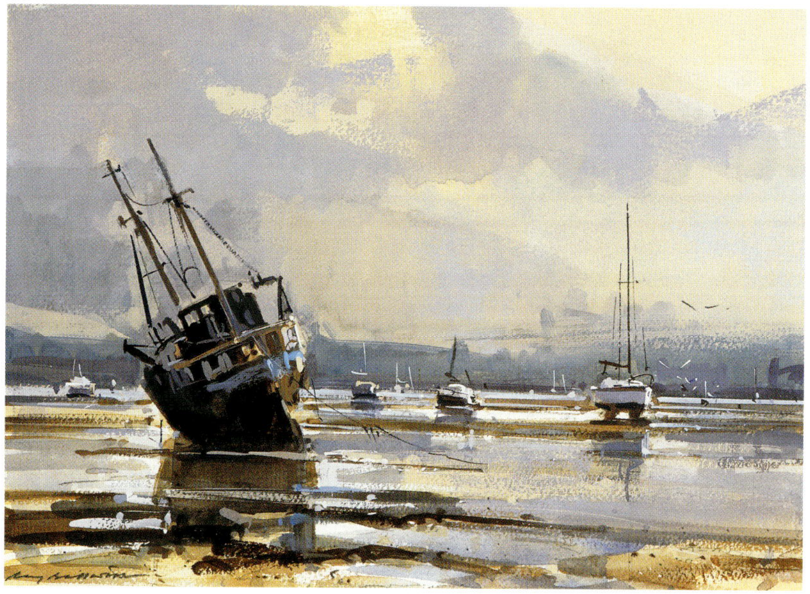

Clockwise, from above:
Bright Light, Shelly Gut
Mixed Media 15.5x17in (39x43cm)

Across the Creek
Mixed Media 13.5x19in (34x48cm)

Dusk on the Exe at Exmouth
Mixed Media 10x14.5in (25x37cm)

There are a thousand and one things to stir the imagination. And it's not only a visual feast: the sound of lapping water, the'popping' mud on a falling tide, the calling of gulls and the smell of seaweed – all this makes it one of the most satisfying subjects to paint.

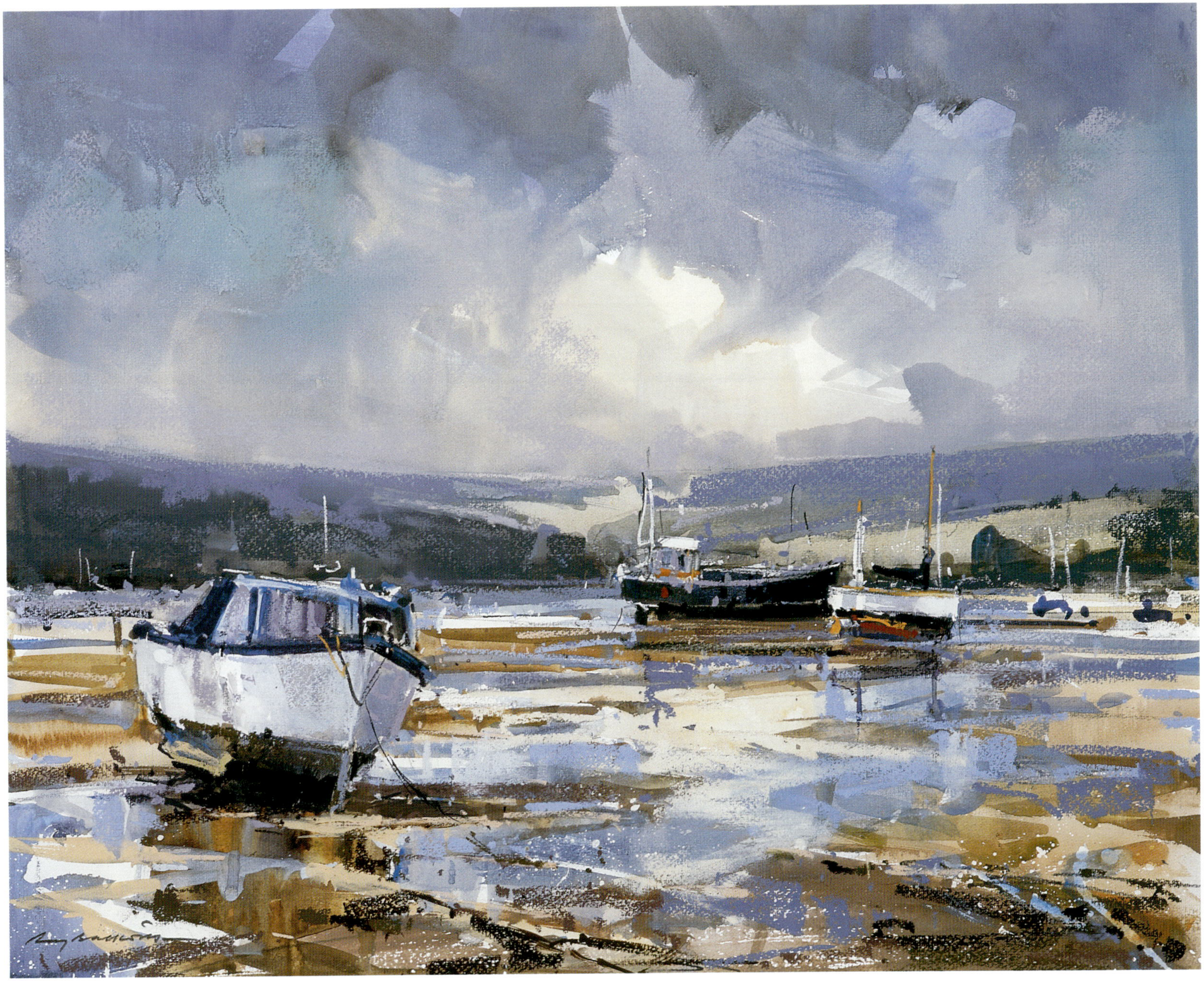

A Break in the Cloud, Exmouth
Mixed Media 16x20in (41x51cm)

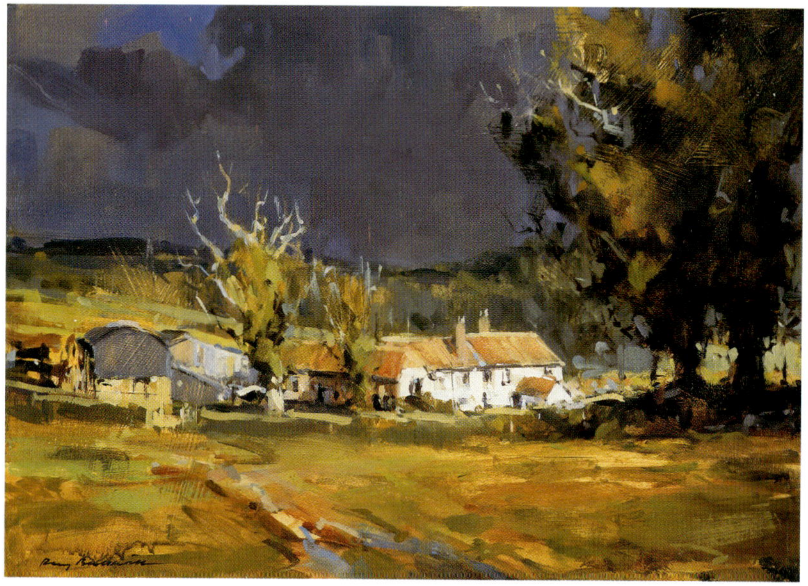

Rain Clouds over Lower Coombe Farm
Oil 10x14in (25x36cm)

Seen here against a dramatic sky, Lower Coombe Farm is set in a deep valley and forms part of the Harefield Estate. The farmhouse is of cob construction and the earliest records go back as far as 1219. As well as running the dairy farm, the Bailey family also provide B&B accommodation.

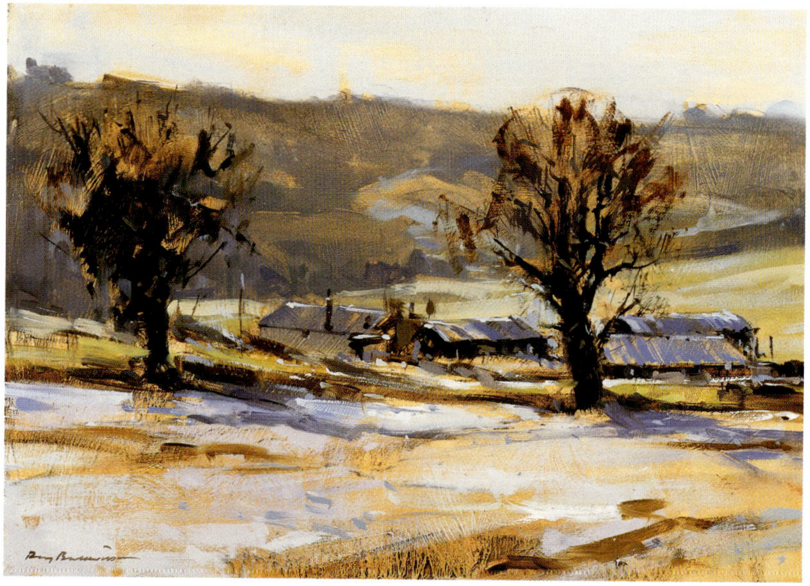

A Dusting of Snow, Lower Coombe Farm
Oil 10x14in (25x36cm)

I love the heightened quiet stillness that always seems to accompany a covering of snow. Here the air was broken only by the 'mewing call' of a soaring buzzard overhead.

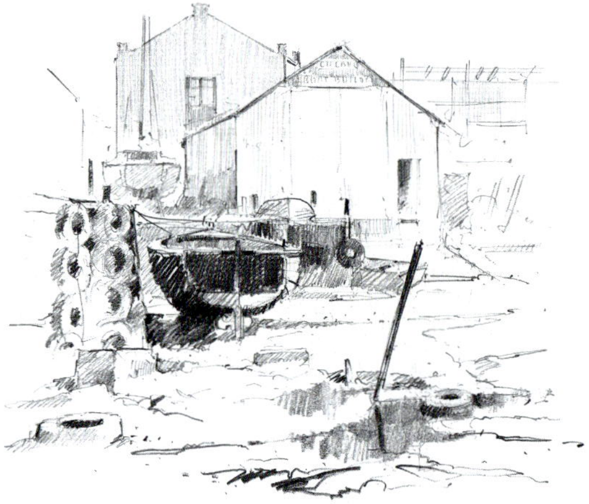

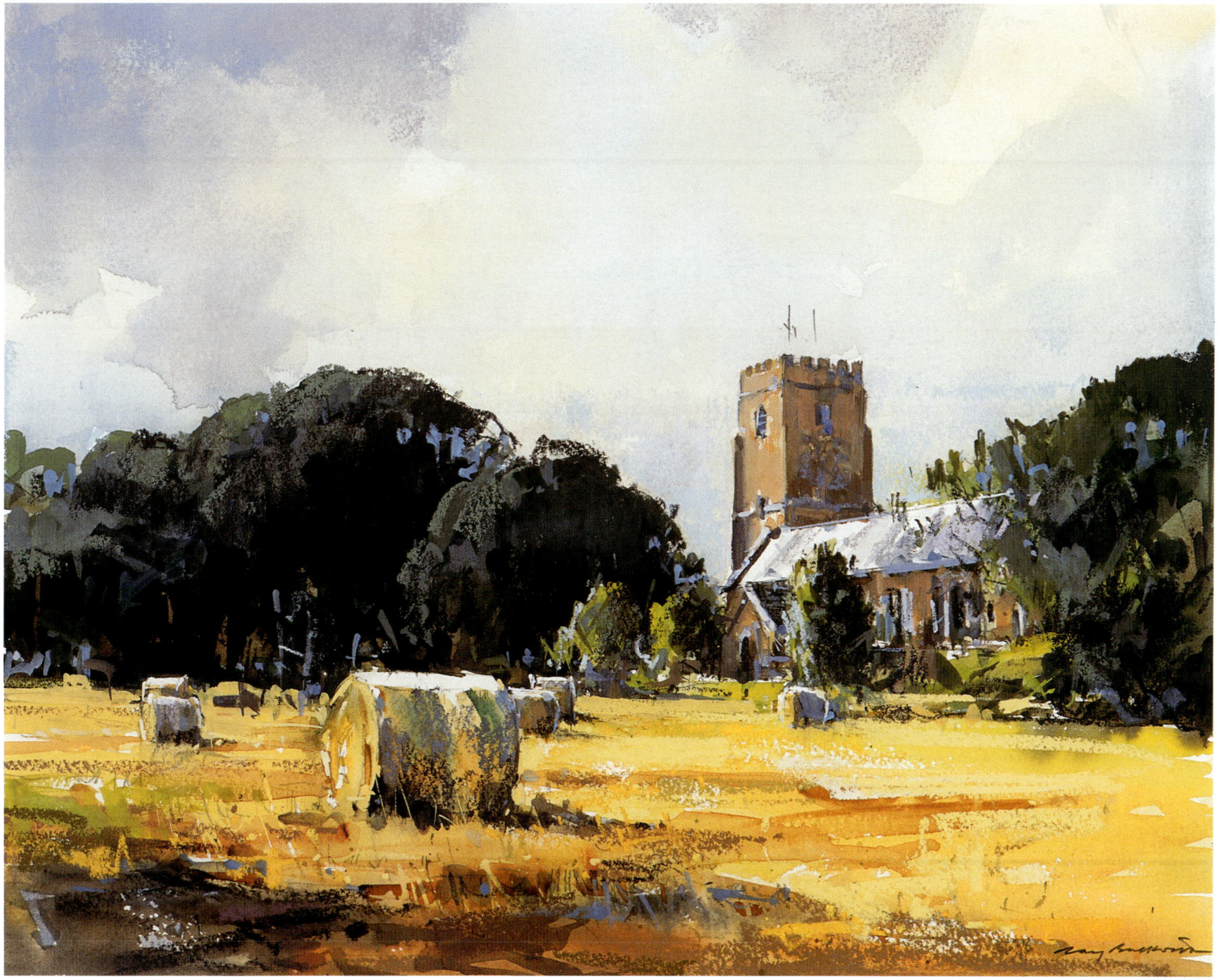

Golden Summer, St Clement's Church, Powderham
Mixed Media 13.5x16in (34x41cm)

St Clement's church is a small and unassuming red sandstone church, built in 1258 and located in a typically English setting close to the estuary and castle. It has a number of interesting features, and because of its position it has to be one of my favourite churches in the county.

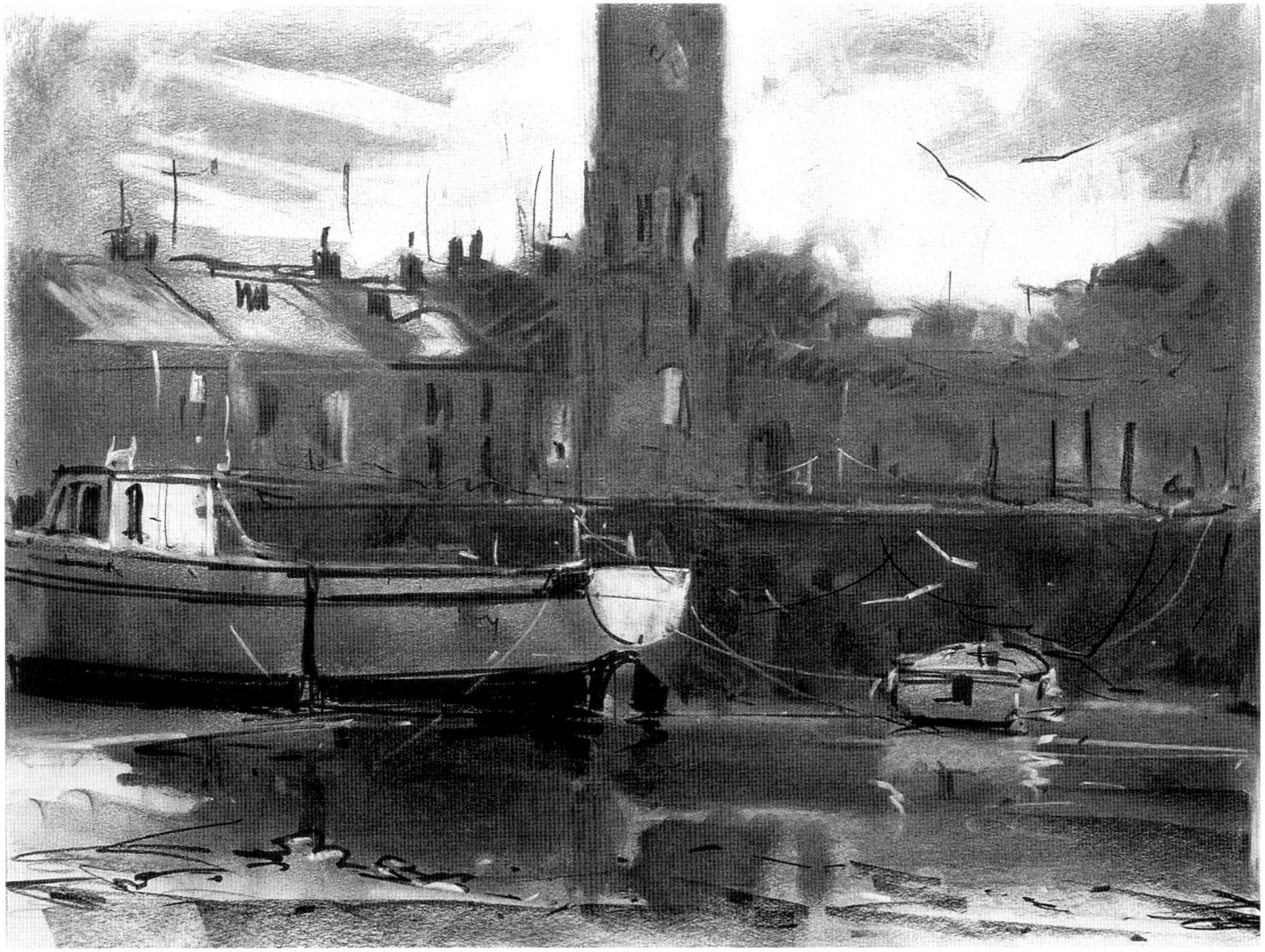

The Harbour, Lympstone
Charcoal Sketch 12x15in (30x38cm)

Sheltered by distinctive red cliffs, the harbour with its quaint fishermen's cottages is always popular with painters and tourists alike. This 36-foot launch was one of four built in Canada in the 1940s for the Antarctic Survey Ship *Endurance*. Because of its unique length Lympstone fisherman Doug Litton purchased it to catch herring.

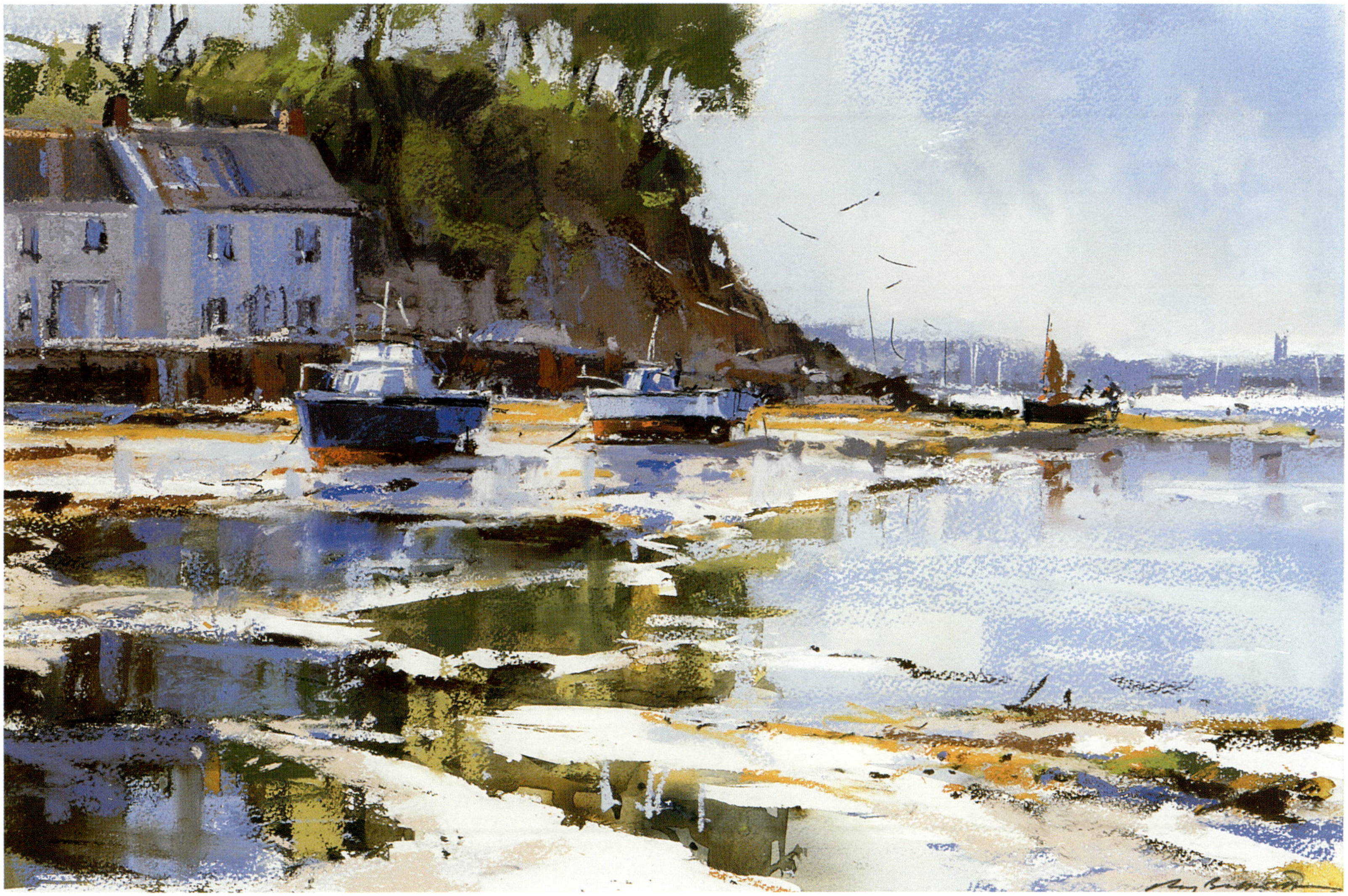

Water's Edge, Lympstone
Mixed Media 14x21in (36x53cm)

Fishermen's tales abound here and 'Snips' Stamp (his father was a tailor) was a master storyteller. He used to say *'…they crows over Cock-ood be educated crows!'* According to 'Snips' the crows would pick up mussels off the foreshore at Cockwood, fly to a great height and drop them on to the railway line, successfully breaking them open every time!

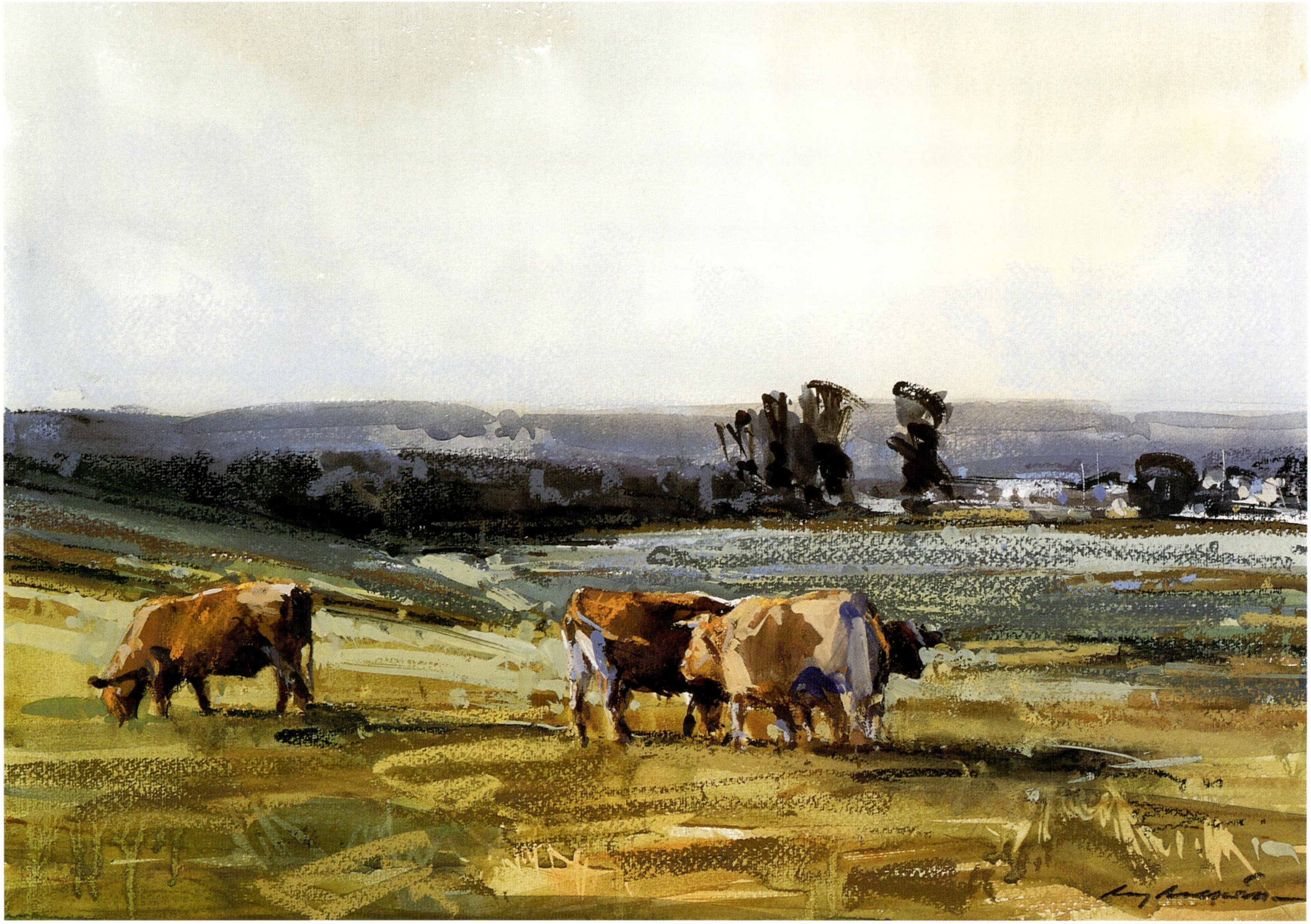

South Devon Reds at Powderham
Mixed Media 13x16.5in (33x42cm)

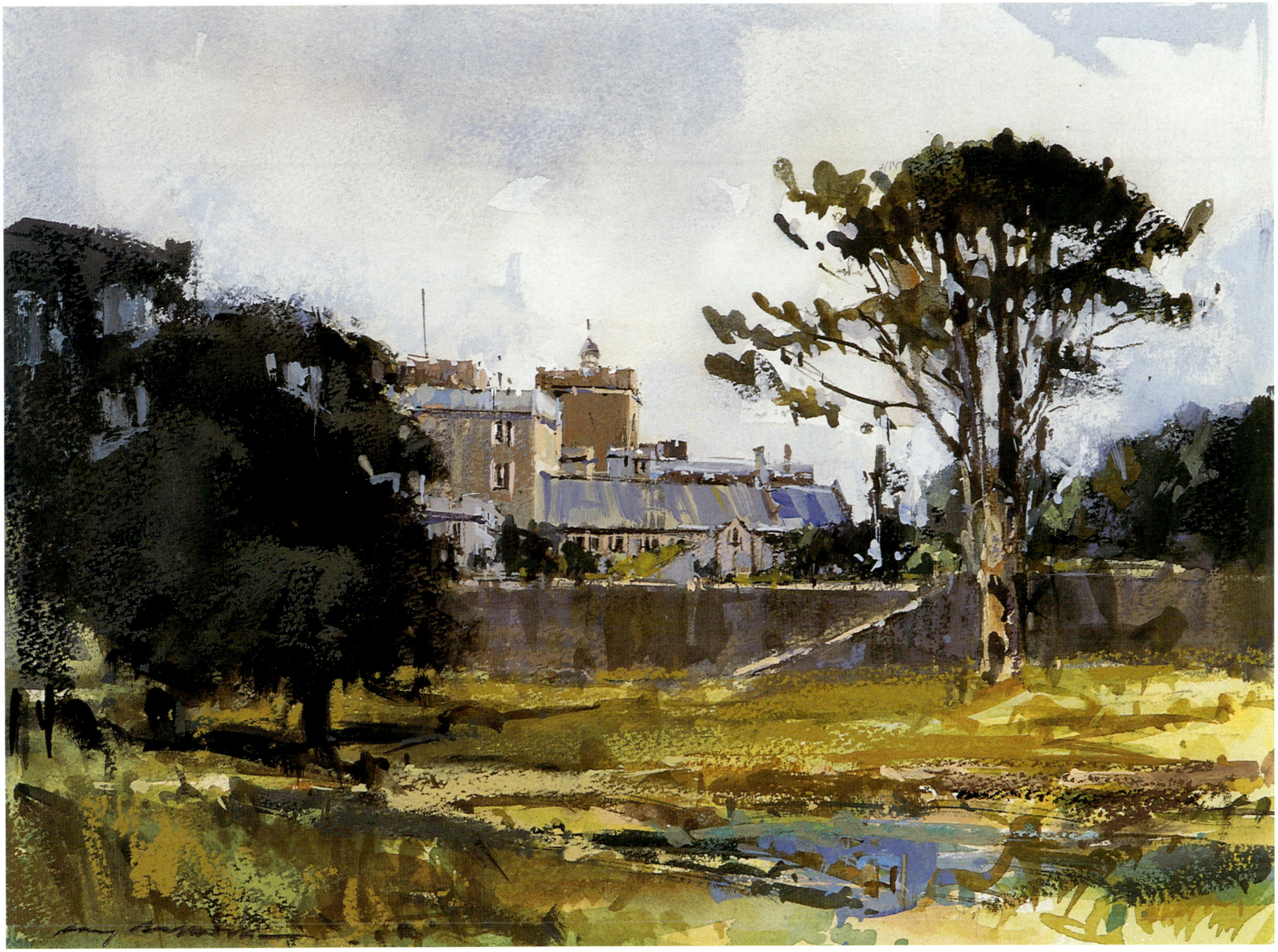

Powderham Castle
Mixed Media 9x12.5in (23x32cm)

Built by Sir Philip Courtenay, ancestor of the present 18th Earl of Devon in 1391, the castle withstood the ravages of the Civil War and was embellished in the eighteenth century. One of Devon's top tourist attractions, the castle hosts many functions and events throughout the year.

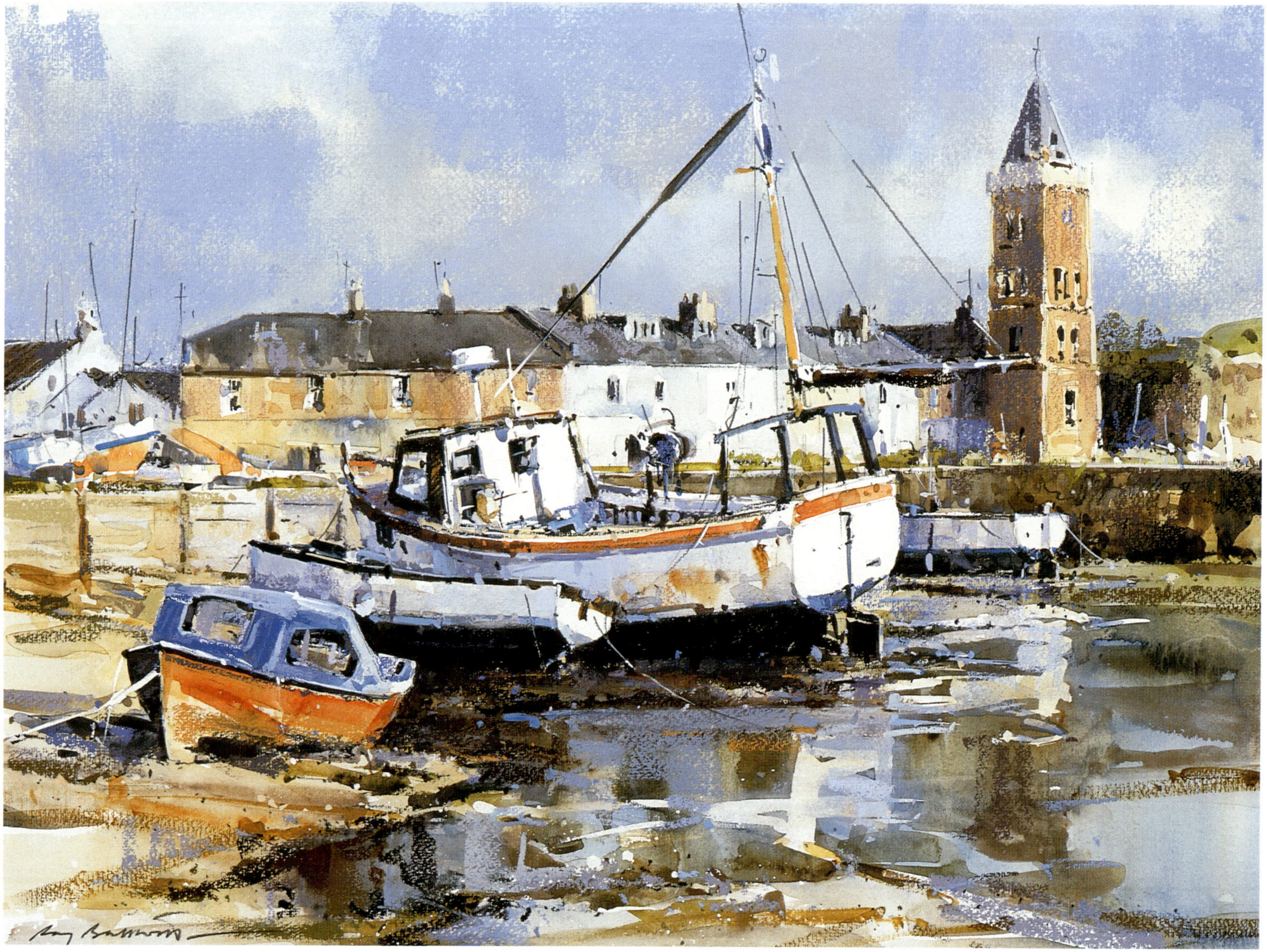

Peaceful Moorings, Lympstone
Mixed Media 13.5x18in (34x46cm)

A local landmark is the Italianate red brick clock tower built in 1885 by General Peters of Harefield House, as a memorial to his wife to mark her kindness to the poor.

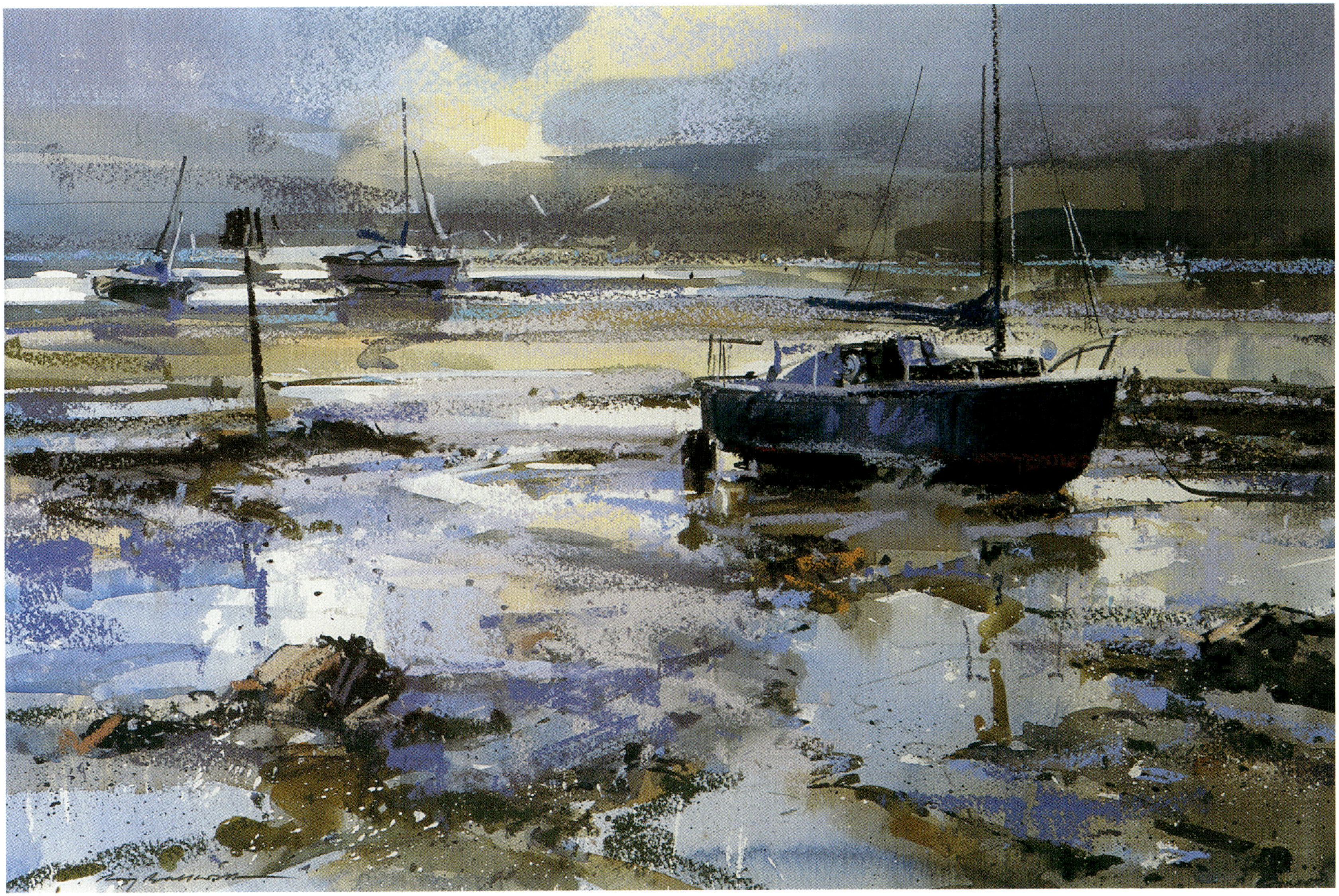

Low Tide, Lympstone
Mixed Media 14.5x21.5in (37x55cm)

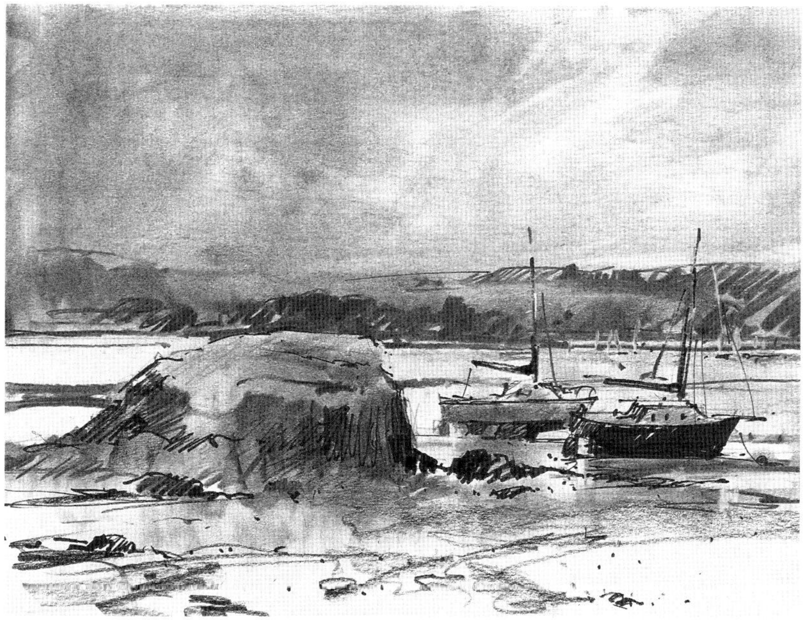

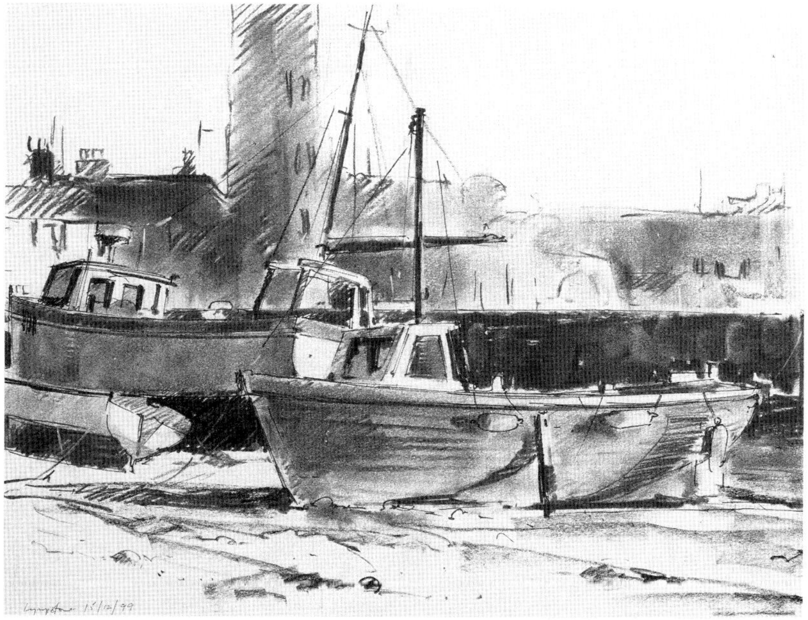

Clockwise, from above:
Darling Rock, Lympstone
Charcoal Sketch 9.5x13in (24x33cm)

Darling rock was once much larger and closer to the cliff than it is today, and it is hard to imagine this isolated stack being the site for cockfights and bonfires, as well as grazing sheep! Now on fuller tides it is almost covered. The are many stories as to the origin of its name but one story tells of how the wives of the fishermen once gathered on the rock, singing songs to guide the fishing fleet back to port in a thick fog. As the fleet came within earshot one man shouted in relief *'...there's me darling!'* and thus the rock acquired its name.

Boats in Lympstone Harbour
Charcoal Sketch 12x15in (30x38cm)

The Harbour
Charcoal Sketch 12x16in (30x40cm)

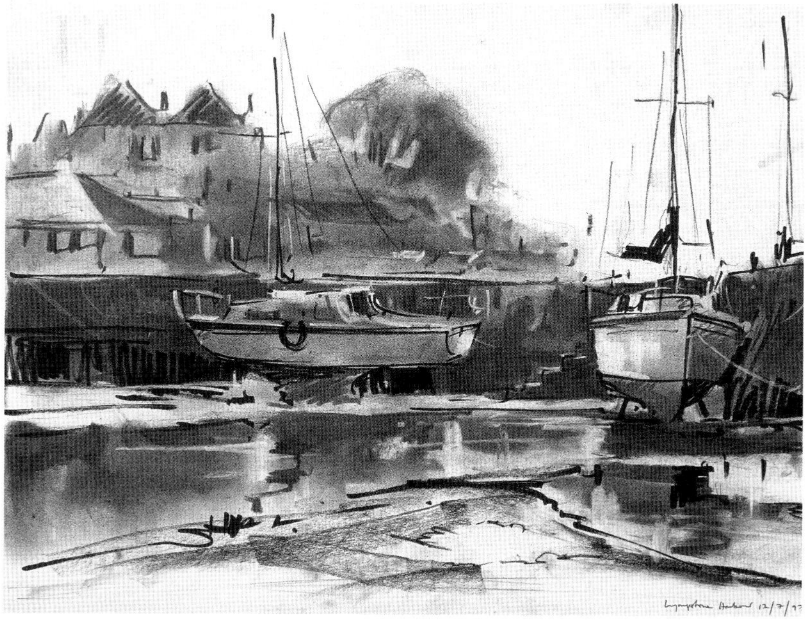

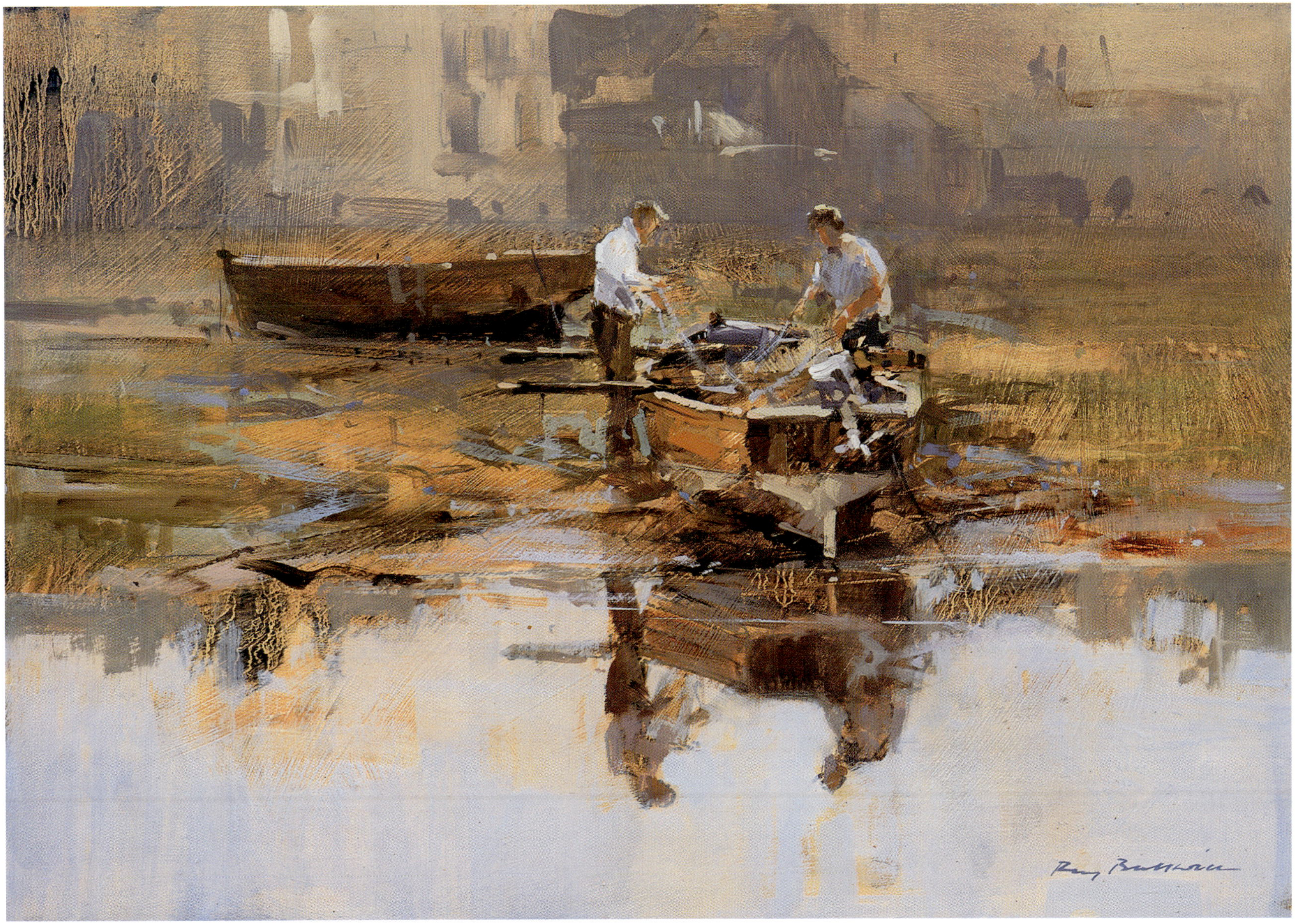

Cleaning the Nets
Oil 10x14in (25x36cm)

Here is another old Lympstone yarn. In the days of sail the mackerel fishermen of Lympstone would arise at 3am and hold a lighted candle out of the window. If it blew out then there was too much wind and if it did not then there wasn't enough. So they didn't go out at all!

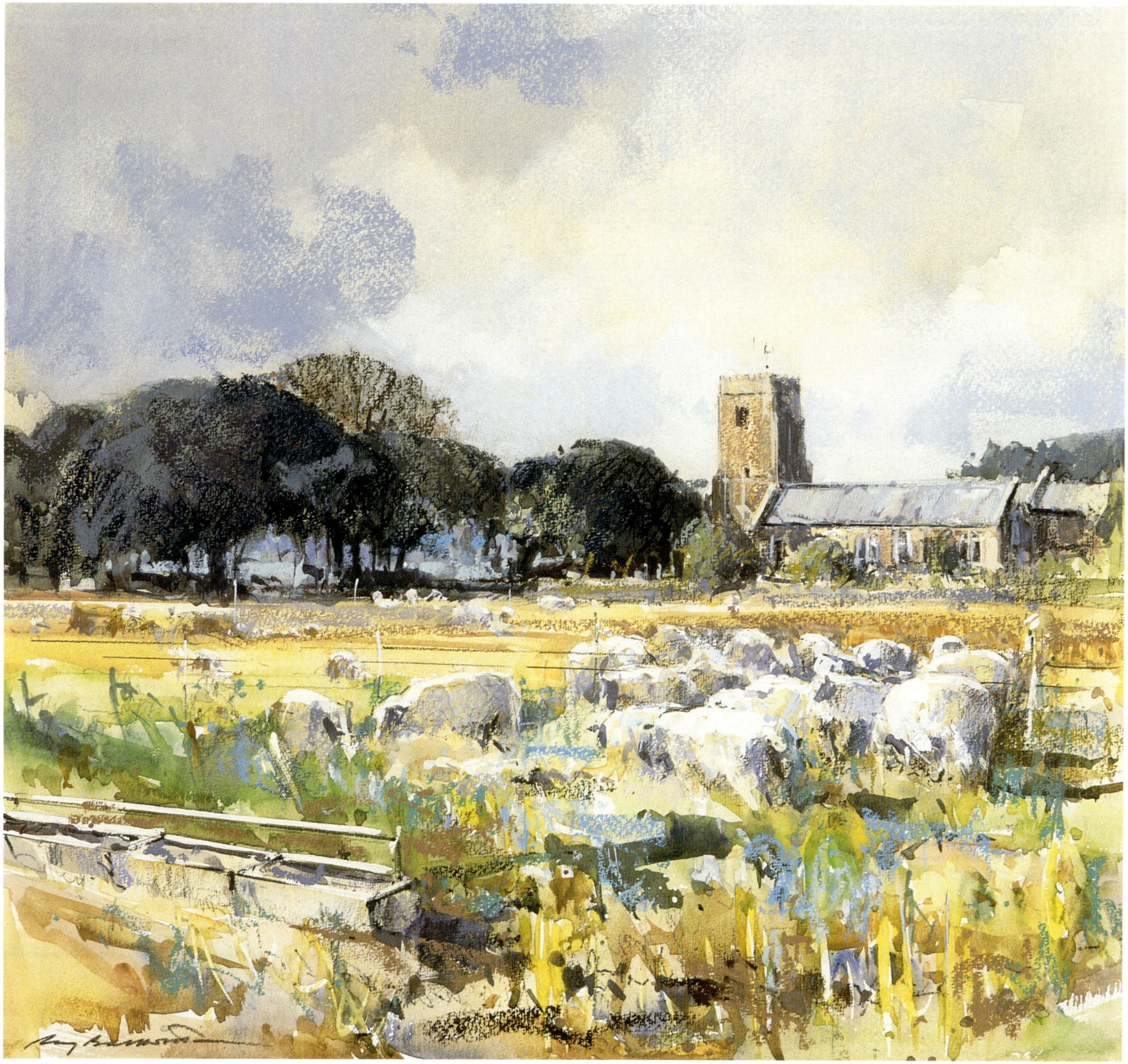

Sheep Feeding on Kale at Powderham
Mixed Media 13.5x14in (34x36cm)

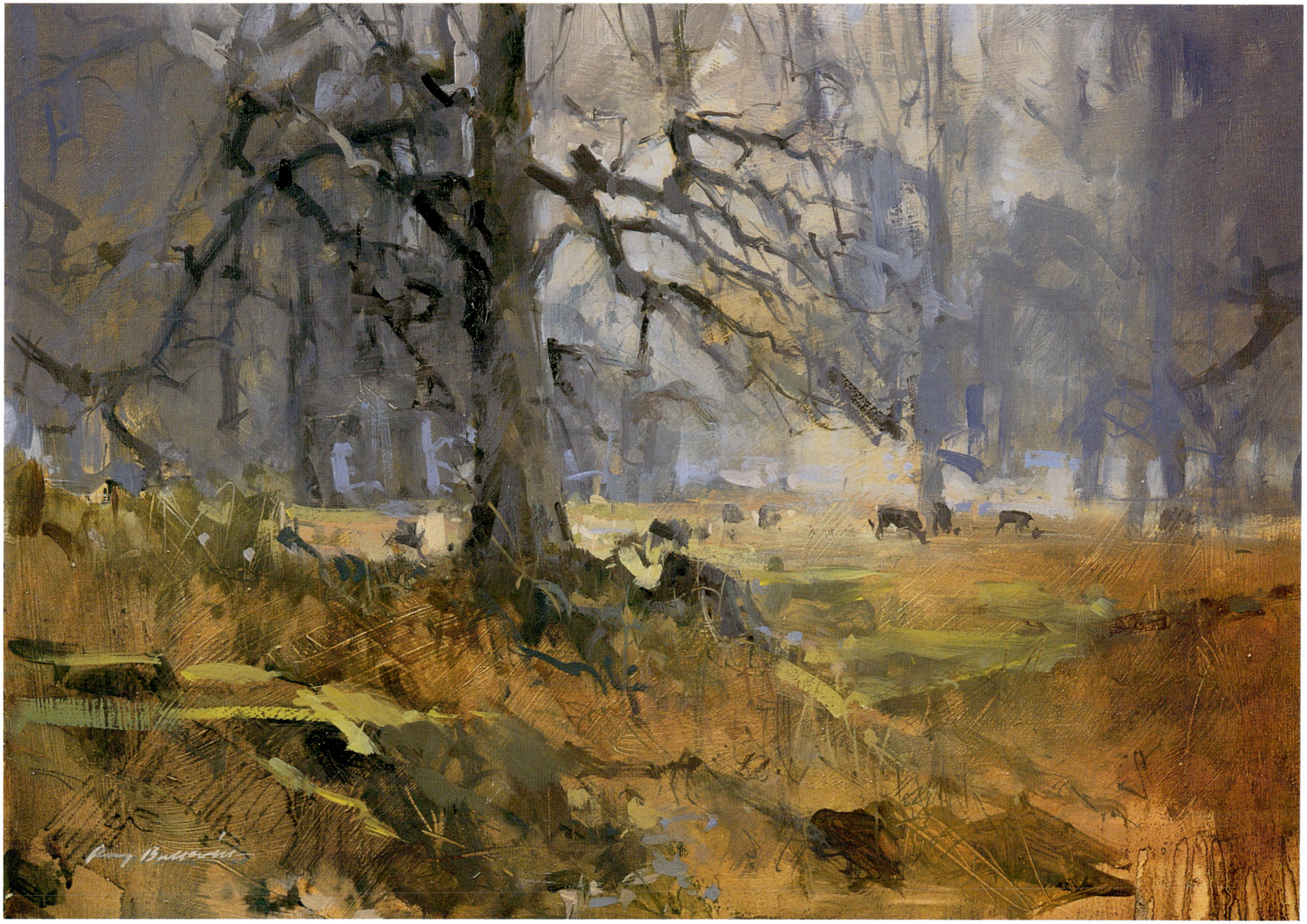

Fallow Deer at Powderham
Oil 10x14in (25x36cm)

Autumn has a passing beauty all of its own; the harvest and hunter's moon, woodsmoke, falling leaves, dew-laden cobwebs and pheasants scurrying amongst the bracken and brambles. The herd of fallow deer at Powderham Castle can be traced back to at least the seventeenth century.

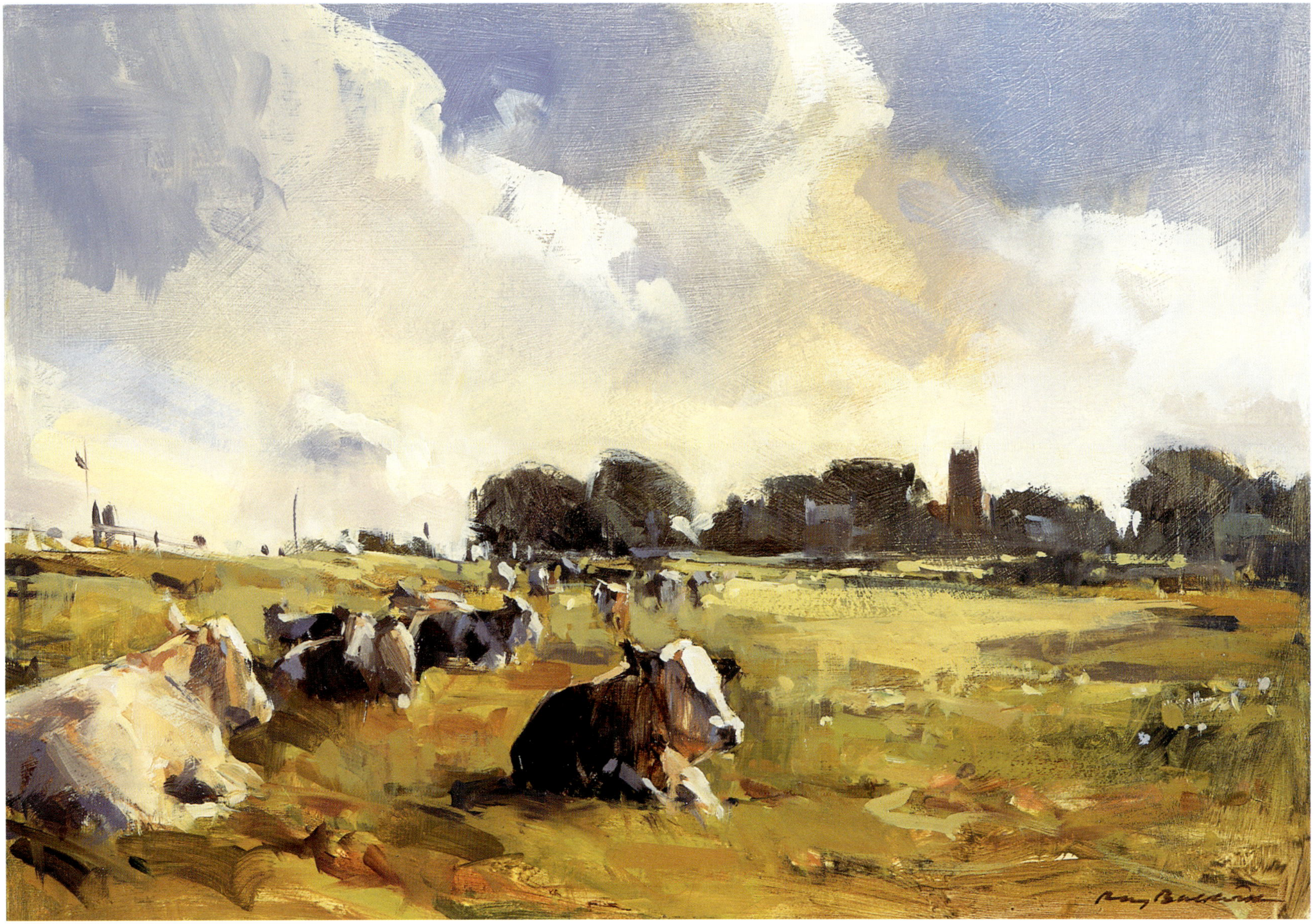

Billowing Sky over Powderham
Oil 10x14in (25x36cm)

The enormous oak trees that shade the church entrance have yielded up many cannon balls – relics of the Civil War, when Cromwell's troops besieged and occupied both castle and church.

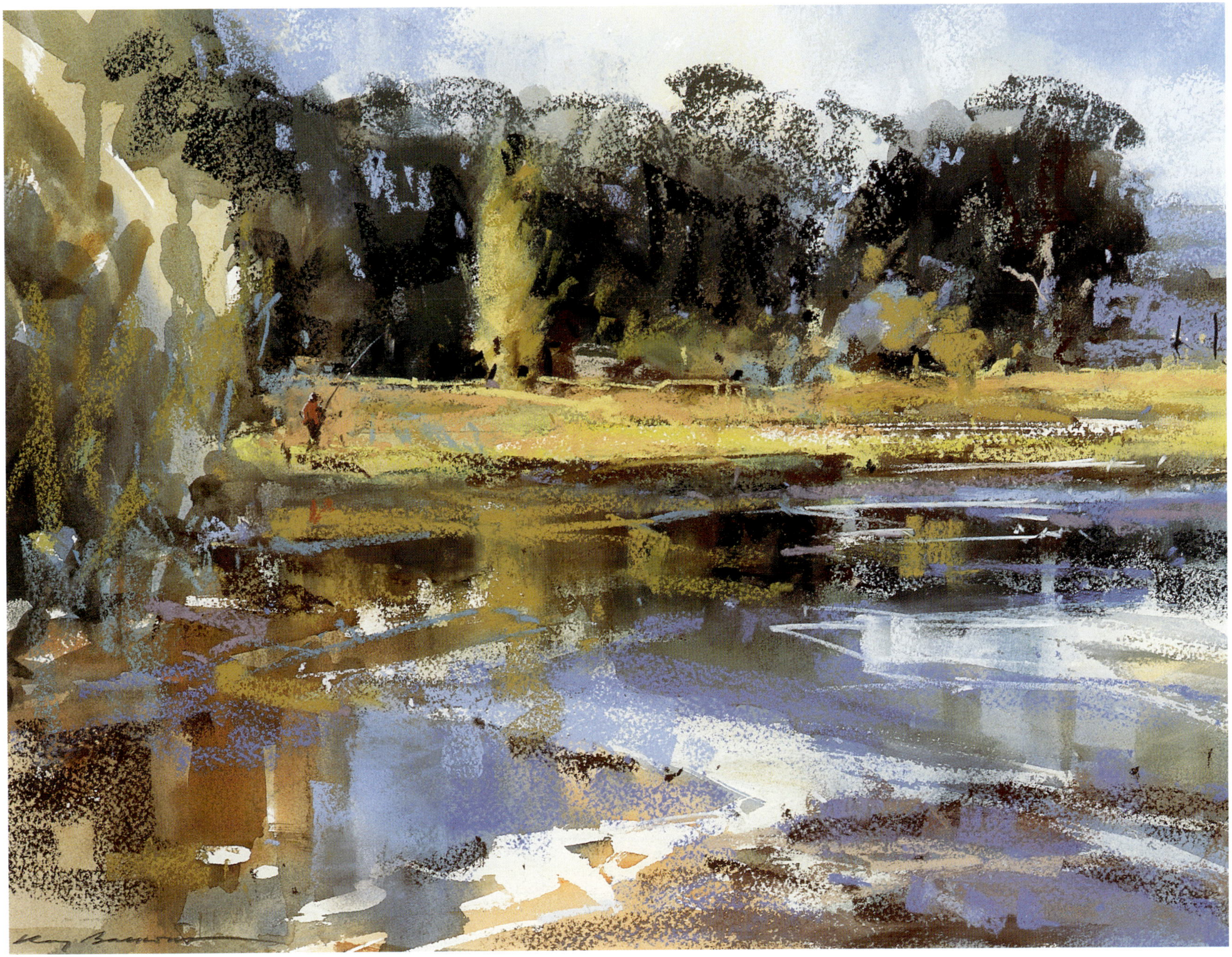

The Lake, Powderham Castle
Mixed Media 13.5x17.5in (34x45cm)

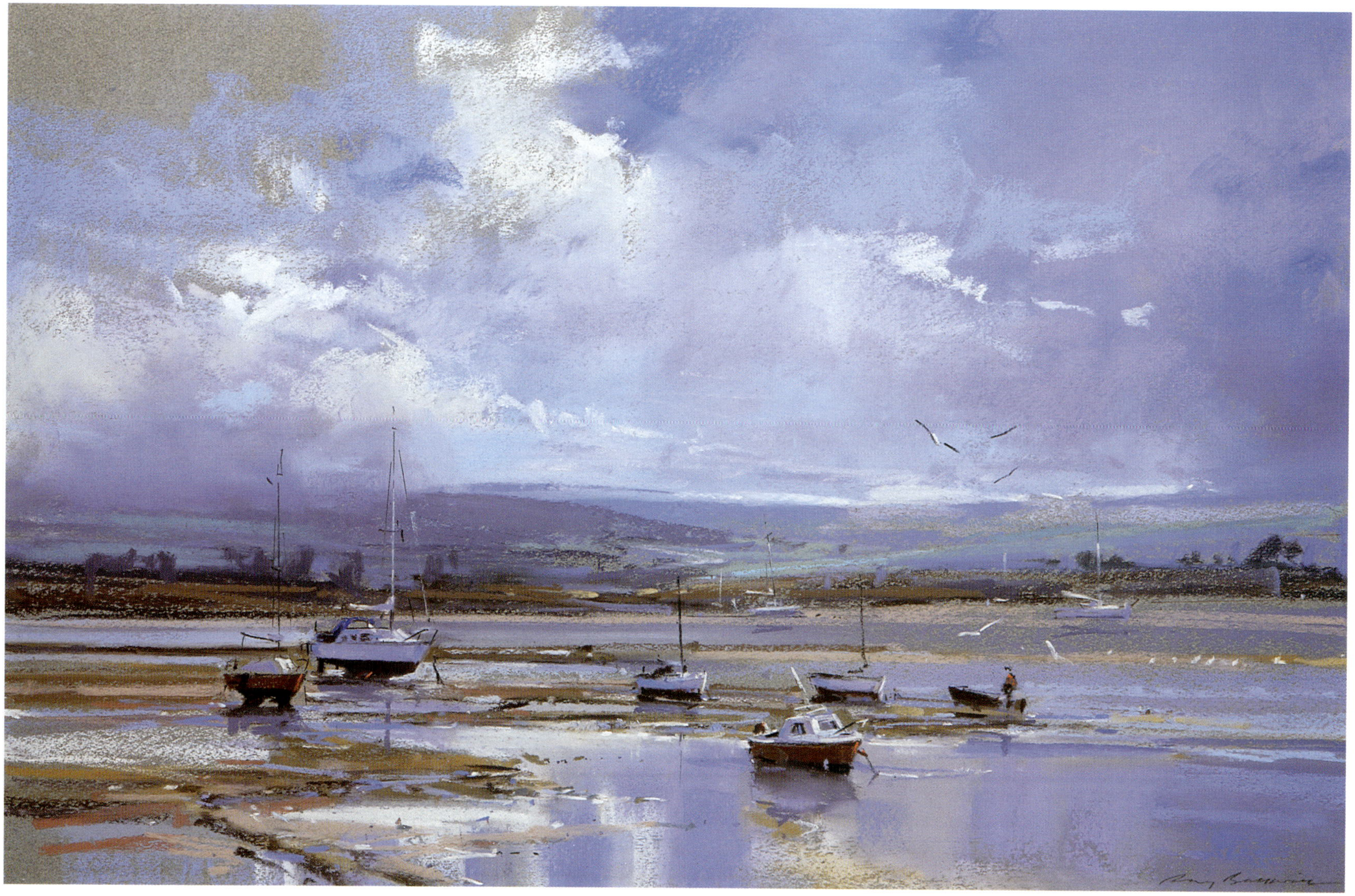

Across the Estuary from Lympstone
Pastel 14x21in (36x53cm)

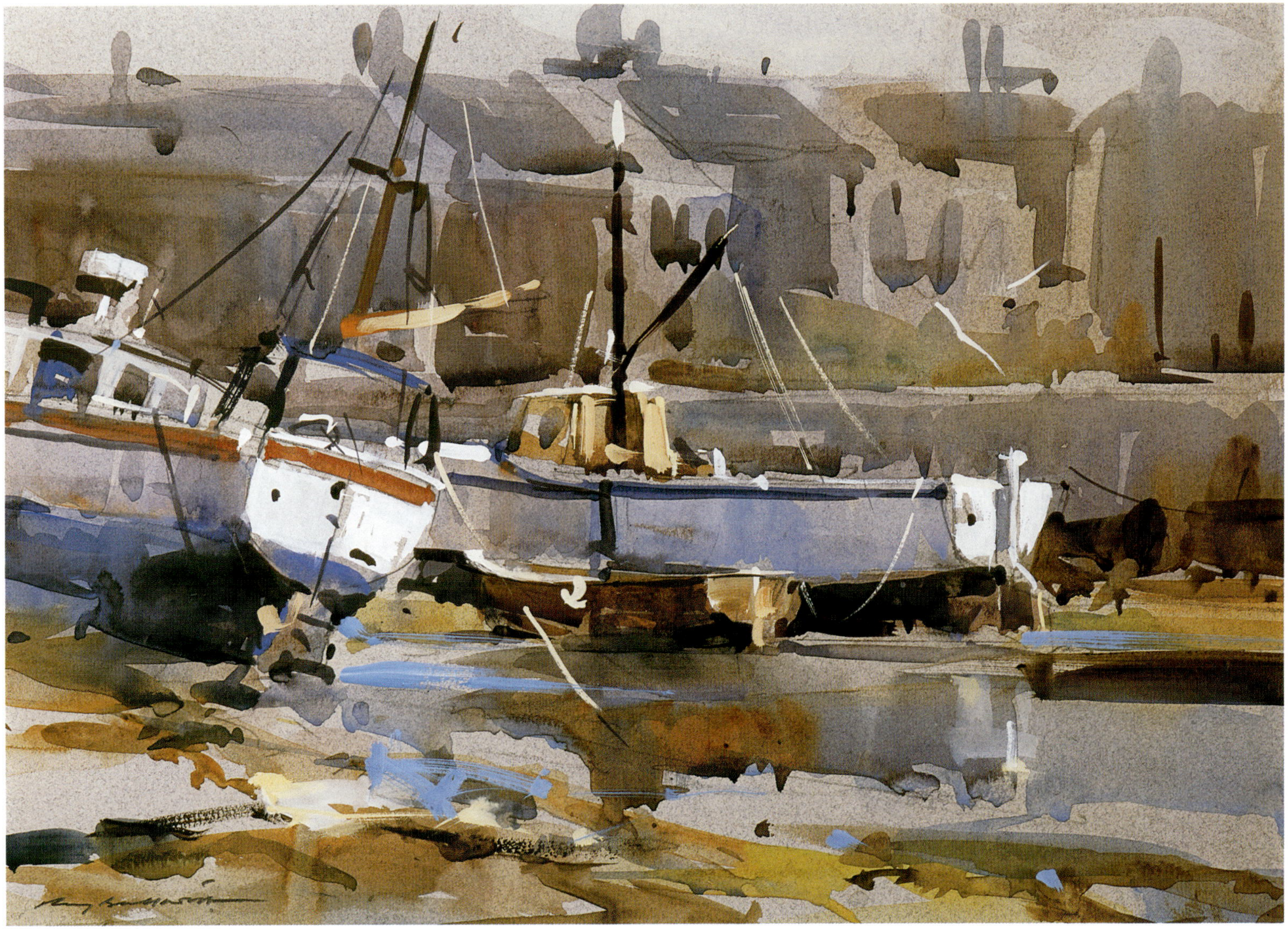

Lympstone Harbour
Watercolour/Gouache Location Study 12x14in (26x36cm)

This quick location sketch, done on a tinted paper, shows the *Compass Rose* on the left, a Cornish crabber built in Polruan, Cornwall. Lympstone was once an important shipbuilding and fishing port and records show that the village was accessible to larger ships in those days. By 1846 the largest vessels to use Lympstone were the coal lighters, with a draft of six feet, which used to moor up to Darling Rock.

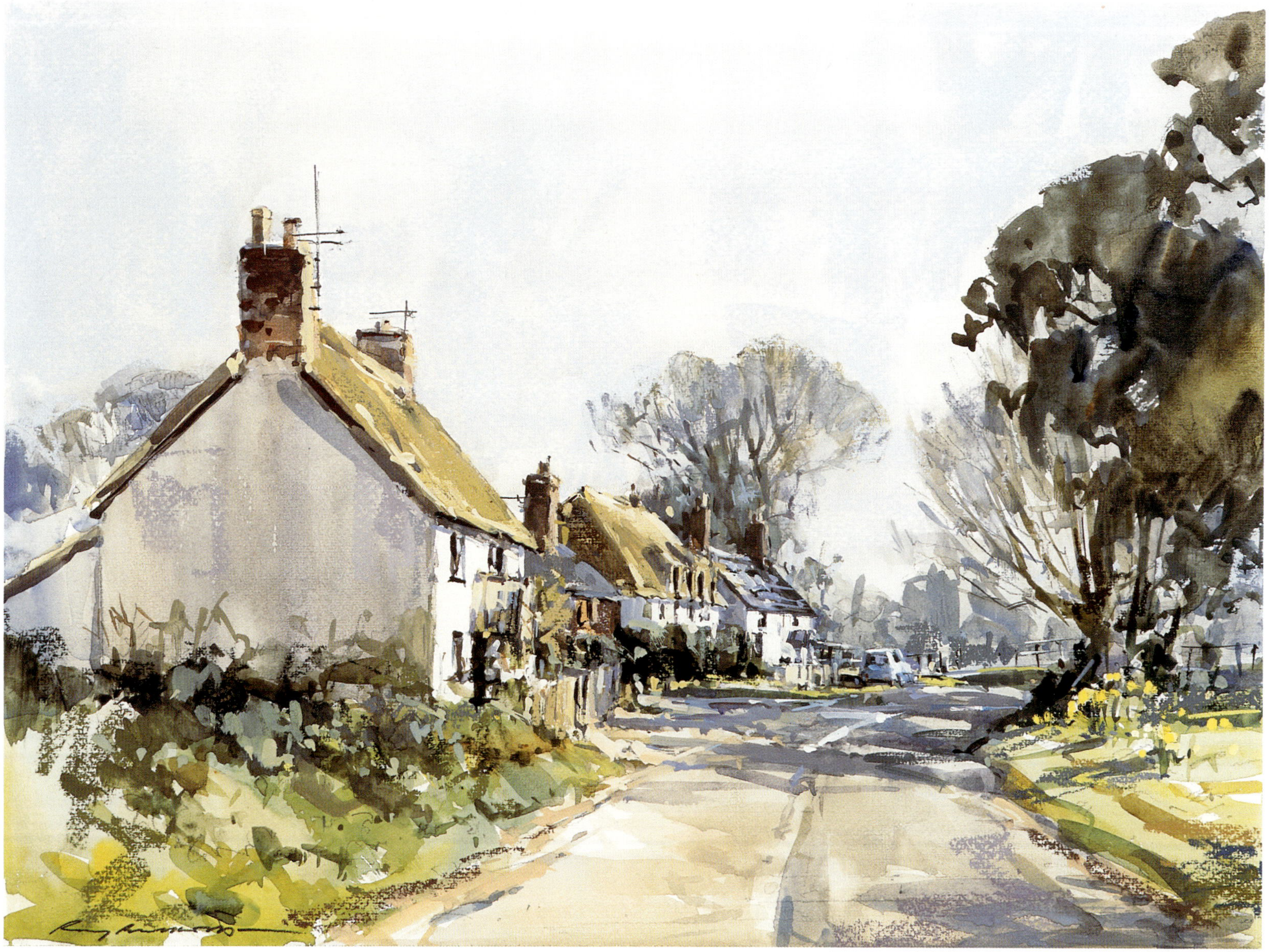

First Signs of Spring, Powderham
Mixed Media 12x16in (30x41cm)

Spring is my favourite season, the fresh vibrant new growth contrasting with the rich-red ploughed fields and the arrival of the Swallows. A small number of typical cob and thatch cottages make up this pretty hamlet that derives its name from John de Powderham who held the castle in the reign of Edward I.

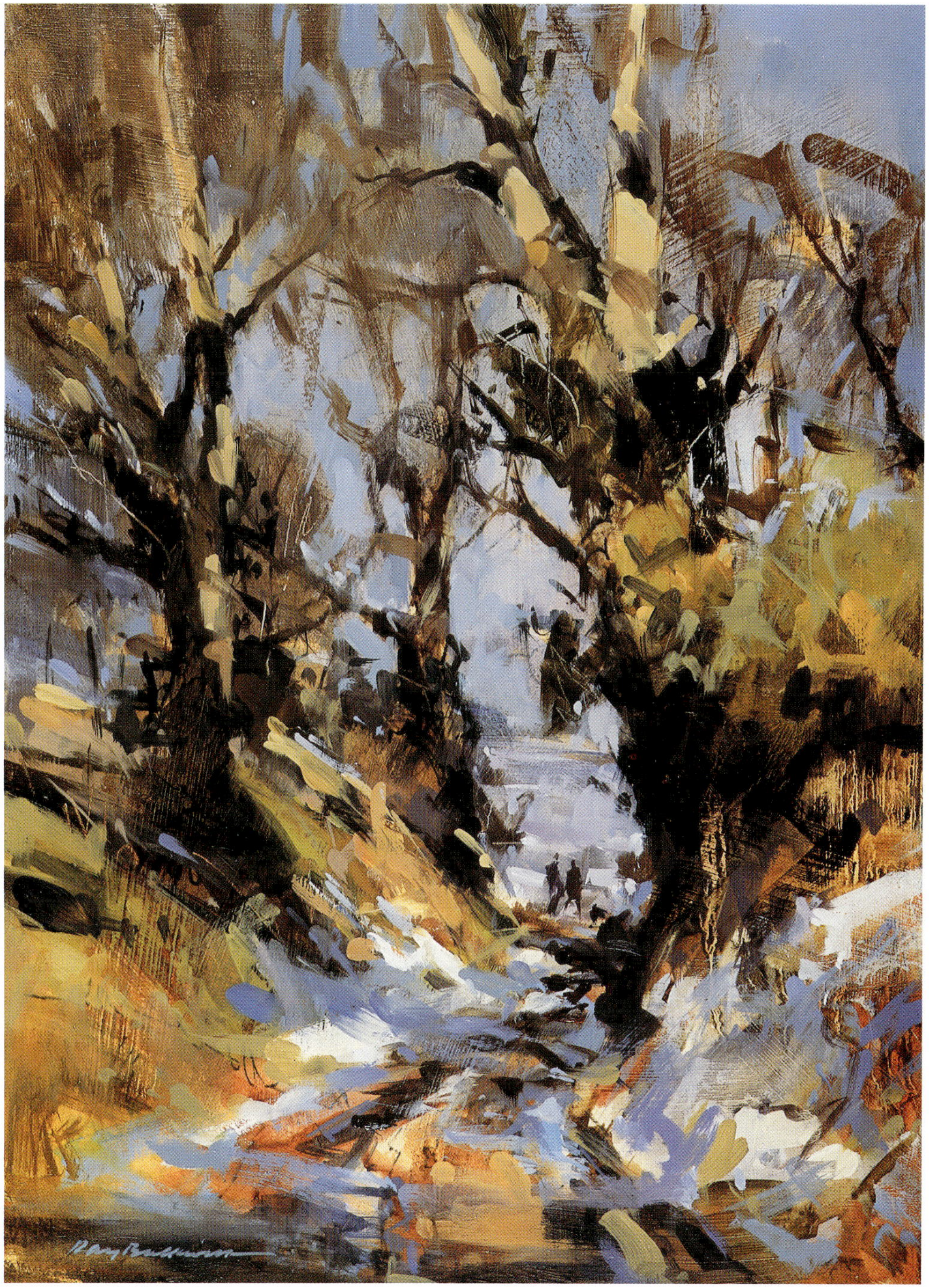

Snow Flurries near Woodbury
Oil 10x14in (25x36cm)

The most prominent and characteristic feature of the present-day Devon landscape is the high-banked lanes. Many of these may be of Norman origin when the county was made a royal forest and deer were protected as game for the king. To keep deer off their crops farmers banked, or hedged in their fields, some of these being up to ten feet high and eight feet across.

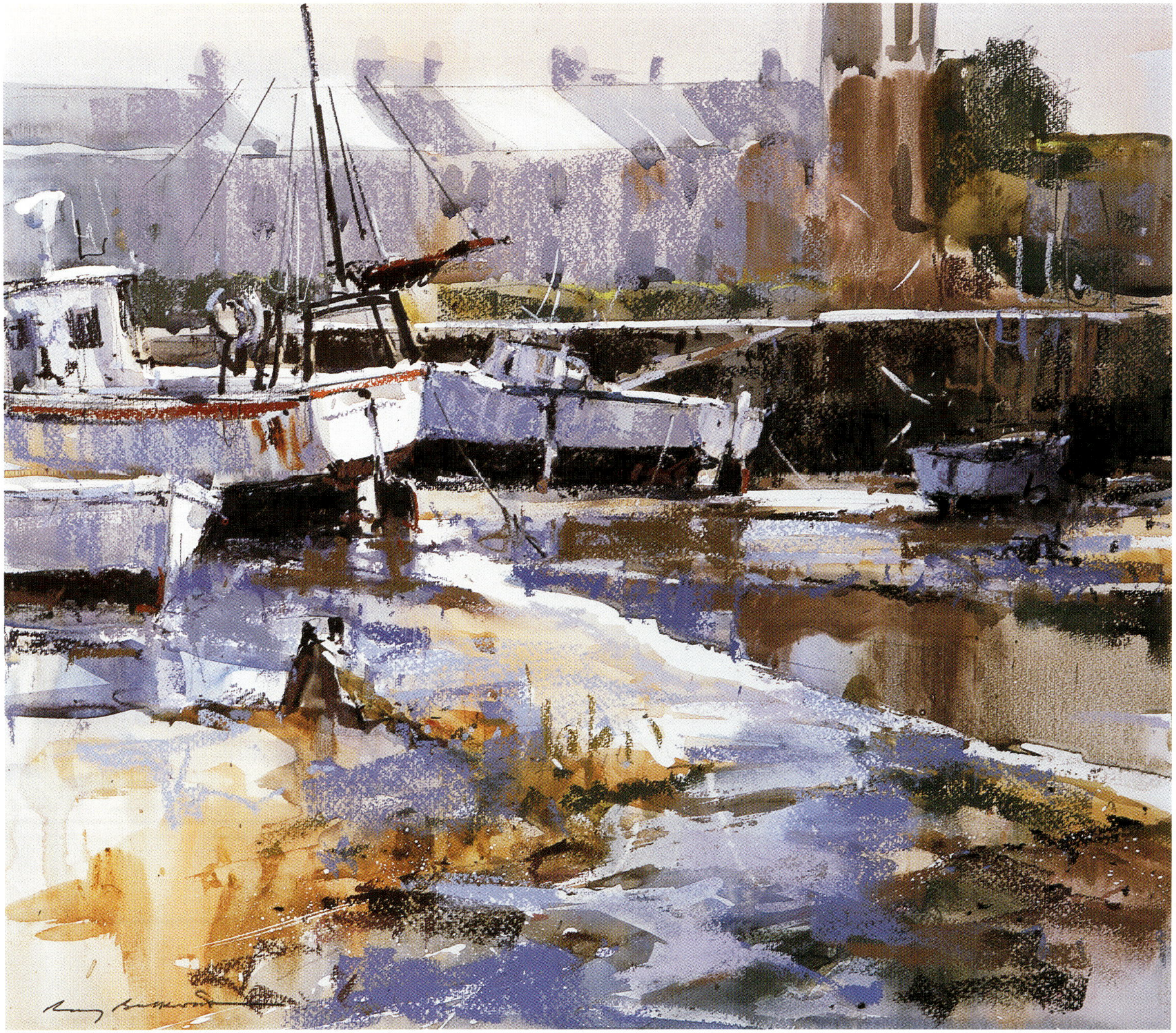

Wet Mud, Lympstone
Mixed Media 16.5x18.5in (42x47cm)

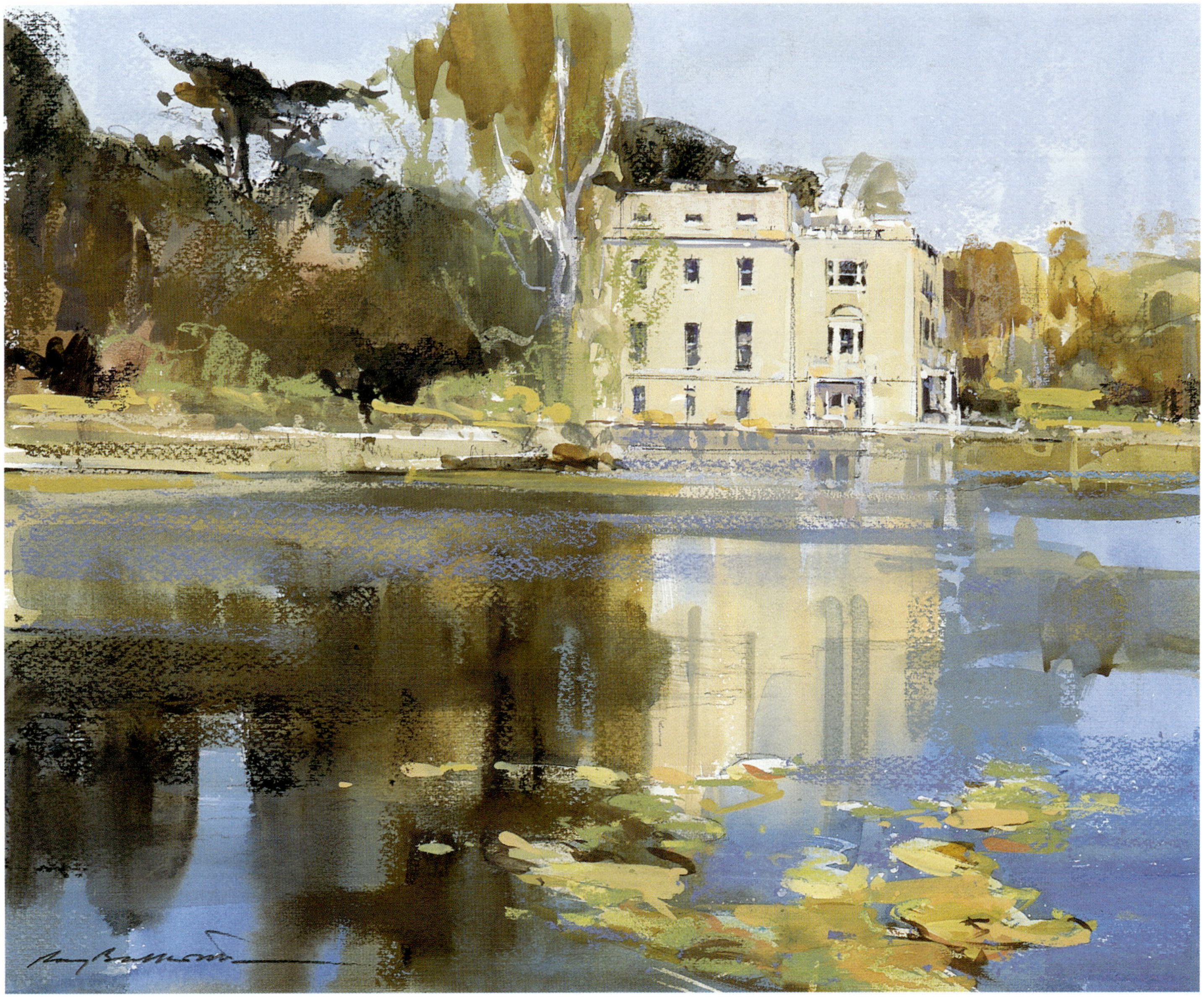

Spring Reflections, Nutwell Court
Mixed Media 12.5x15in (32x38cm)

Tucked away in superb grounds that sweep down to the estuary, a house has been in existence here since Domesday. Once owned by the Drake family, parts of the present house date back to the fourteenth century, with additions in the eighteenth century. It is now a private house.

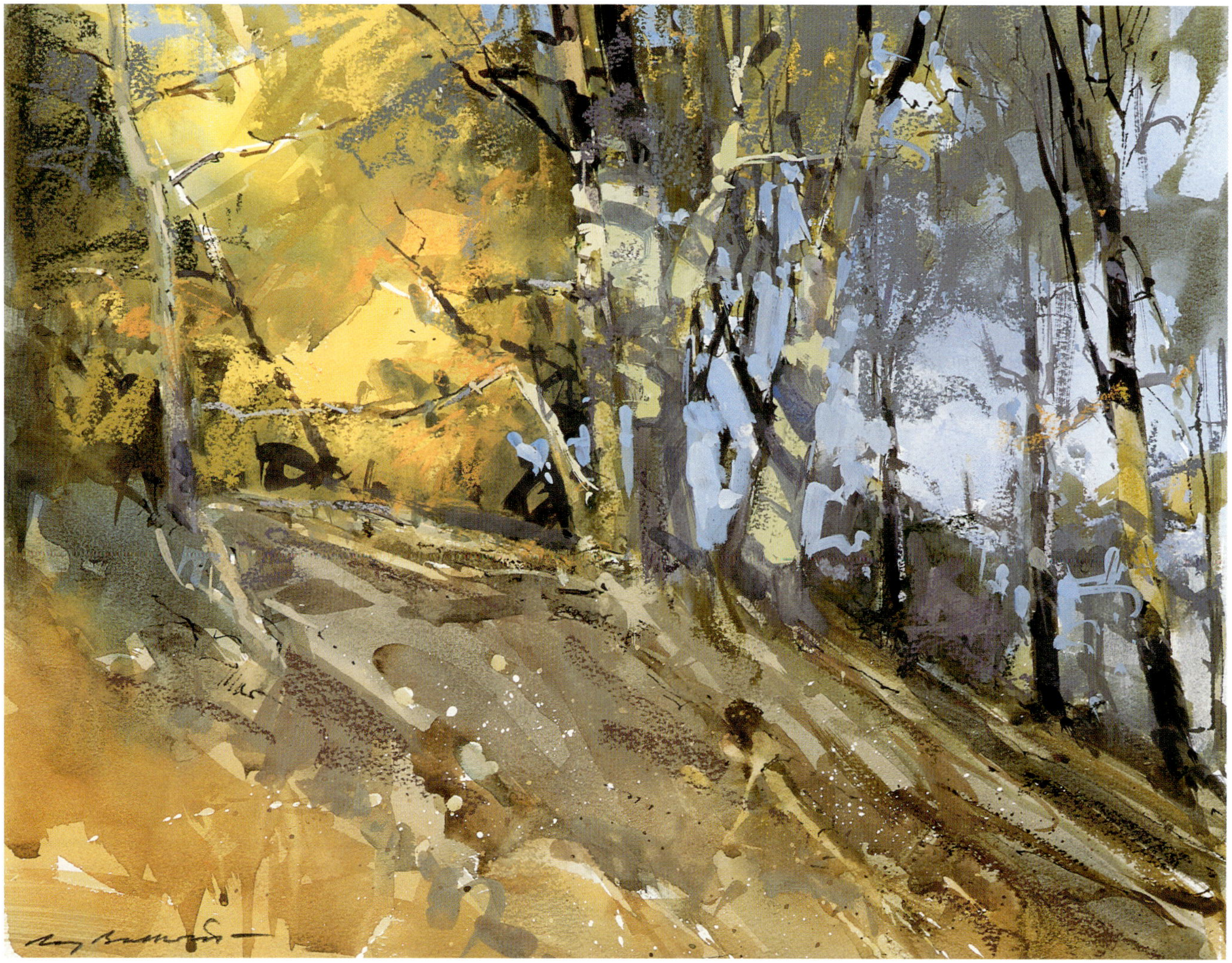

Autumn Colours, Woodbury Castle
Mixed Media 13x16.5in (33x42cm)

Inland from the Exe is a long barren ridge that takes its name from the earthen fort or camp that crowns it. The *'Woodbeorh'* built about four thousand years ago may have witnessed the last resistance in this area to the spread of the Roman Empire.

The views from here are spectacular and on a clear day one can see the whole of the estuary as well as Dartmoor's highest tors. My favourite time of day however is when the sun is setting and the river appears like a sparkling ribbon of silver light against the backdrop of the Haldon hills.

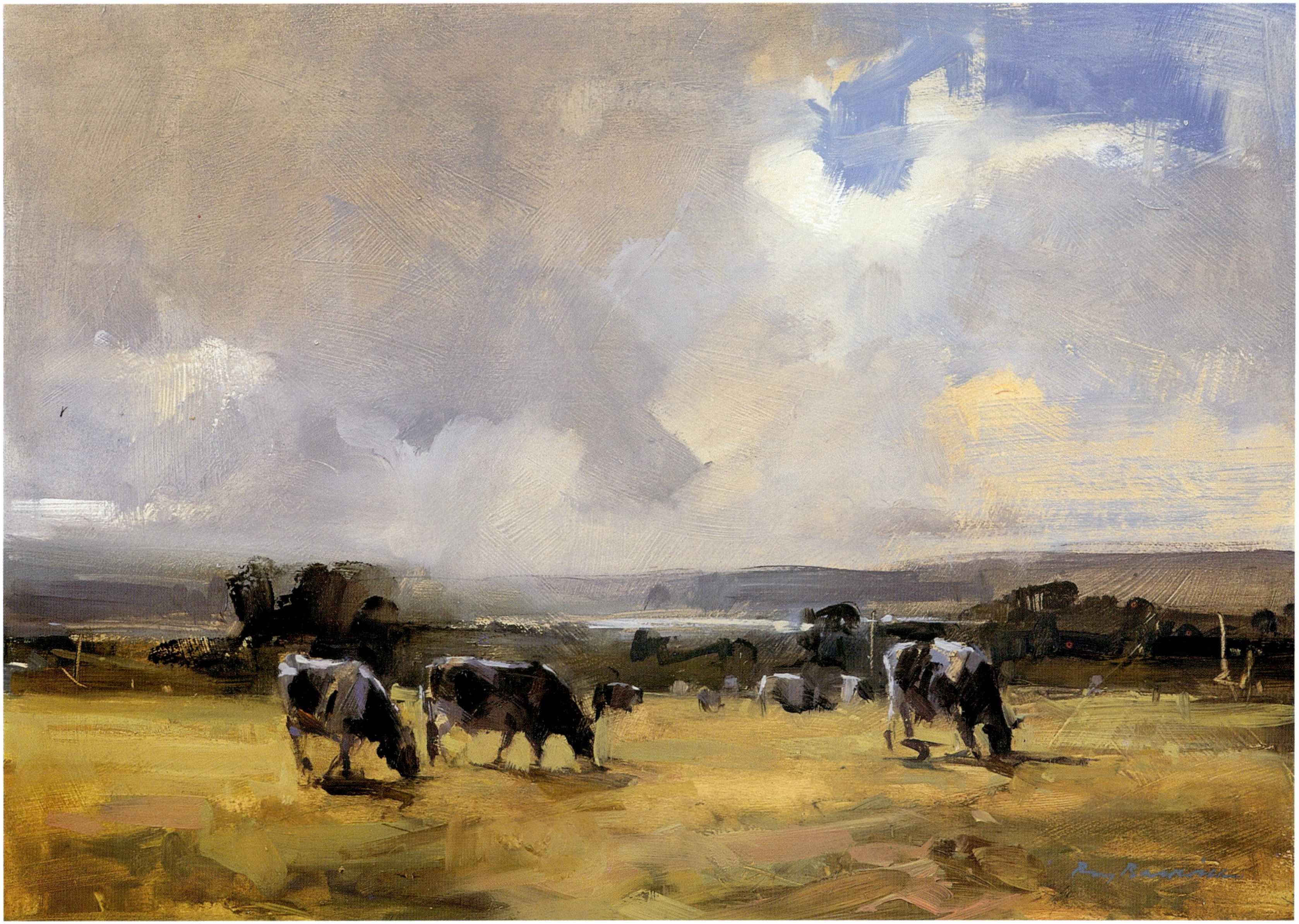

The Estuary from Woodbury Common
Oil 10x14in (25x36cm)

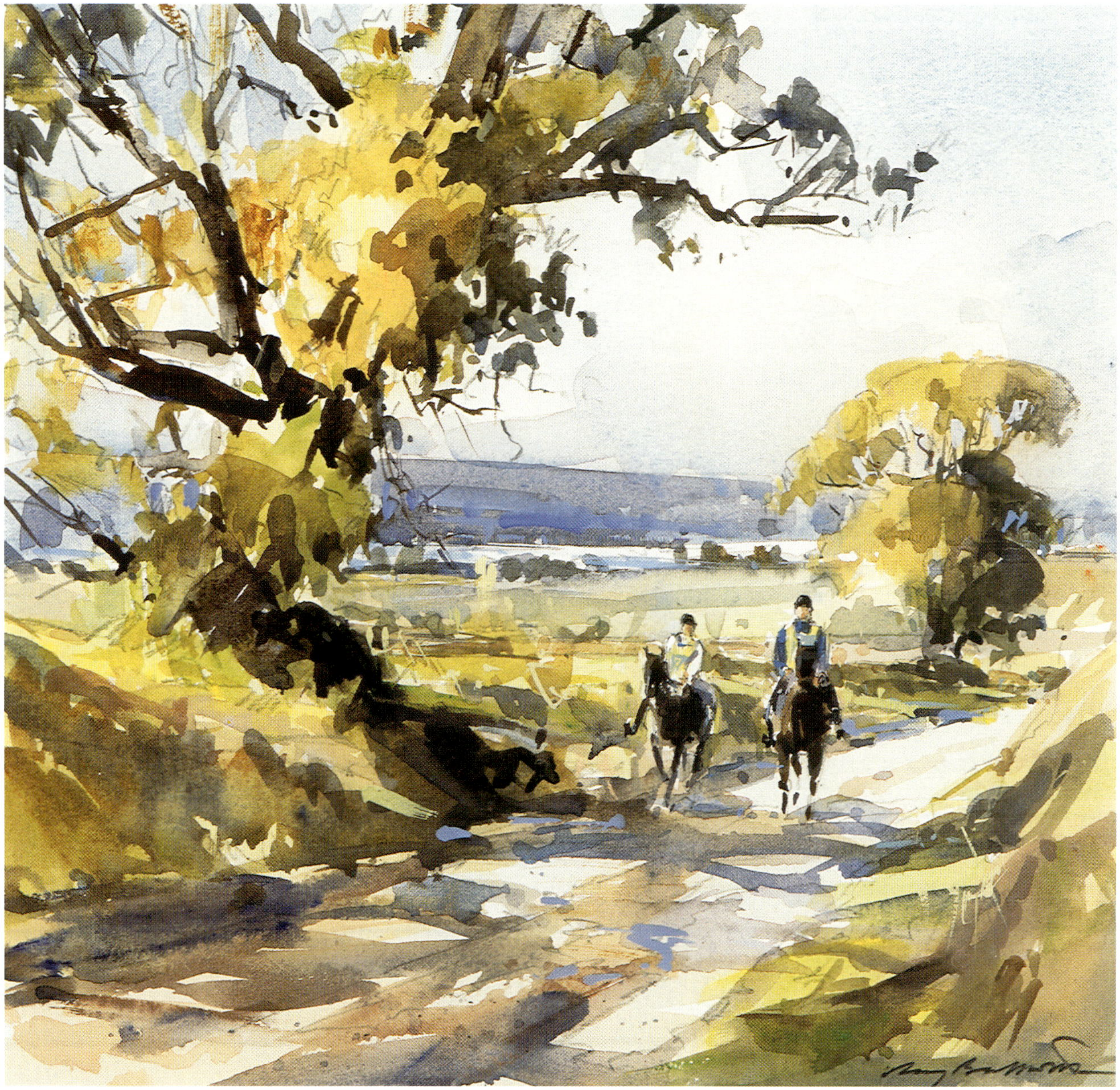

On the Edge of the Common
Watercolour 9.5x9.5in (24x24cm)

This epitomises the 'typically English' scene for me. The sounds of horse's hooves on a Devon lane, the 'caw' of the rooks in their colony, and church bells ringing across the fields from Woodbury and Lympstone. Devon countryside at its finest!

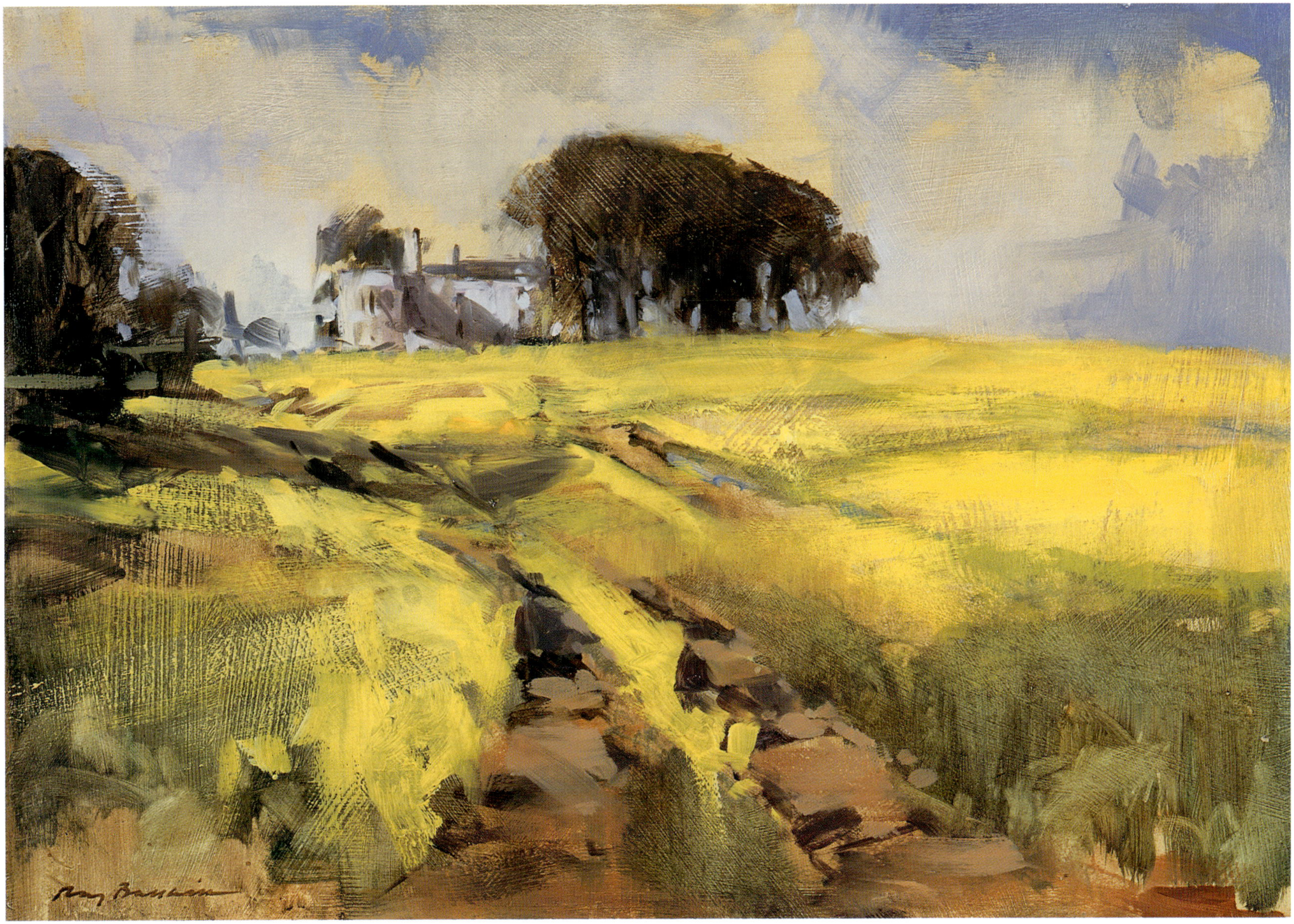

Oilseed Rape in Full Flower, Mount Ebford
Oil 10x14in (25x36cm)

This sea of yellow below Mount Ebford stopped me in my tracks and made for an exciting contrast to the green and red landscape that one expects at this time of year. The fields glow like the brightest sunshine and lighten the landscape from dawn to dusk – and even by moonlight.

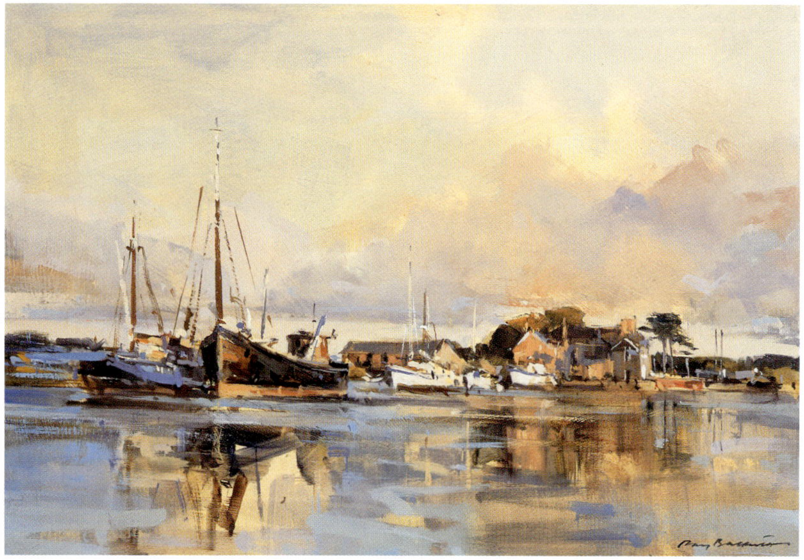

Evening Sky over Turf
Oil 10x14in (25x36cm)

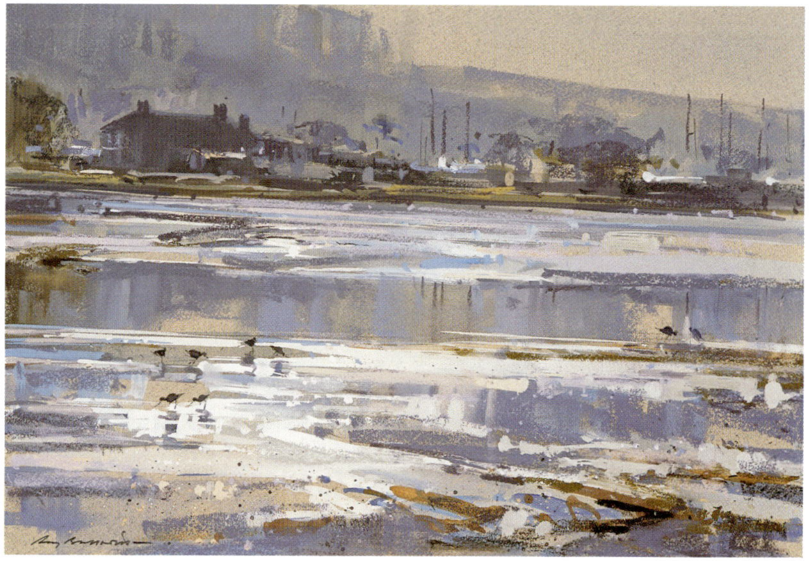

Avocets Feeding off Turf
Watercolour/Gouache Location Study 9.5x13in (24x33cm)

The entrance to the Exeter Ship Canal at Turf is a popular spot for bird-watchers and walkers. The Turf Hotel is in a unique and truly peaceful setting, as one has to approach it, either by foot or boat. This shows the Turf Basin where sailing vessels in the past often lay awaiting fair winds to leave the estuary having offloaded their cargo into lighters for transhipment to Exeter.

Outstanding among the wealth of wintering waders on the river is the elegant Avocet and these can best be seen from November to the end of February. One of the best places to see them is in the narrow channel between Topsham and Powderham, where the freshwater and saltwater mix to provide the ideal feeding grounds.

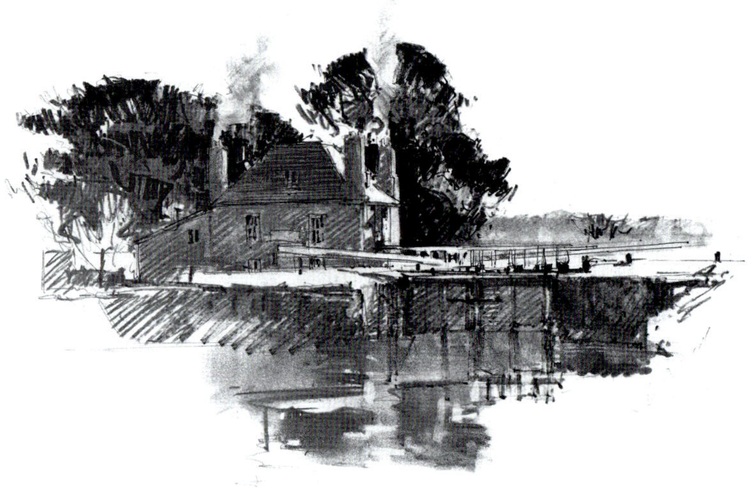

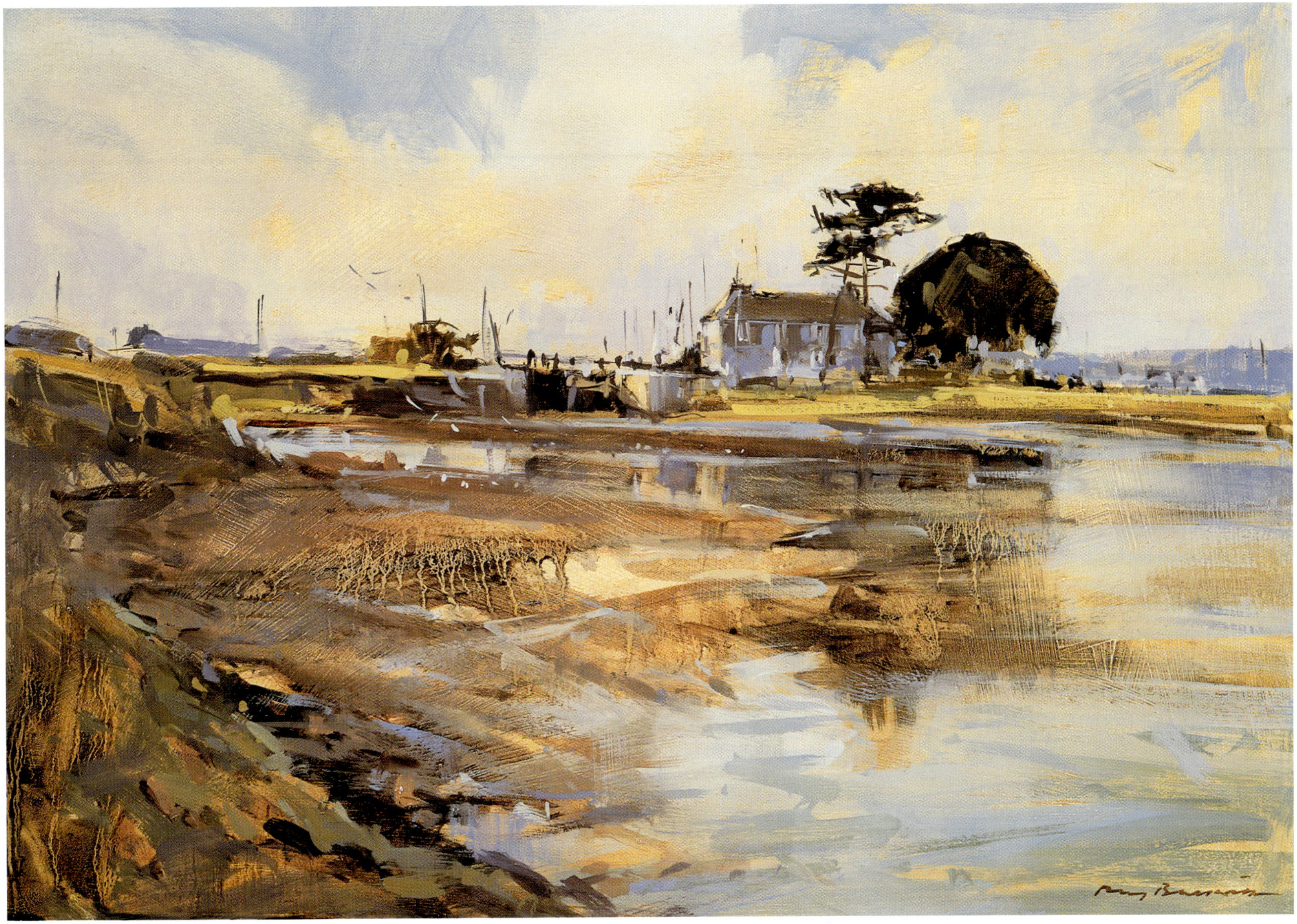

Falling Tide, Turf Lock
Oil 10x14in (25x36cm)

This painting shows the entrance to the ship canal from the river. The canal was extended to Turf in 1827 which enabled sea-going craft able to cross the bar at Exmouth to navigate through the estuary into the canal. The Hotel built by James Green has extensive outbuildings, some of which were used as stabling for the horses that towed the ships up the canal.

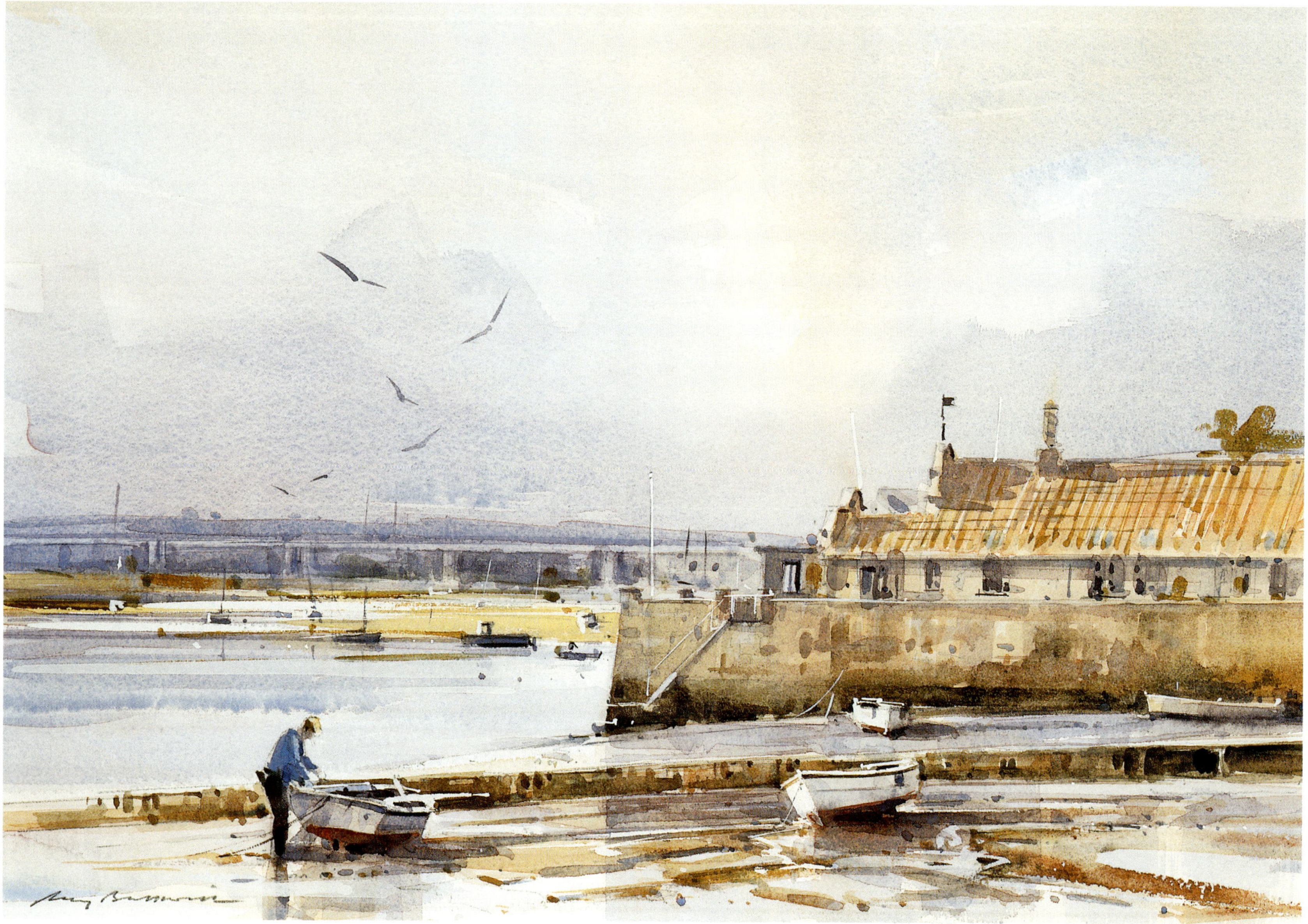

'Wixels', Topsham
Watercolour 10x14in (25x36cm)

Set in its prominent position when looking upriver, this is probably the most painted view in Topsham. It was built on the site of Cox's Quay. The name *'Wixels'* derives from the tenancy in the mid nineteenth century of the Wigzell brothers who ran a nail-making business from the premises. It was converted to a private house in 1920.

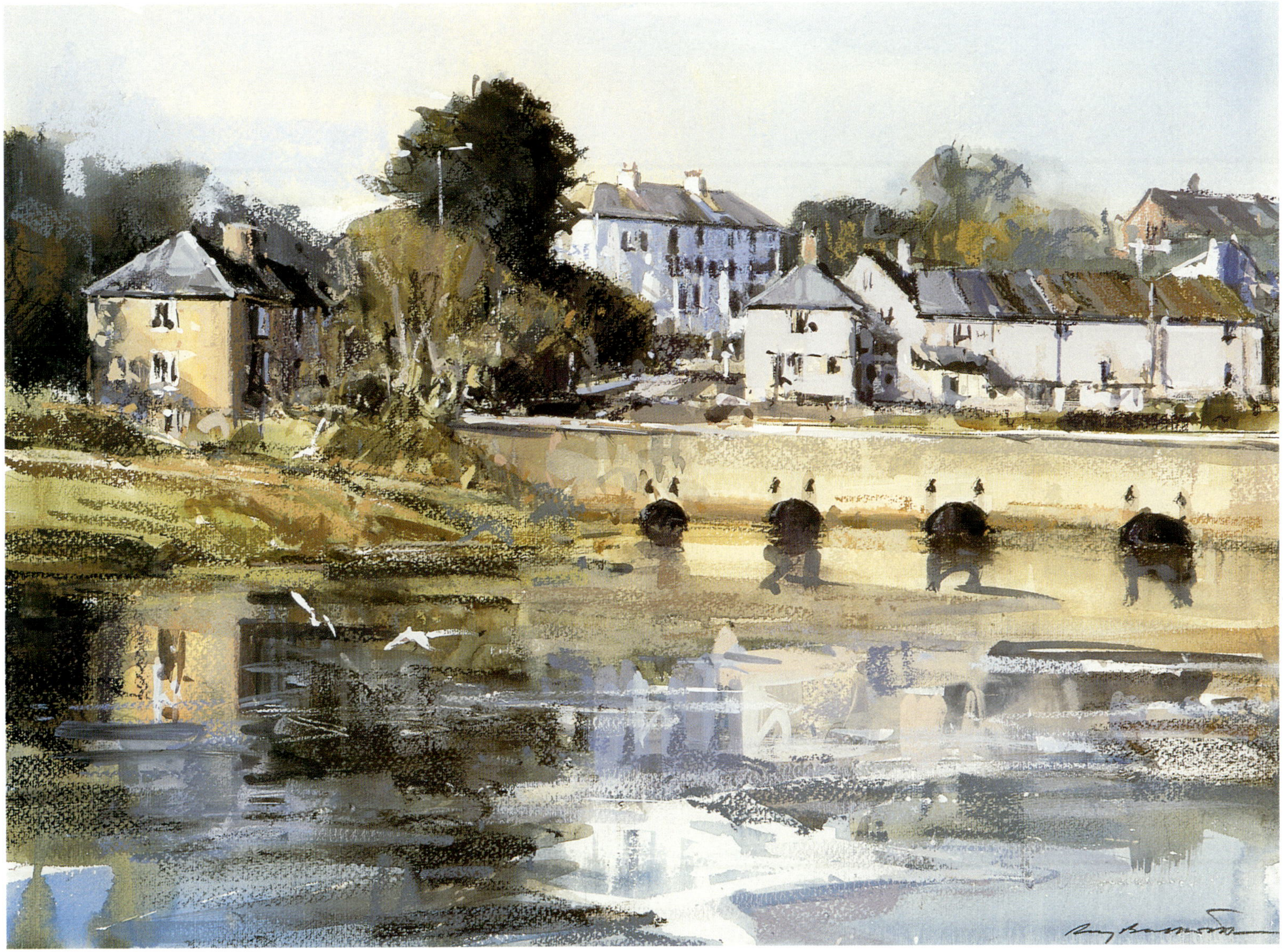

Reflections, Bridge Inn
Mixed Media 13x17.5in (33x45cm)

This 'Real Ale' inn is listed as an ancient monument and is one of Devon's oldest and most interesting inns. It is mentioned in Domesday and is said to have been originally a lodging house for the masons who built Exeter Cathedral. It still retains its old-world character and charm and a recent claim to fame is that it is the only public house ever to be officially visited by the Queen.

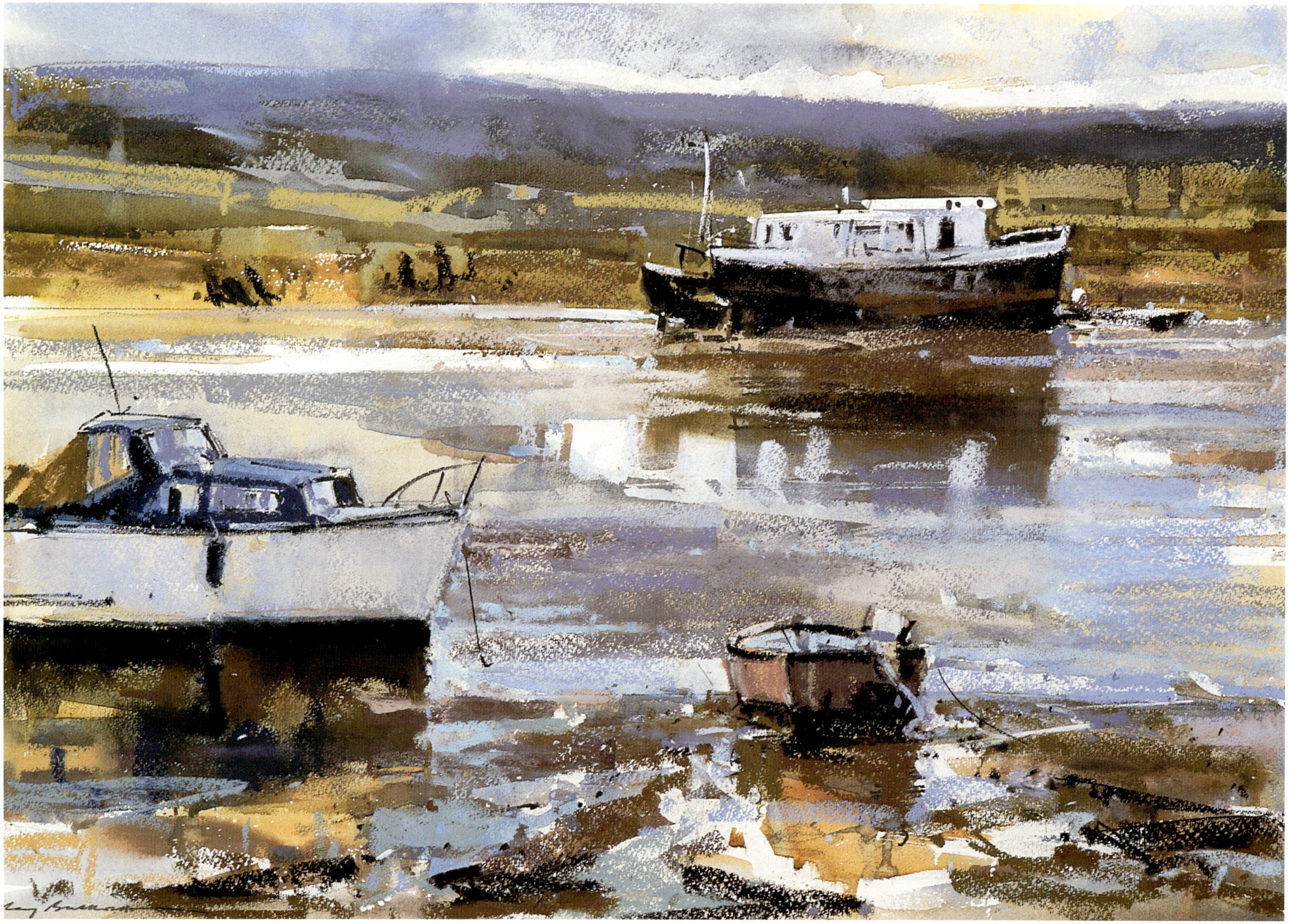

The Houseboat, Topsham
Mixed Media 13.5x19in (34x48cm)

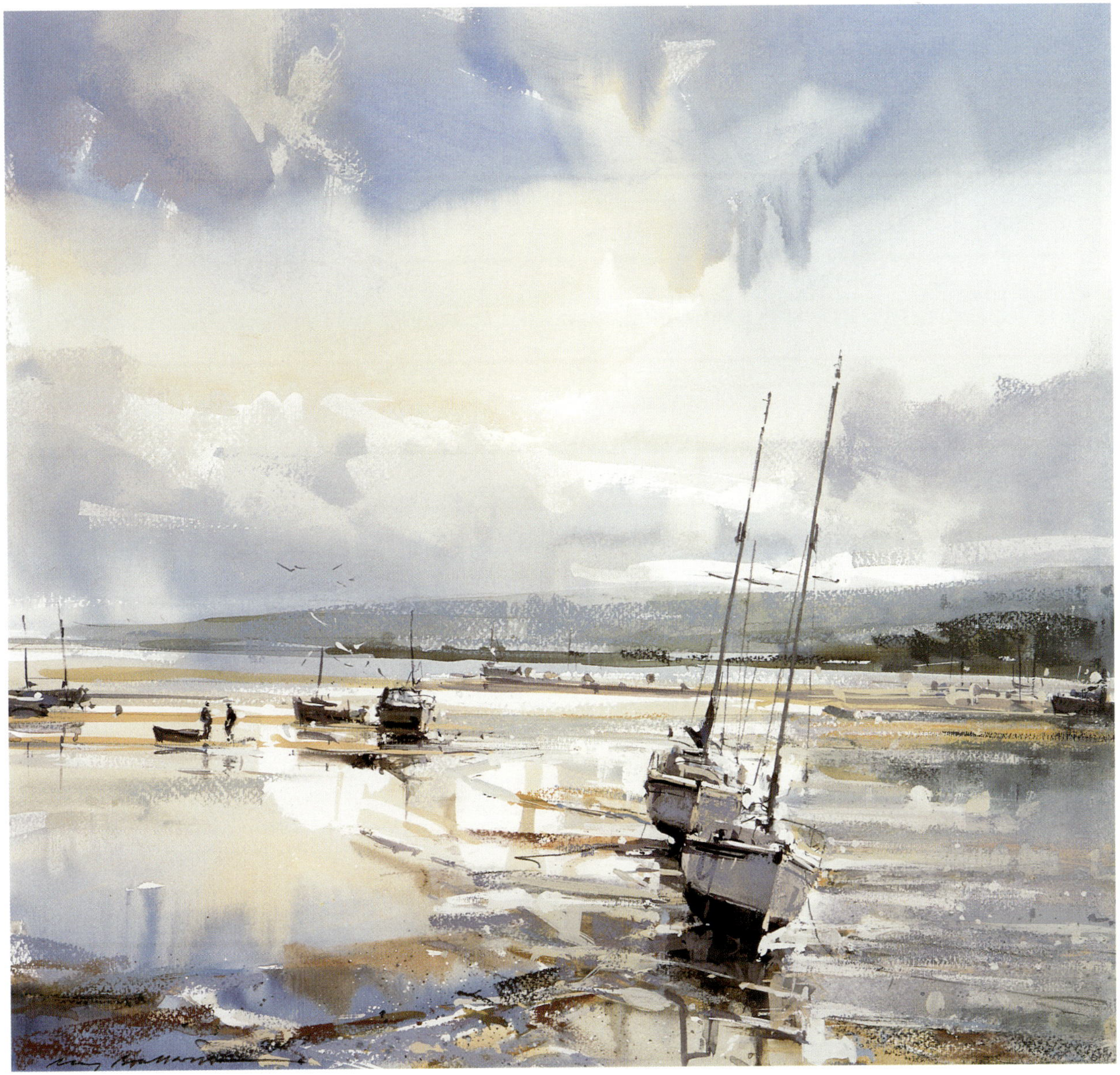

Sunshine After Rain, Topsham
Mixed Media 17.5x17.5in (45x45cm)

Topsham is a favourite painting spot as there is always a tranquillity here despite its close proximity to the town. Only the bubbling calls of Curlew and the high-pitched whistles of Wigeon echo across the broad estuary waters, whilst Herons stalk the muddy shallows.

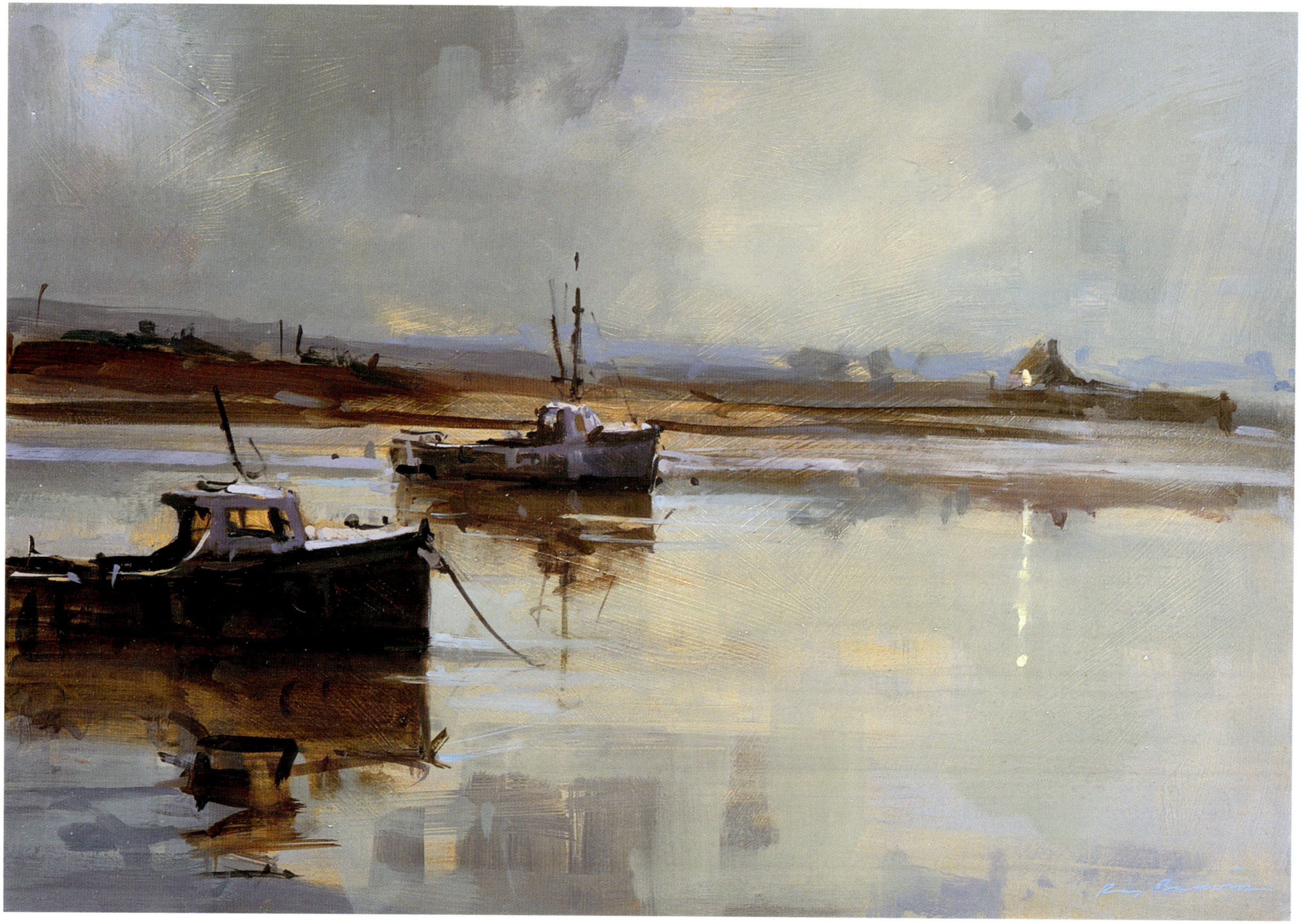

Night Draws On, Topsham
Oil 10x14in (25x36cm)

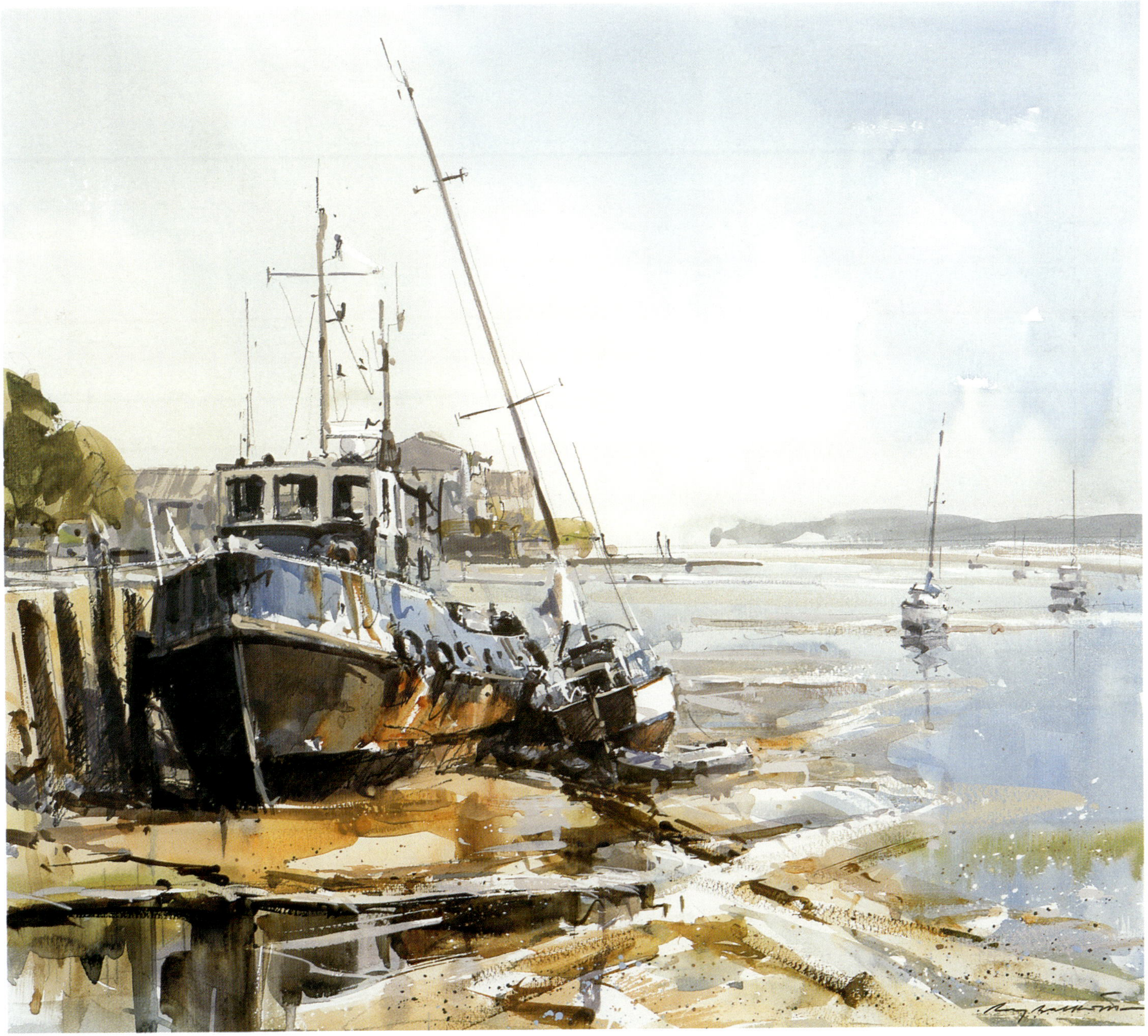

The Old Tug, Topsham
Watercolour 17x19in (43x48cm)

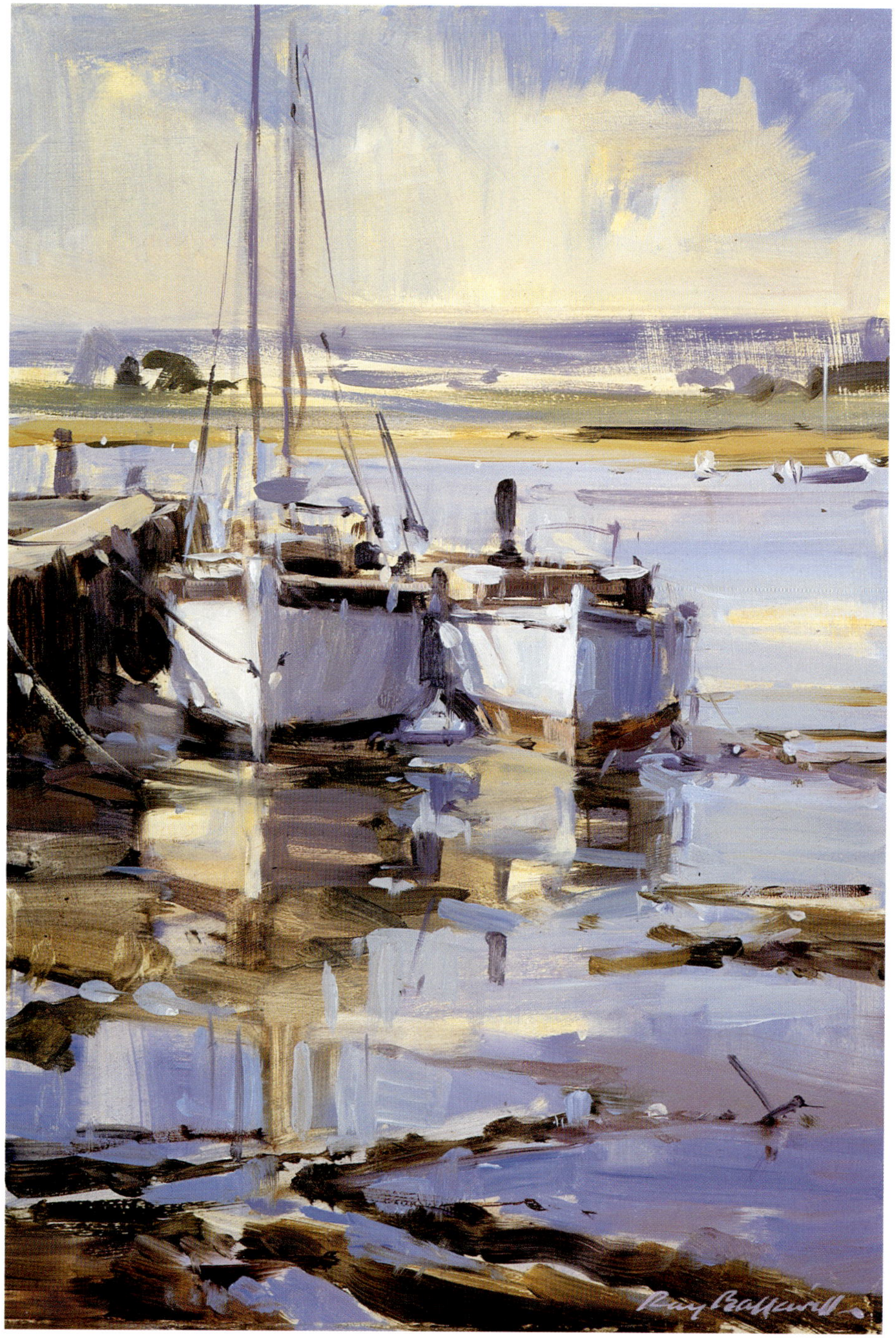

Quiet Anchorage, Topsham
Oil 12x8in (30x20cm)

This painting has fond memories for me as it was done in the company of a friend and fine painter from Australia, John Shave. When he visits, I always enjoy our painting trips together. In this scene it was the reflections and reflected light on the side of the boats that caught my attention. Strangely one feels more like a 'real' artist painting oils *en plein air*. I think the smock and box easel have something to do with it! However, this usually attracts onlookers which I never mind, but I tell my students, if they are concerned, to put down a hat with some coins in it, and that usually does the trick!

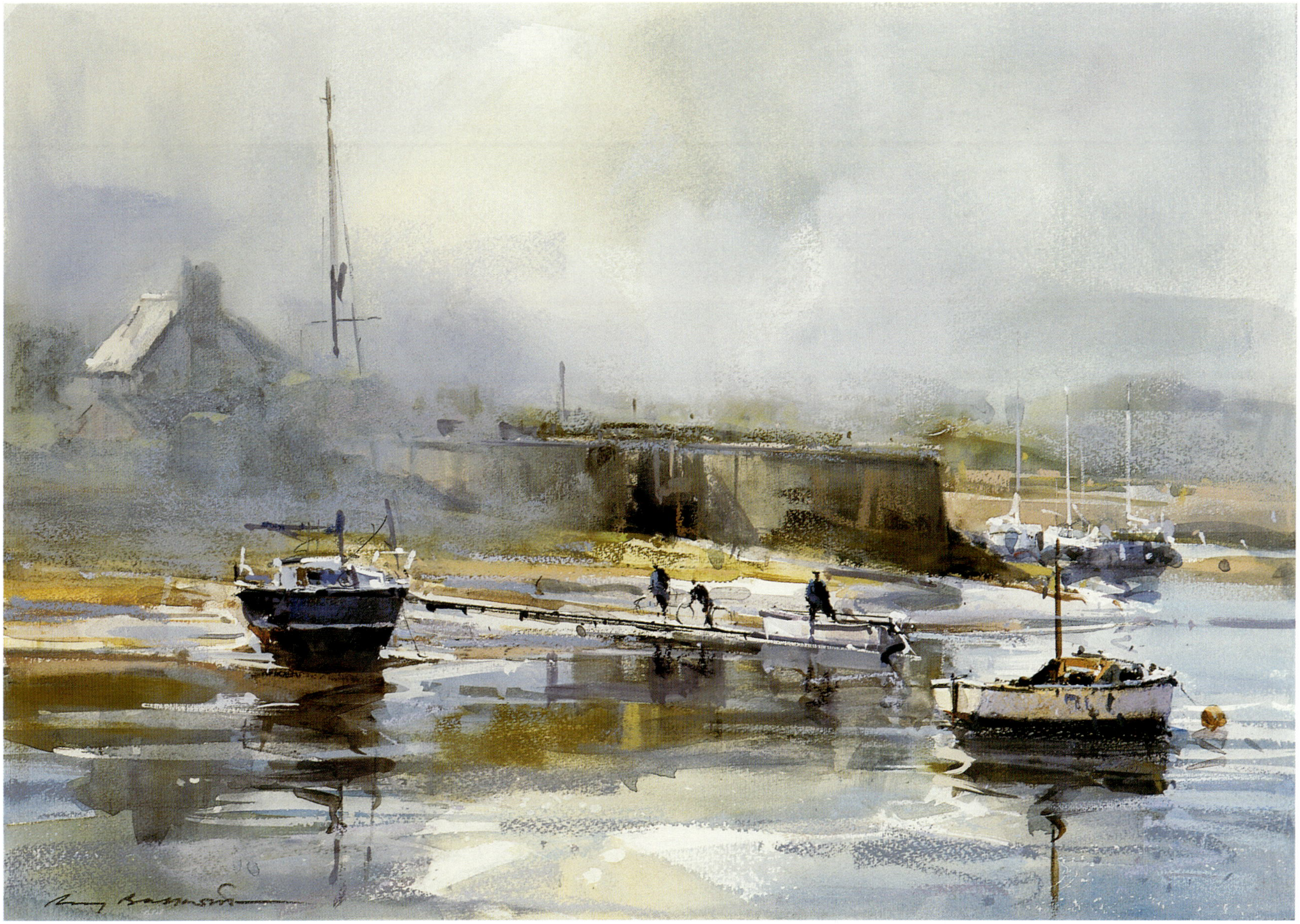

Rising Mist, Topsham
Mixed Media 13x18.5in (33x47cm)

As the morning mist lifts it reveals the old lock and the ferryman who still takes foot passengers across the river. A ferry has been established at Topsham for centuries and it is believed that monks ran a ferry here on their route from Sherborne Abbey into the South West peninsula.

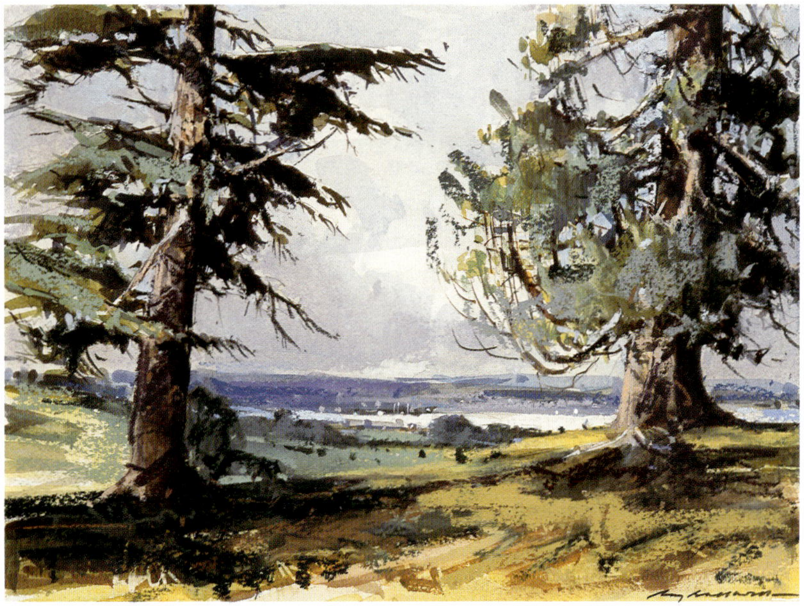

View from Pigeon Vale, near Powderham
Mixed Media 8x11in (20x28cm)

Set in rich Devon farmland the vale sweeps down to Turf and the estuary. I love the voluptuous countryside on this side of the river particularly in mid July when dark trees ride against golden fields of ripening oats and barley.

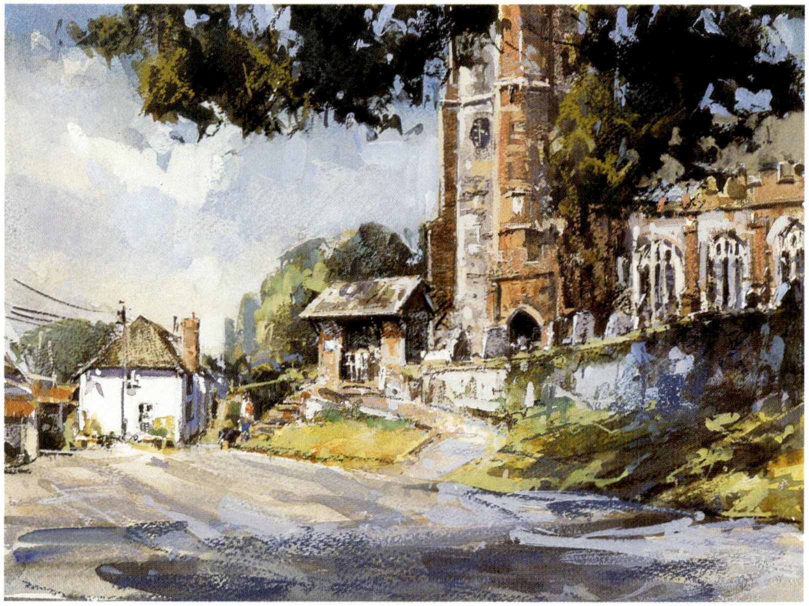

St Andrew's Church, Kenn
Mixed Media 9x12.5in (23x32cm)

Set amidst stunning countryside is the pretty village of Kenn with its lovely church. During the Black Death in East Devon every parish for miles around lost its parson. The deanery of Kenn was the worst-hit in the whole of England, losing altogether eighty-six parsons from its seventeen churches in just two years.

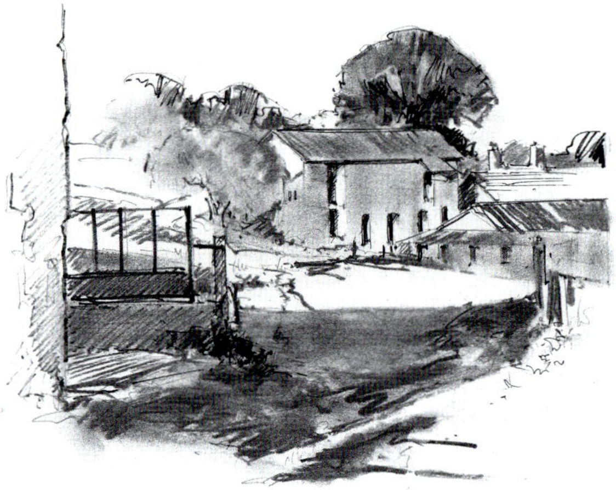

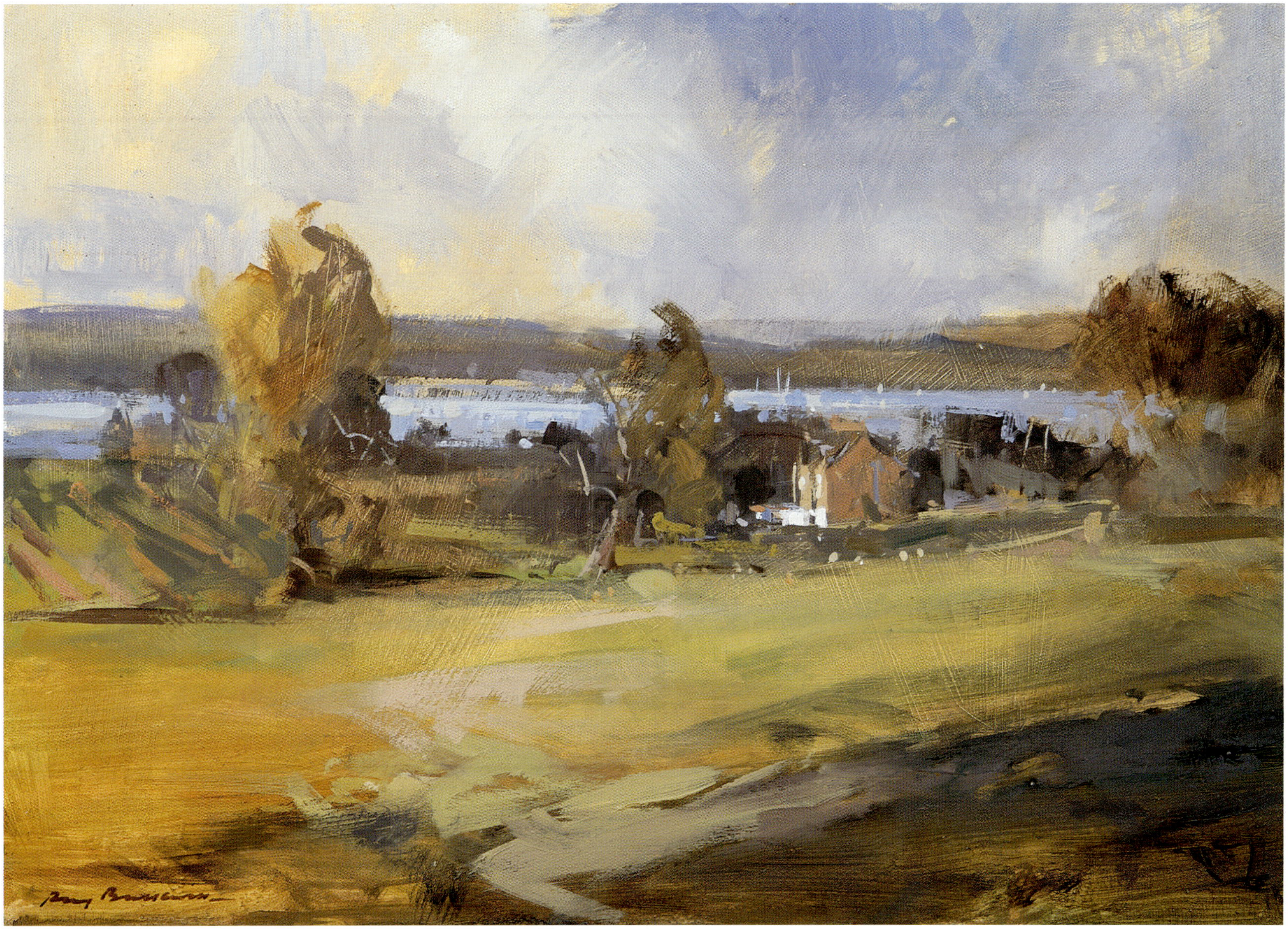

Towards Exwell Barton and the Estuary
Oil 10x14in (25x36cm)

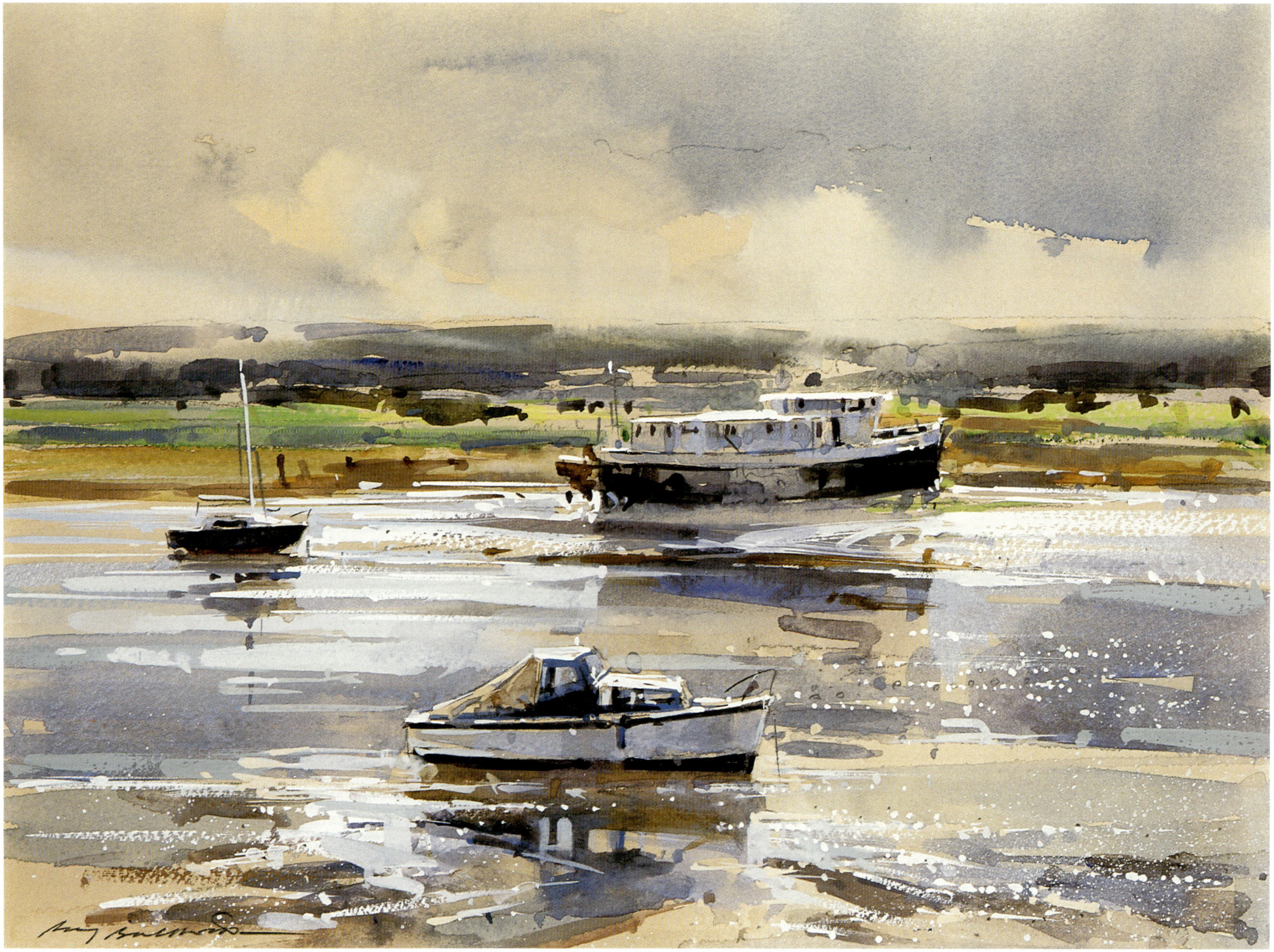

Fair and Bright, Topsham
Watercolour/Gouache 10x14in (25x36cm)

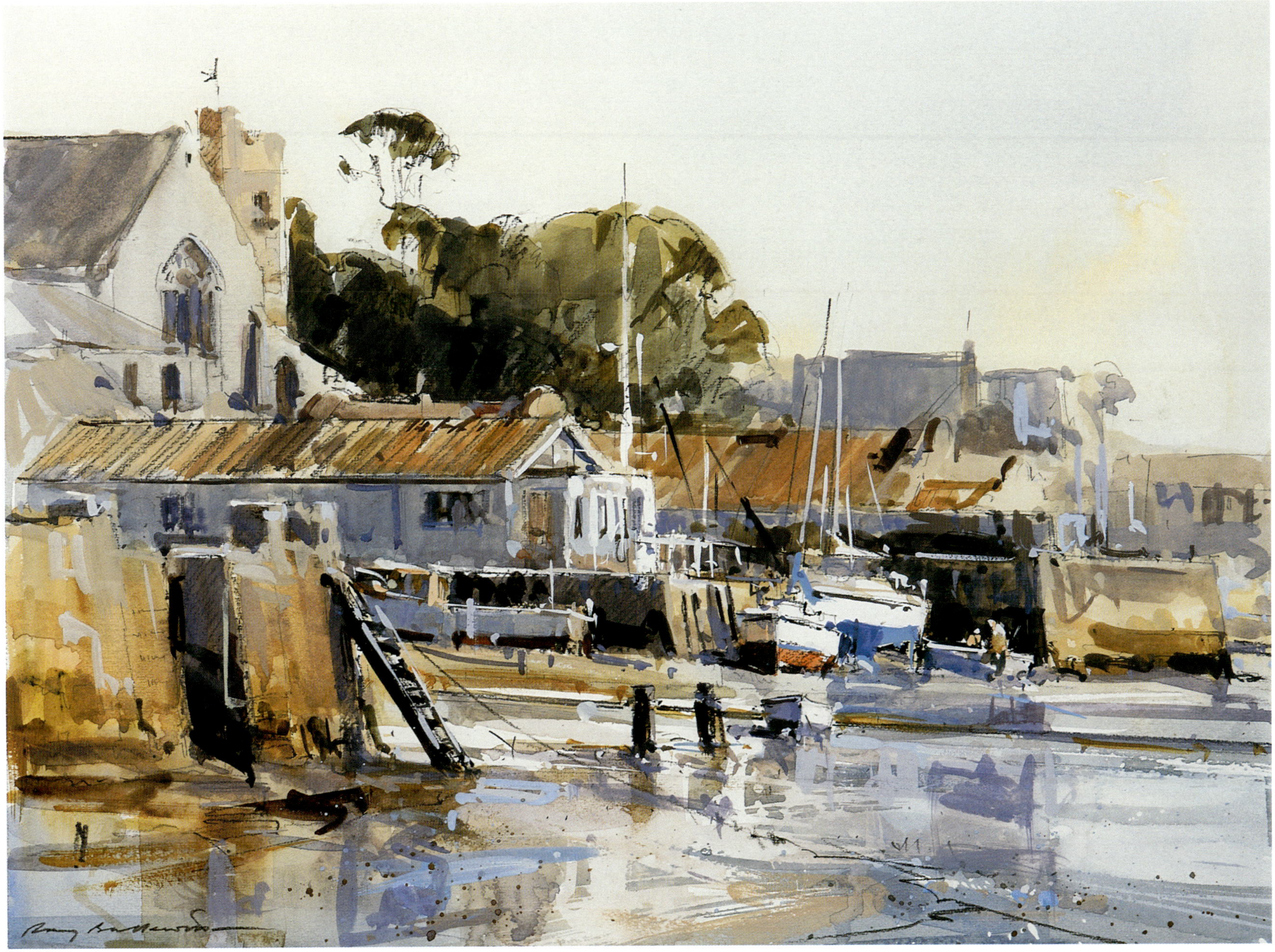

The Waterfront, Topsham
Watercolour 12x16in (30x40cm)

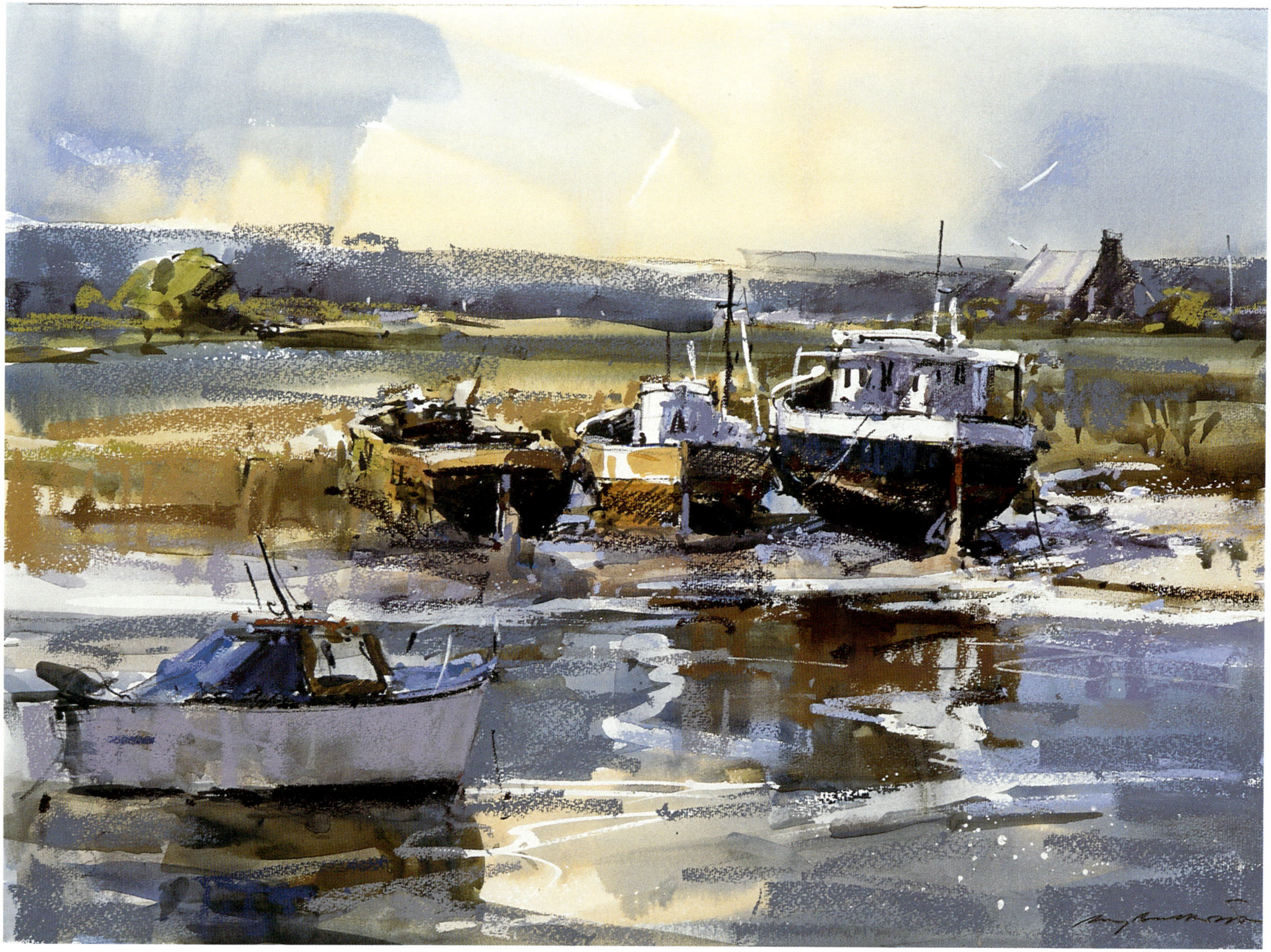

Across the River, Topsham
Mixed Media 13x17.5in (33x44cm)

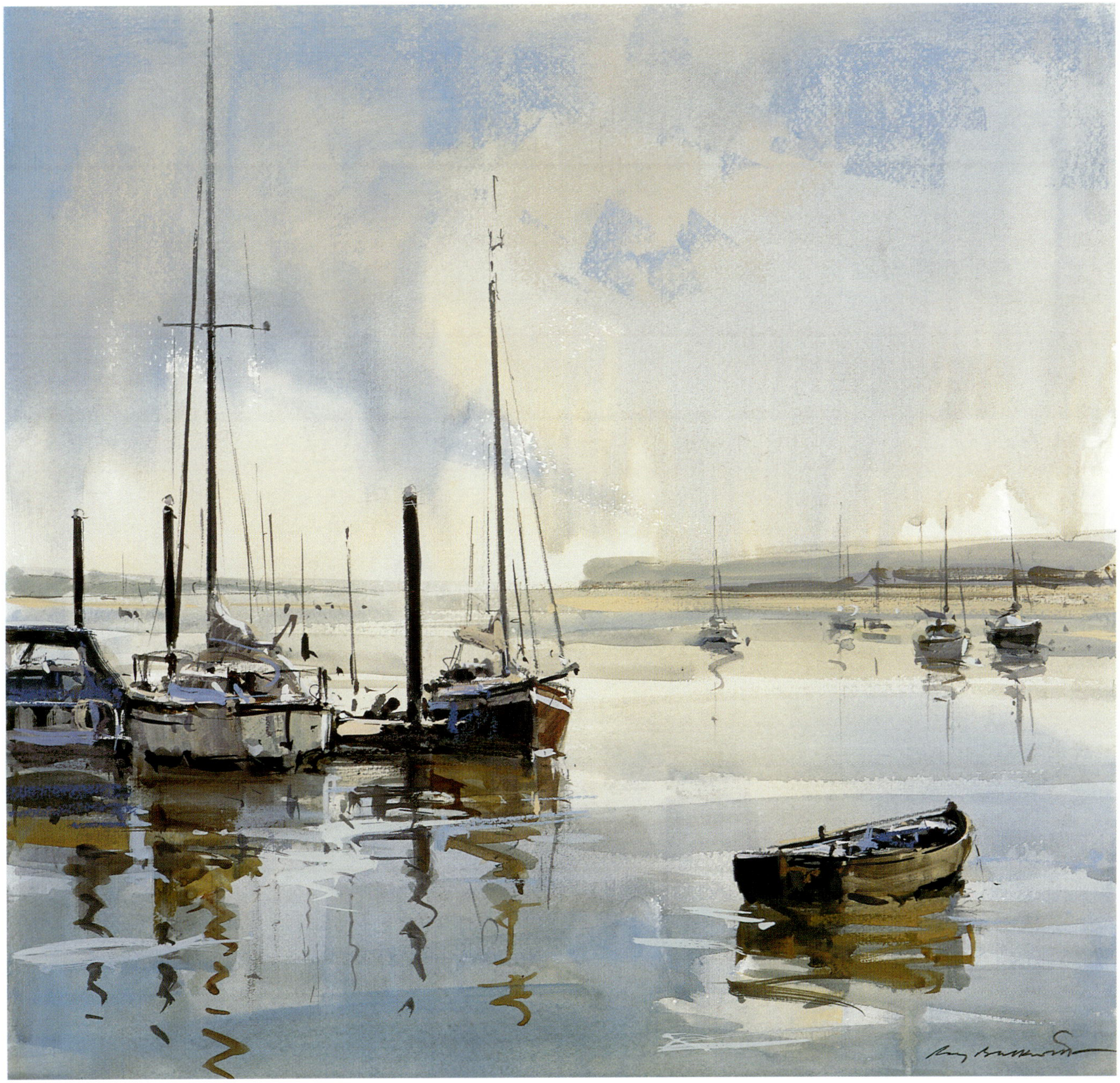

Passing Shower, Topsham
Mixed Media 17x17in (43x43cm)

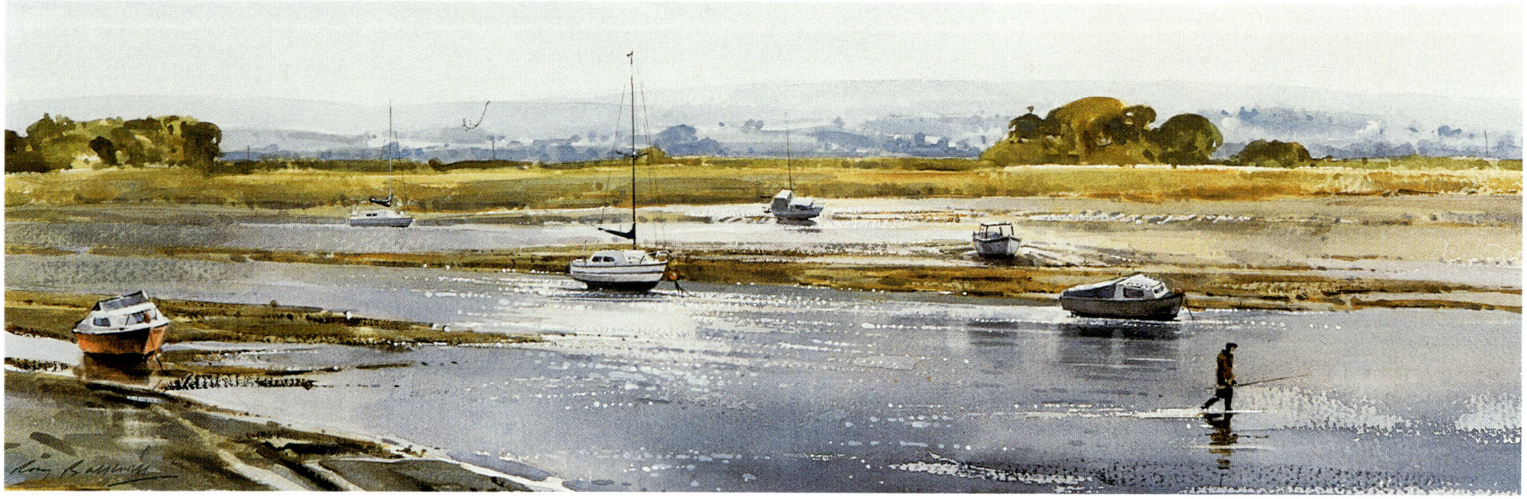

Sunlit Shallows, Topsham
Watercolour 10x21in (26x53cm)

For a number of years I was a member of Exeter Art Society and this painting was shown in the 1990 exhibition, held in the Royal Albert Memorial Museum. It won the Howard Williams Trophy for the most popular painting, voted on by the public.

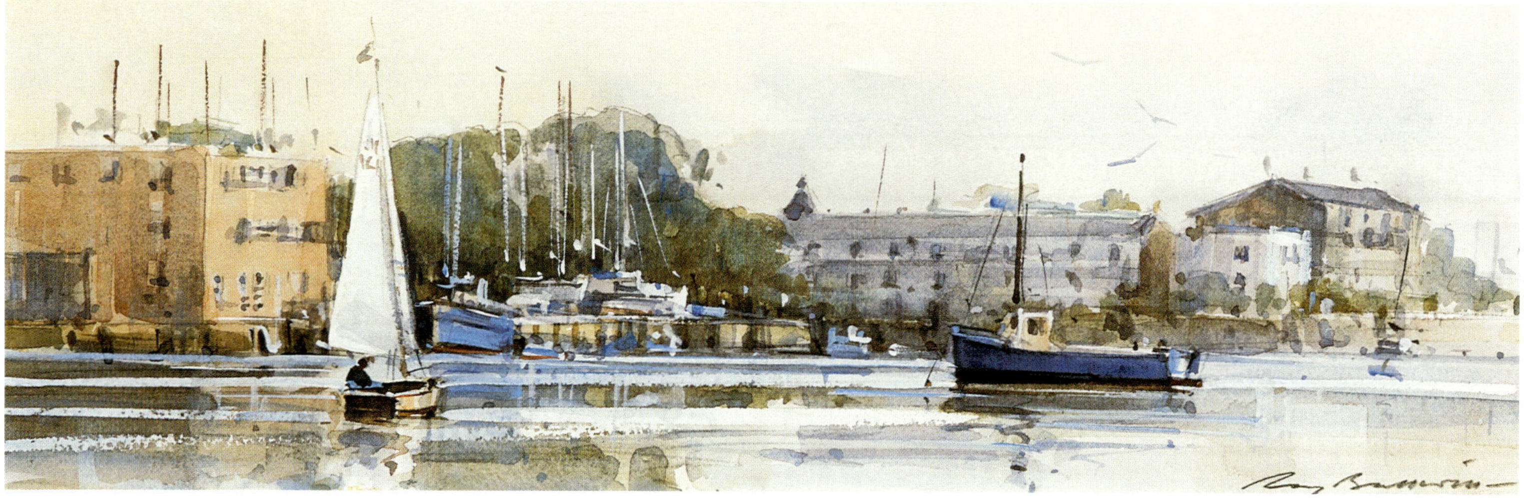

Fair Wind, Topsham
Watercolour 5x14.5in (13x36cm)

This is the view from the Topsham Lock, looking downriver towards Town Quay and Strand Court on the right, which was built on the former Holman's shipyard. Now the dry dock holds a different mode of transport, as it is the underground car park for the flats!

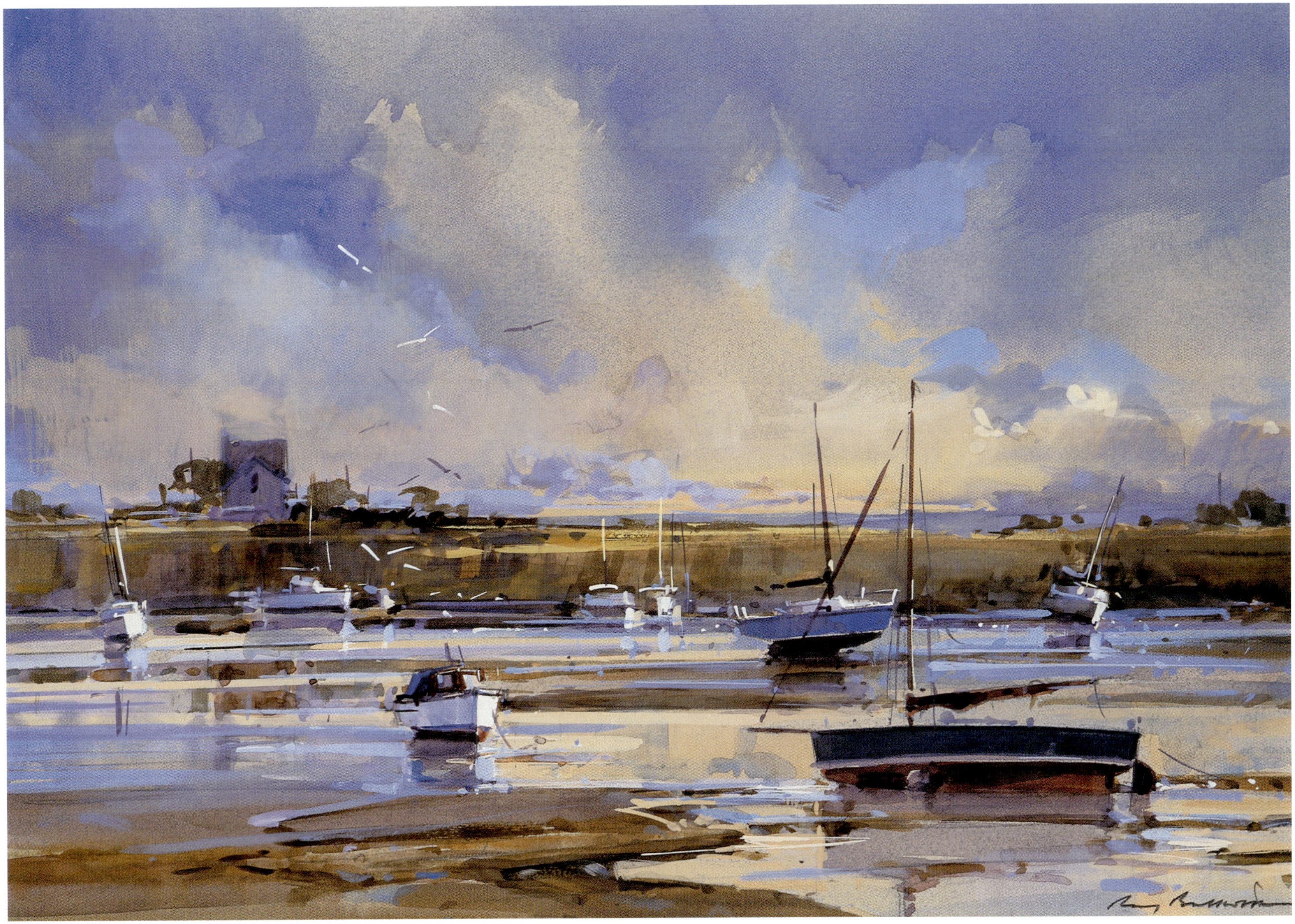

Evening Sky, Topsham
Watercolour/Gouache 10x14in (25x36cm)

This view from below Retreat House is looking downriver towards Topsham Lock. Beside the disused lock is the fairly complete hulk of the wooden barge *Nancy* which plied her trade between Topsham and the Humber with cargoes of coal and fertiliser.

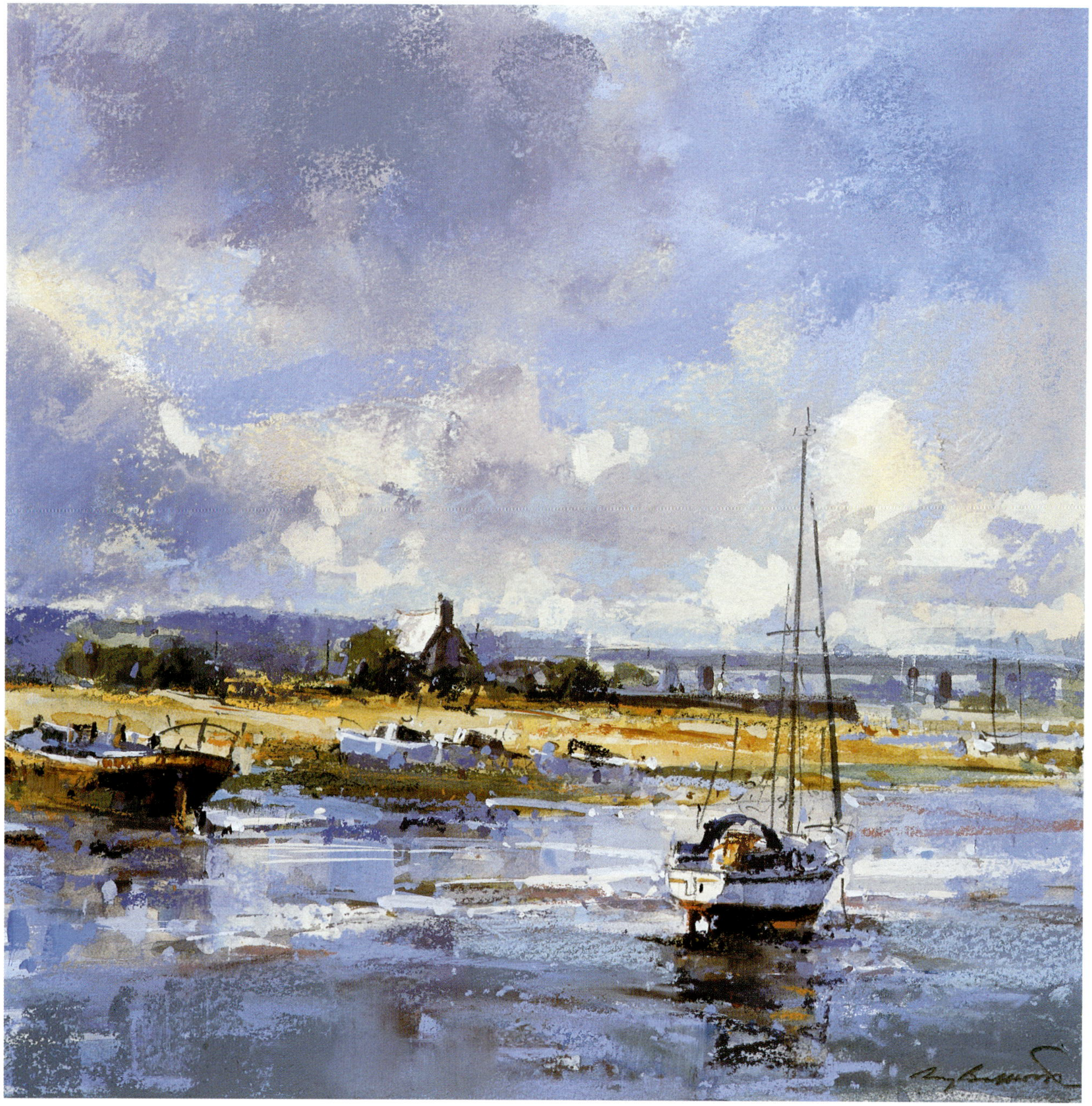

Bright Day, Topsham
Mixed Media 10x10in (25x25cm)

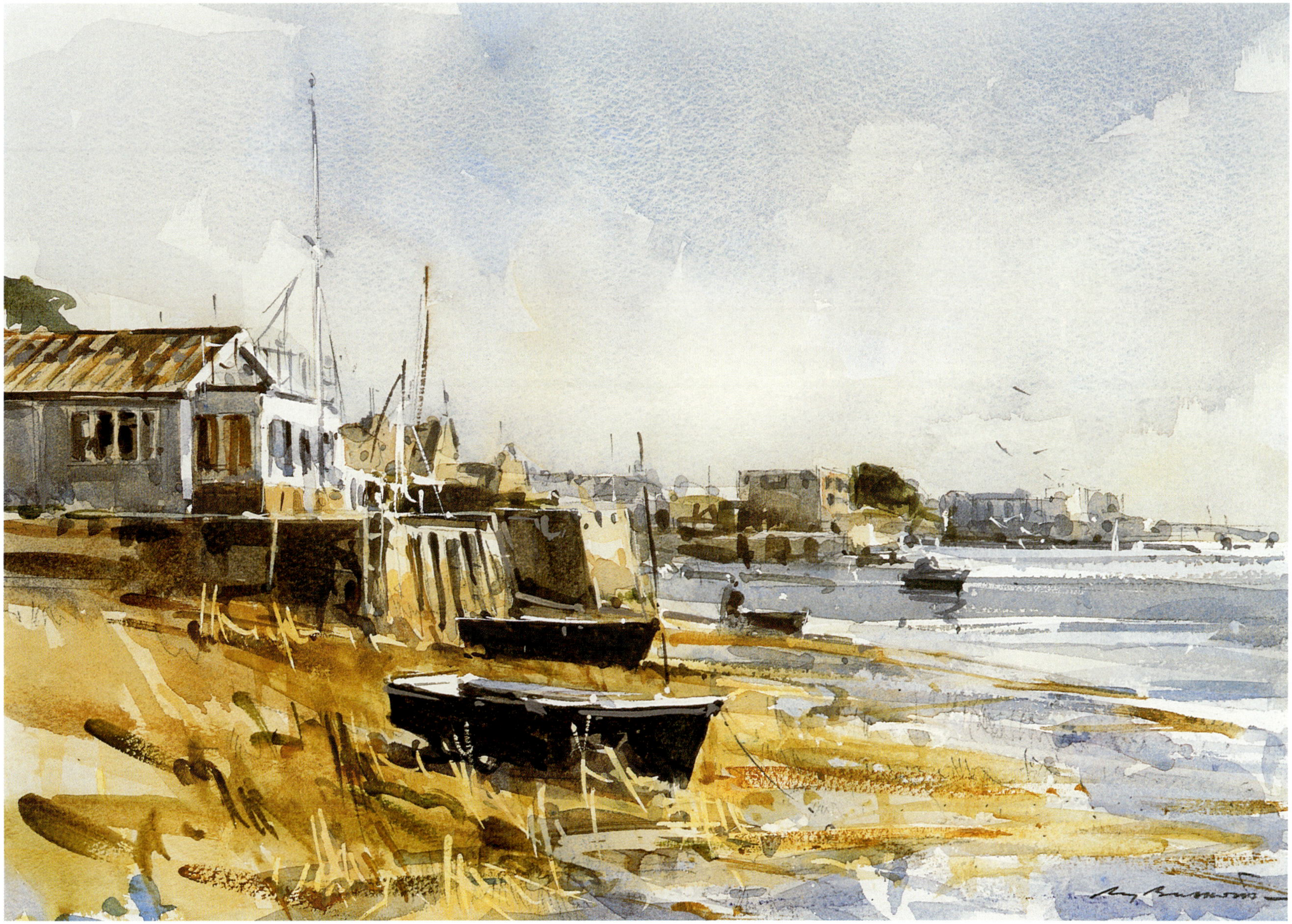

Topsham, on the Mud!
Watercolour 10x14in (25x36cm)

The old folk of Topsham used to say; *'tis the last place the good Lord made, and He didn't stop to finish it, or we would have had sand, not mud!'* The name of the town derives from a personal Saxon name – *'Topa's Ham'* and therefore is correctly pronounced 'Tops-ham.'

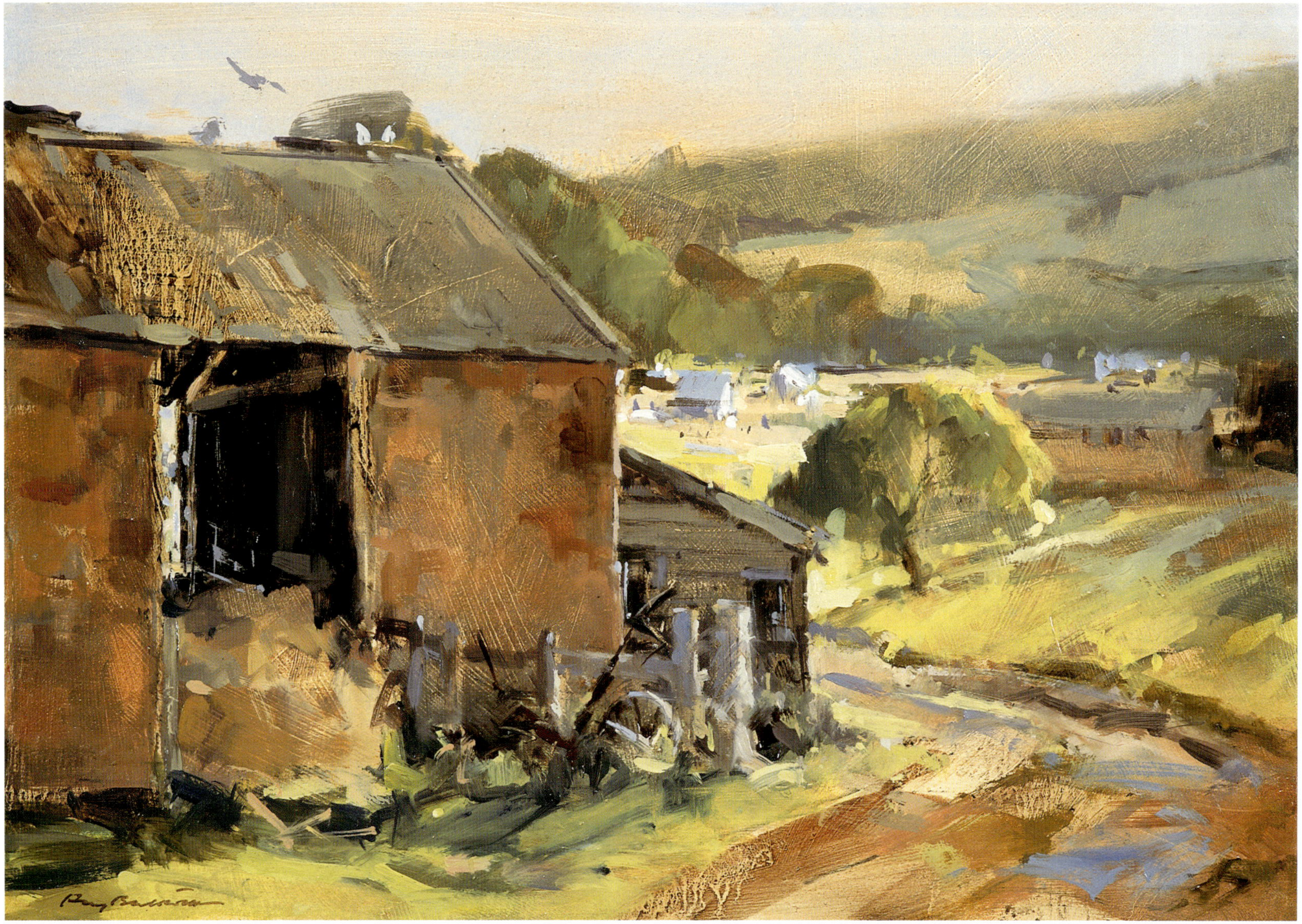

The Old Barn at Bickham, Kenn
Oil 10x14in (25x36cm)

This unique two-storey old barn was once a Victorian powerhouse containing horse-powered agricultural machinery including a thresher, grinder, wurzel-beater and cider press. No longer a hive of agricultural activity, but now more a busy summer home to Swifts, Swallows House-Martins and Sand-Martins! (It is very rare indeed to have all four nesting in the same location).

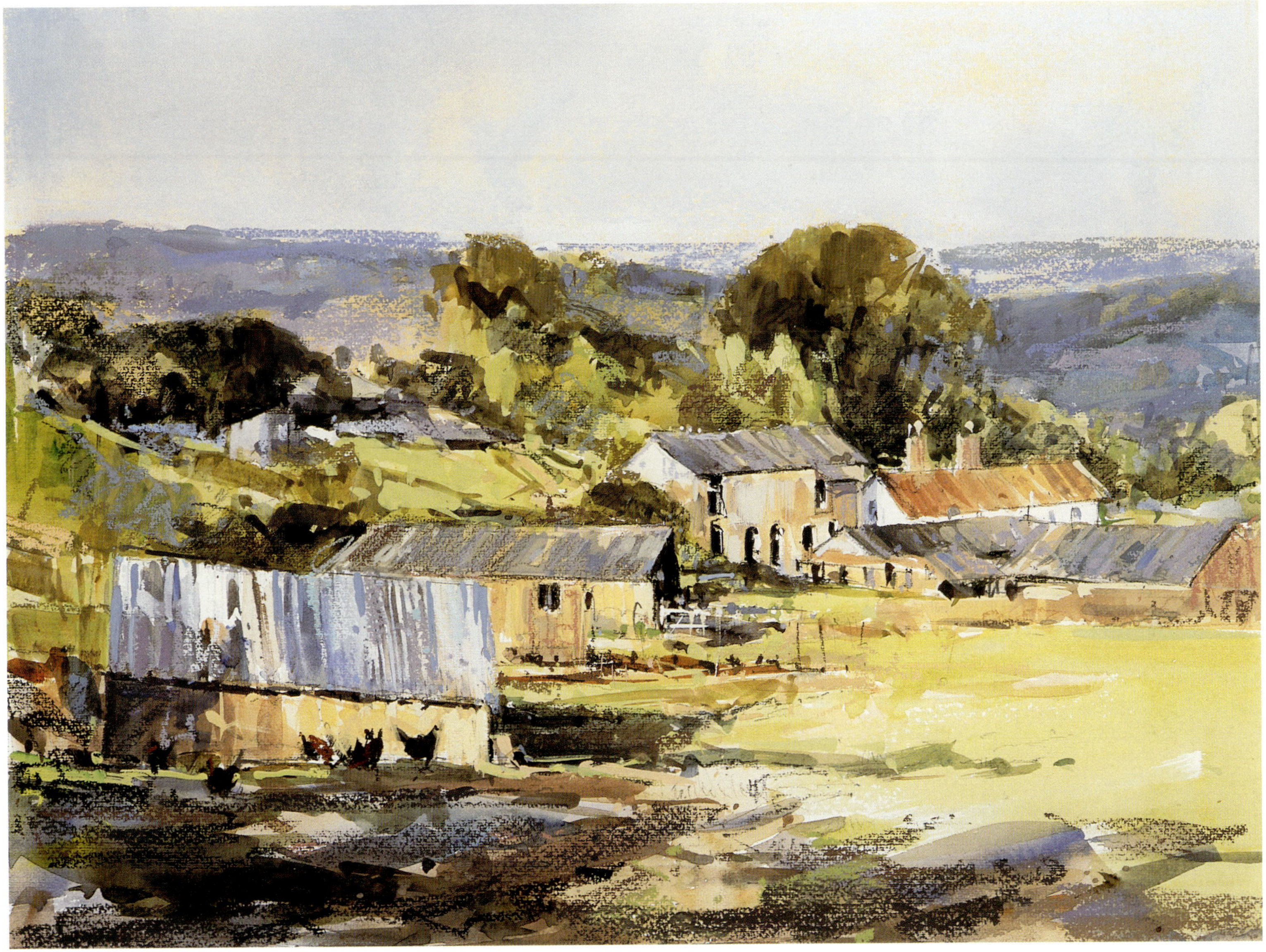

'Rod and Ben's', Bickham Farm
Mixed Media 12x16in (30x41cm)

Bickham Farm is stunningly set on the edge of the Haldon hills and it is here Rod and Ben run a hundred-acre organic farm with Dexter cows, sheep, Black Rock hens, Bronze turkeys as well as growing organic vegetables for their box scheme. They take a real pride in the environment and in producing organic food for the people of the Exe estuary.

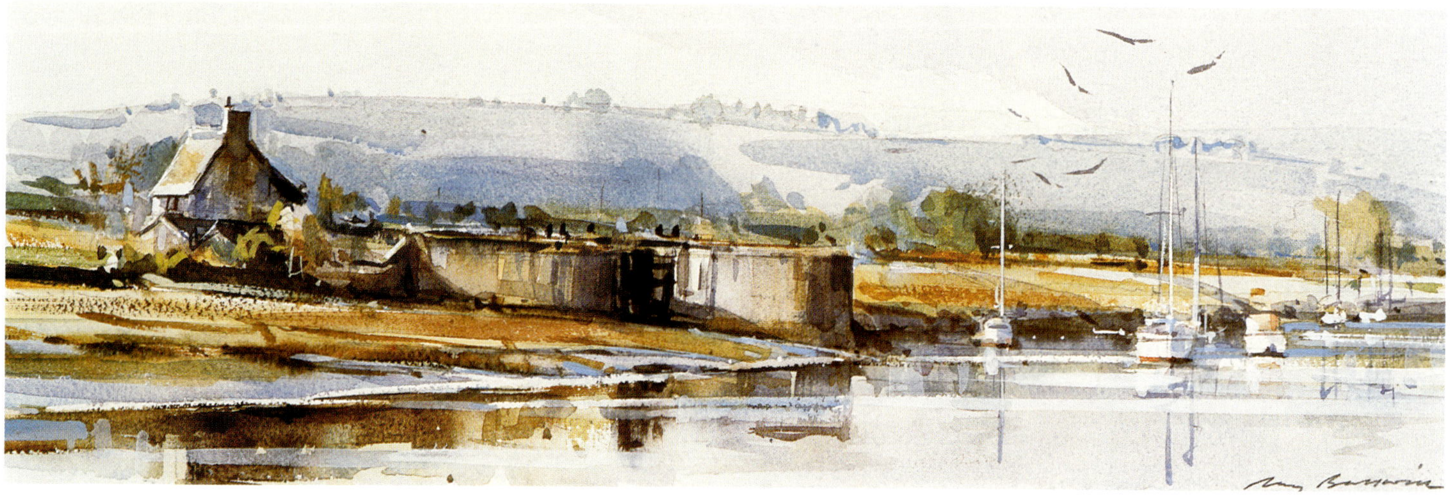

Mary's Cottage, Topsham Lock
Watercolour 5x14.5in (13x37cm)

The isolated location of the lock cottage meant that there was no electricity or gas, and water had to be fetched from a courtyard across the river at Topsham. One lock keeper was Mary Howard and the nature of her lifestyle meant that she certainly had to be a very tough woman to live there.

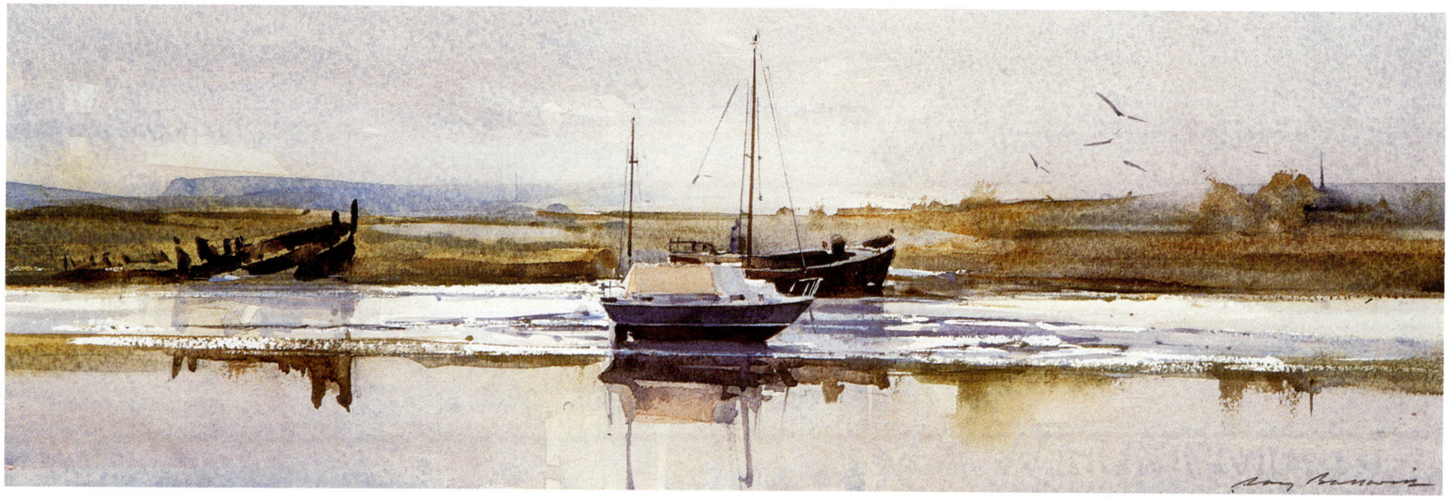

The Old Hulks, Topsham
Watercolour 5x14in (13x36cm)

Across the river from Topsham, rising out of the mud like skeletons, are the ribs of trawlers and barges. In fact there are remains of about twelve vessels on this bank altogether, many being coal ships of yester-year, when the coal trade flourished around our coasts.

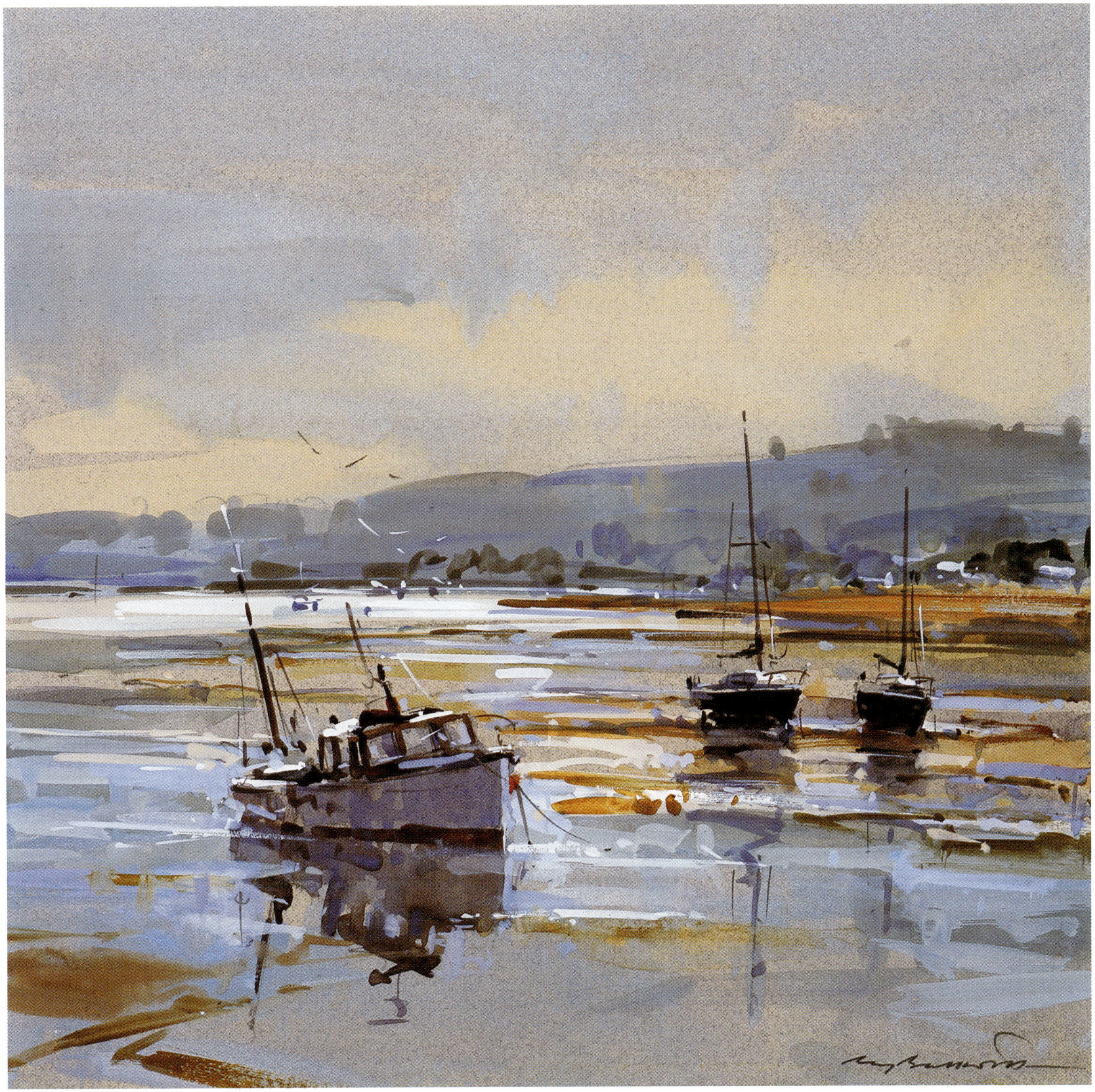

Towards Turf
Watercolour/Gouache 10x10in (25x25cm)

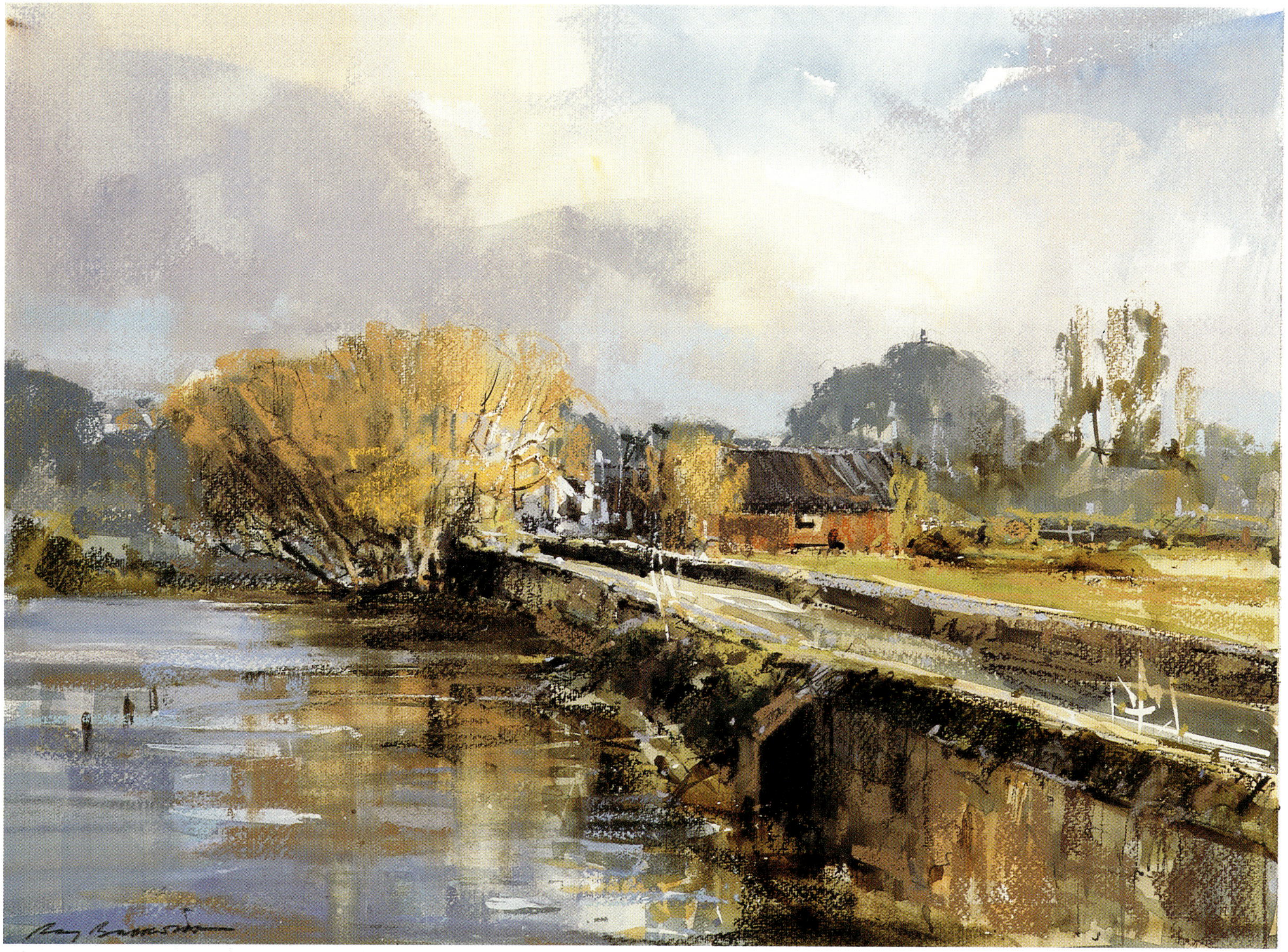

Spring Floods, Clyst Bridge
Mixed Media 13x17.5in (33x45cm)

Next to the busy main road at Clyst St Mary stands Clyst Bridge or 'Clisbrigge', Devon's oldest surviving bridge and river crossing with records of its existence going back as far as 1238. It is hard to imagine that it was once the scene of a bloody battle during the time of the Wars of the Roses between the Courtenays of Powderham and the Bonvilles. It is now an ancient monument.

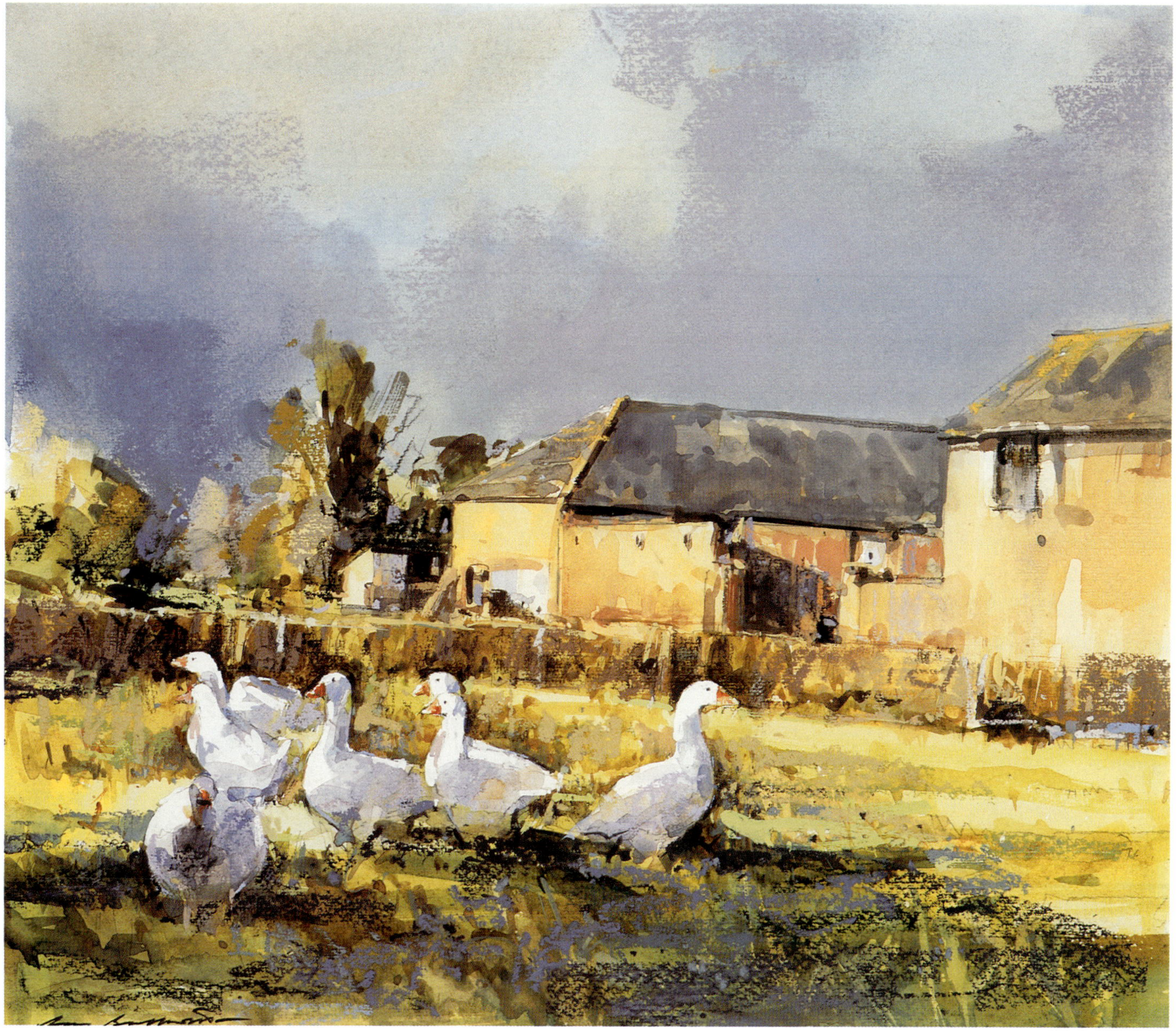

Geese at Marianne Pool Farm, Clyst St George
Mixed Media 11x12in (28x30cm)

Perhaps the title for this painting should be 'Christmas Dinner!' The traditional cob and thatch farmhouse dates back to 1781 and once formed part of the Wraxall Estate. The Bragg family now run a dairy farm of 200 acres, along with B&B accommodation.

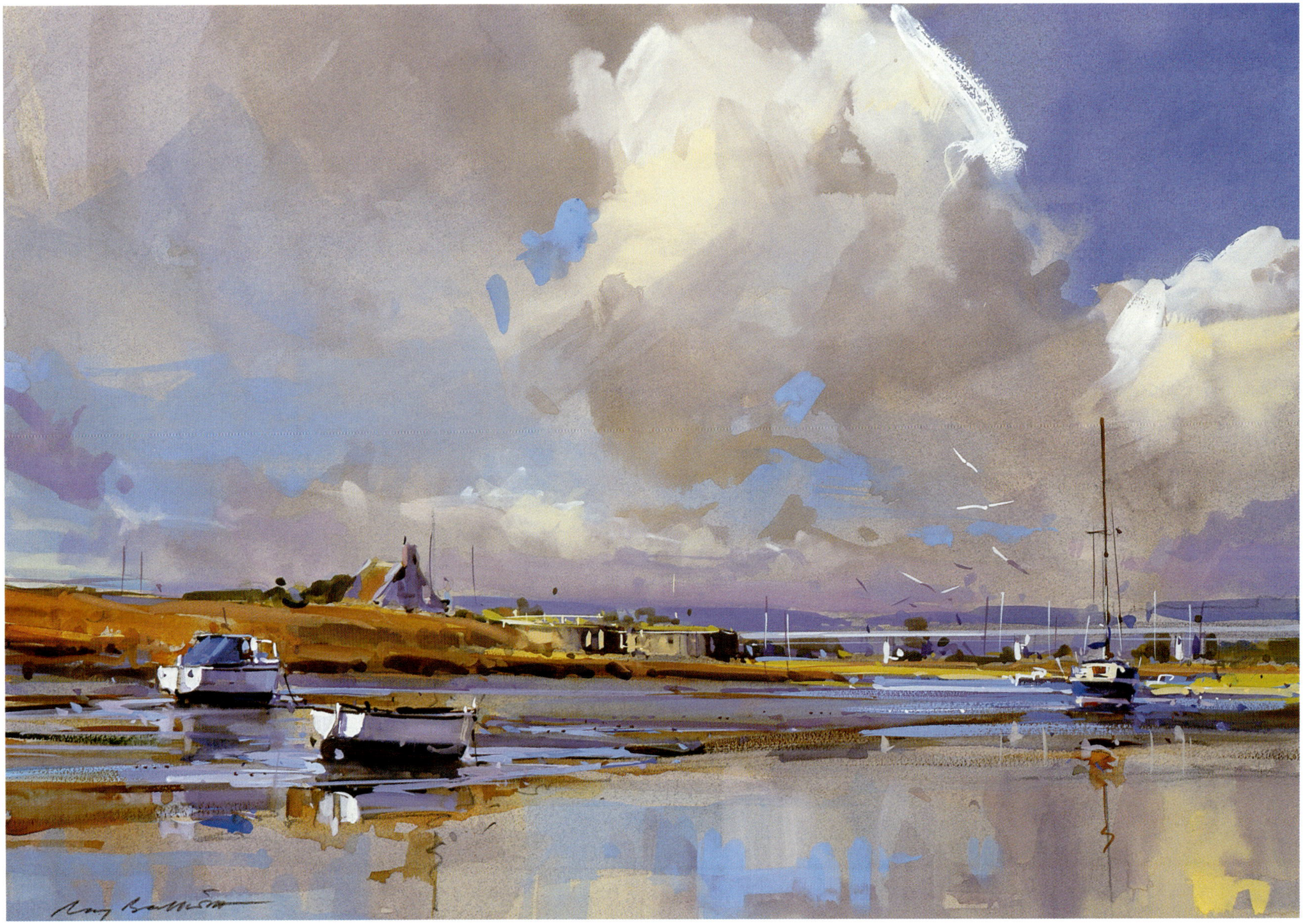

Billowing Clouds, Topsham
Watercolour/Gouache 10x14in (25x36cm)

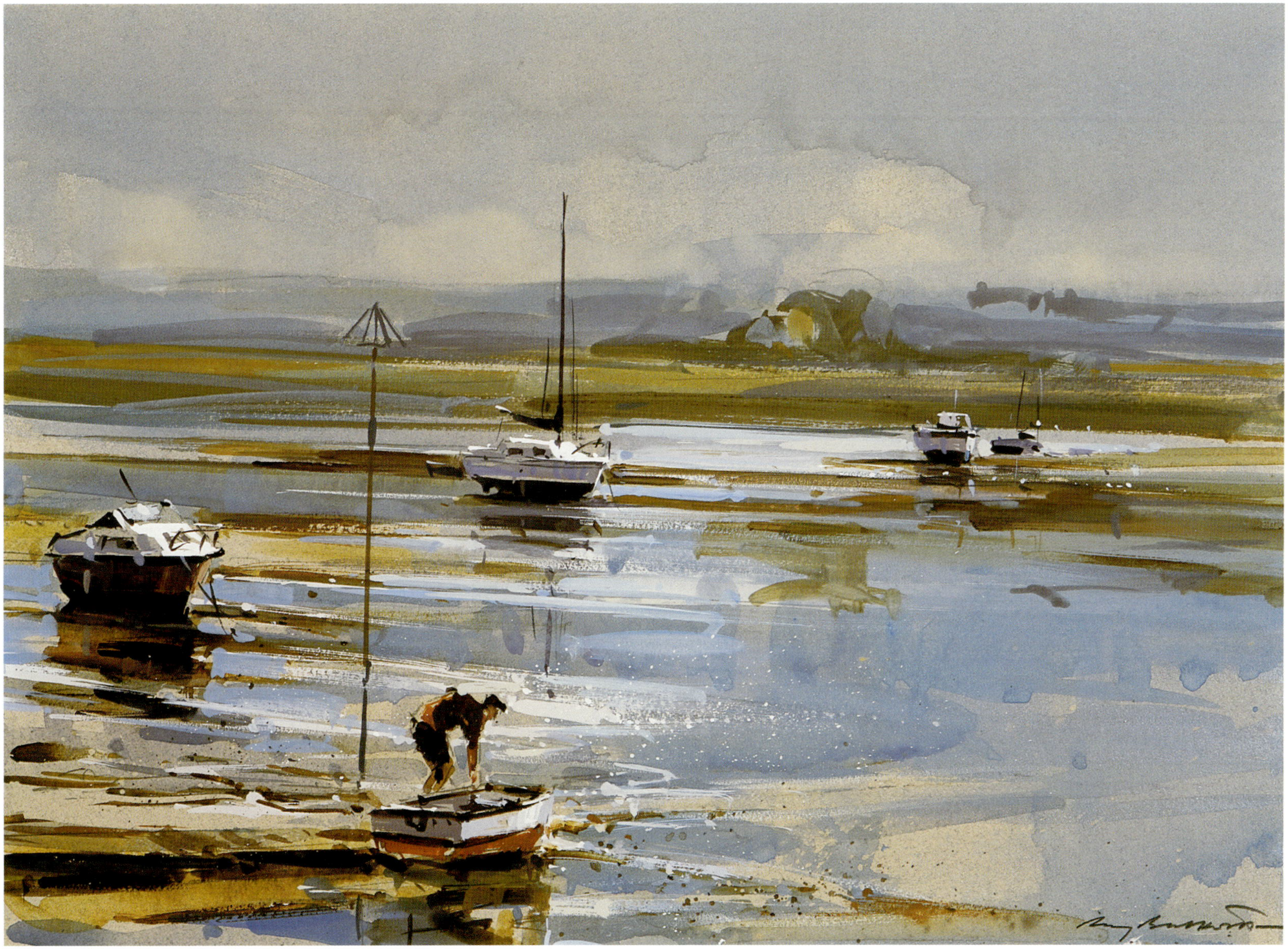

Tranquil Waters, Topsham
Watercolour/Gouache 10x14in (25x36cm)

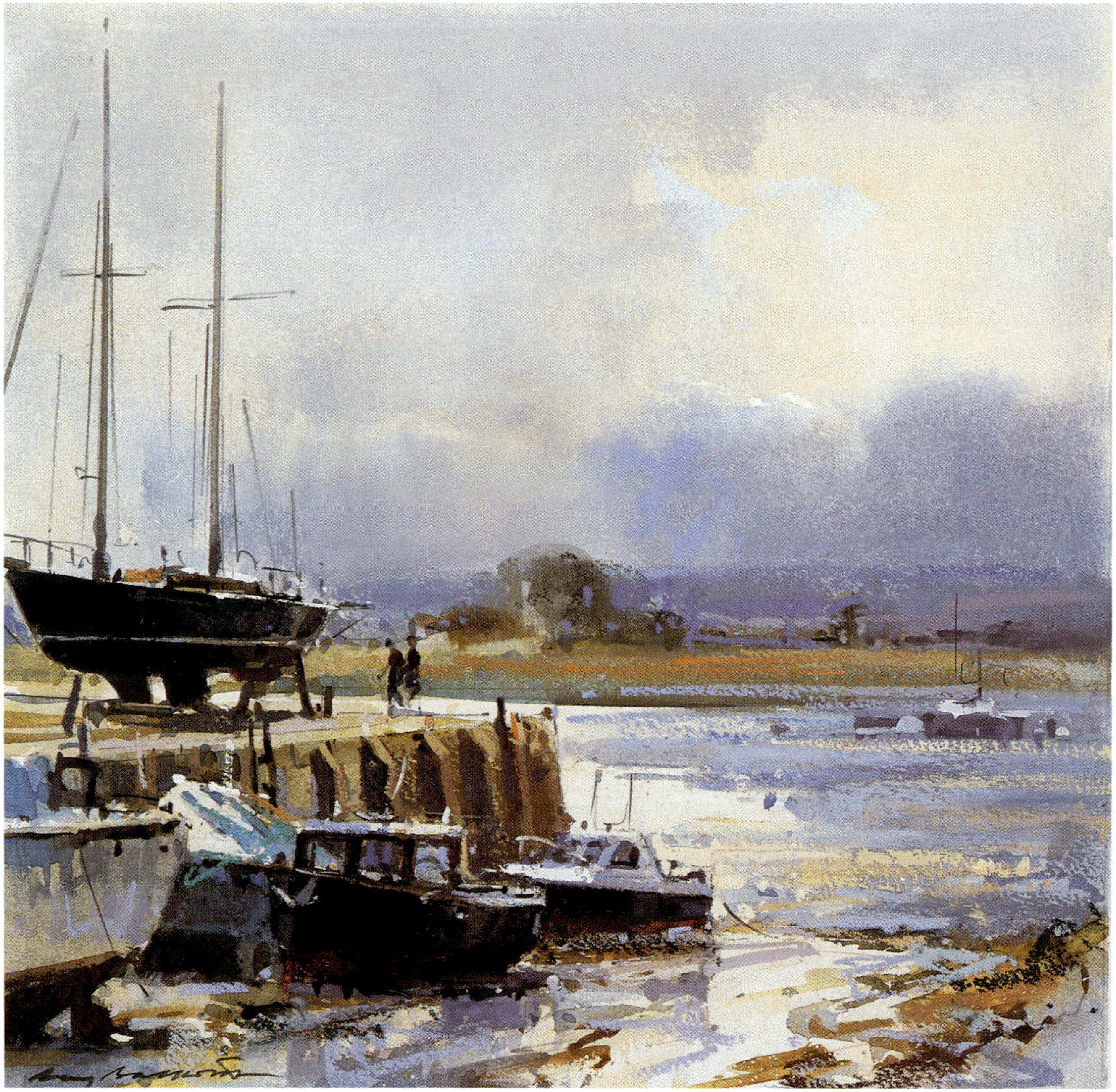

High and Dry, Town Quay
Mixed Media 10x10in (25x25cm)

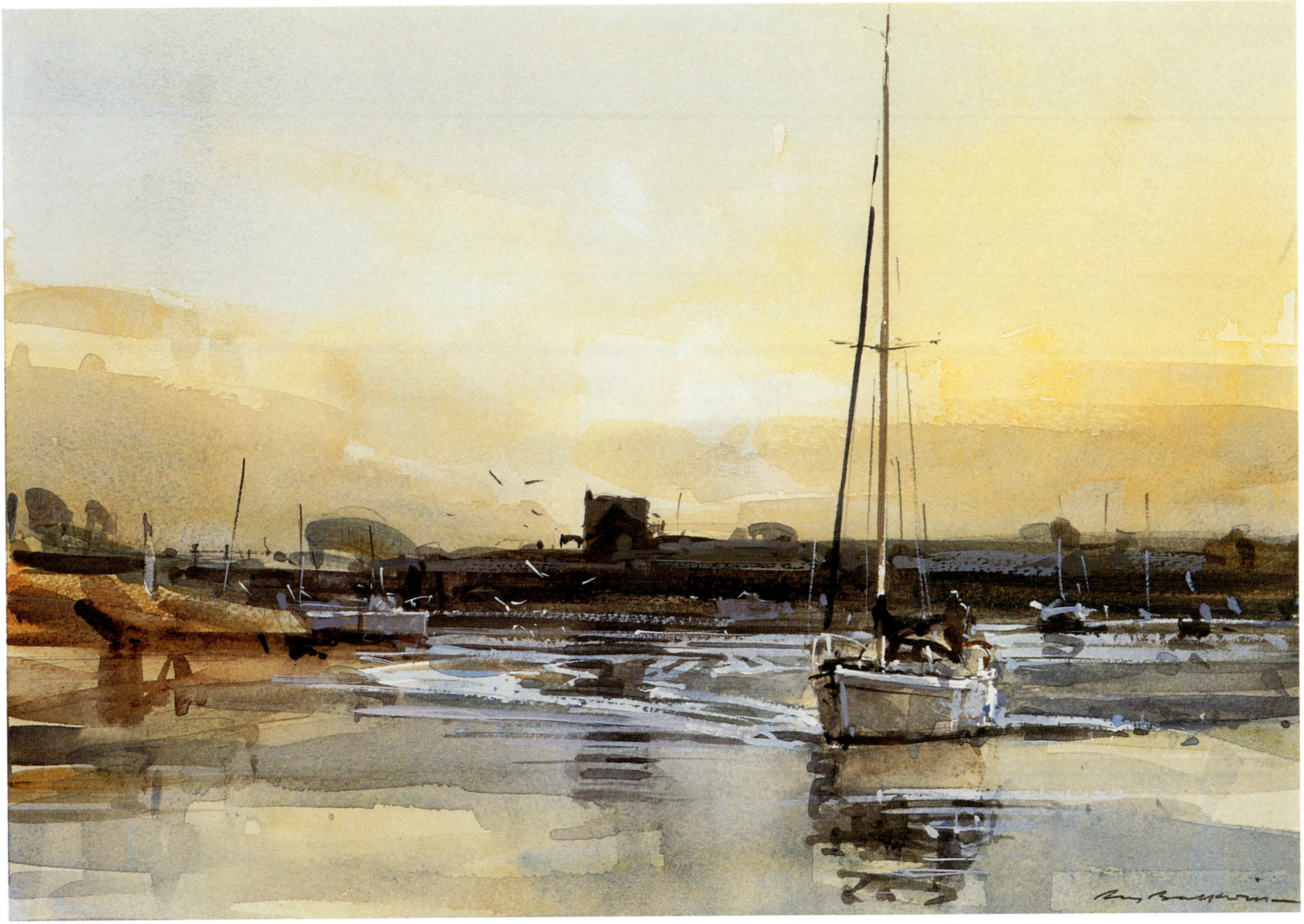

Homeward Bound, Topsham
Watercolour 10x14in (25x36cm)

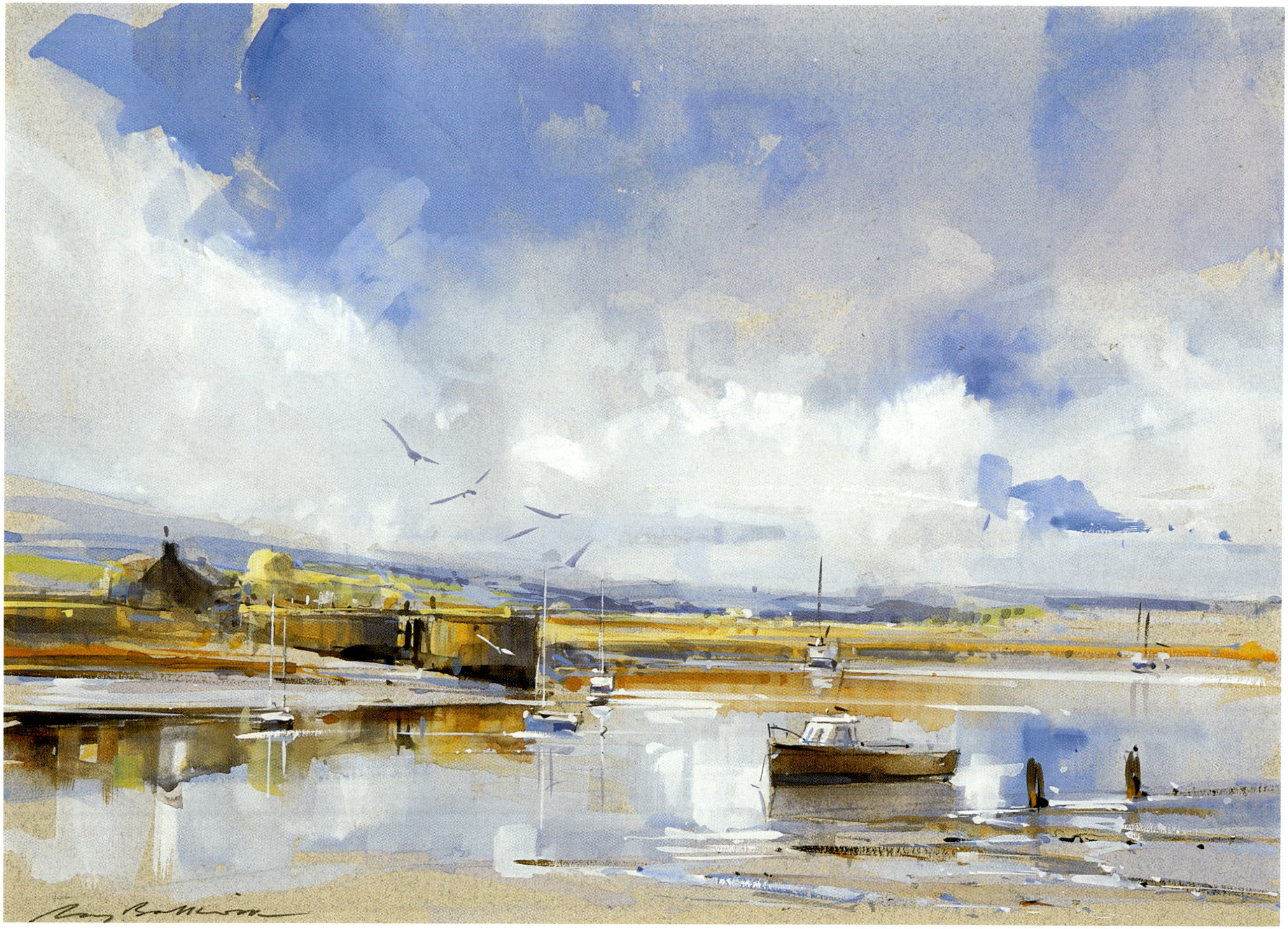

Topsham Lock
Watercolour/Gouache 10.5x14.5in (27x37cm)

The now disused Topsham Lock was built after the canal had been extended to Turf. The merchants at Topsham feared a decline in trade, so the side lock was added in 1832.

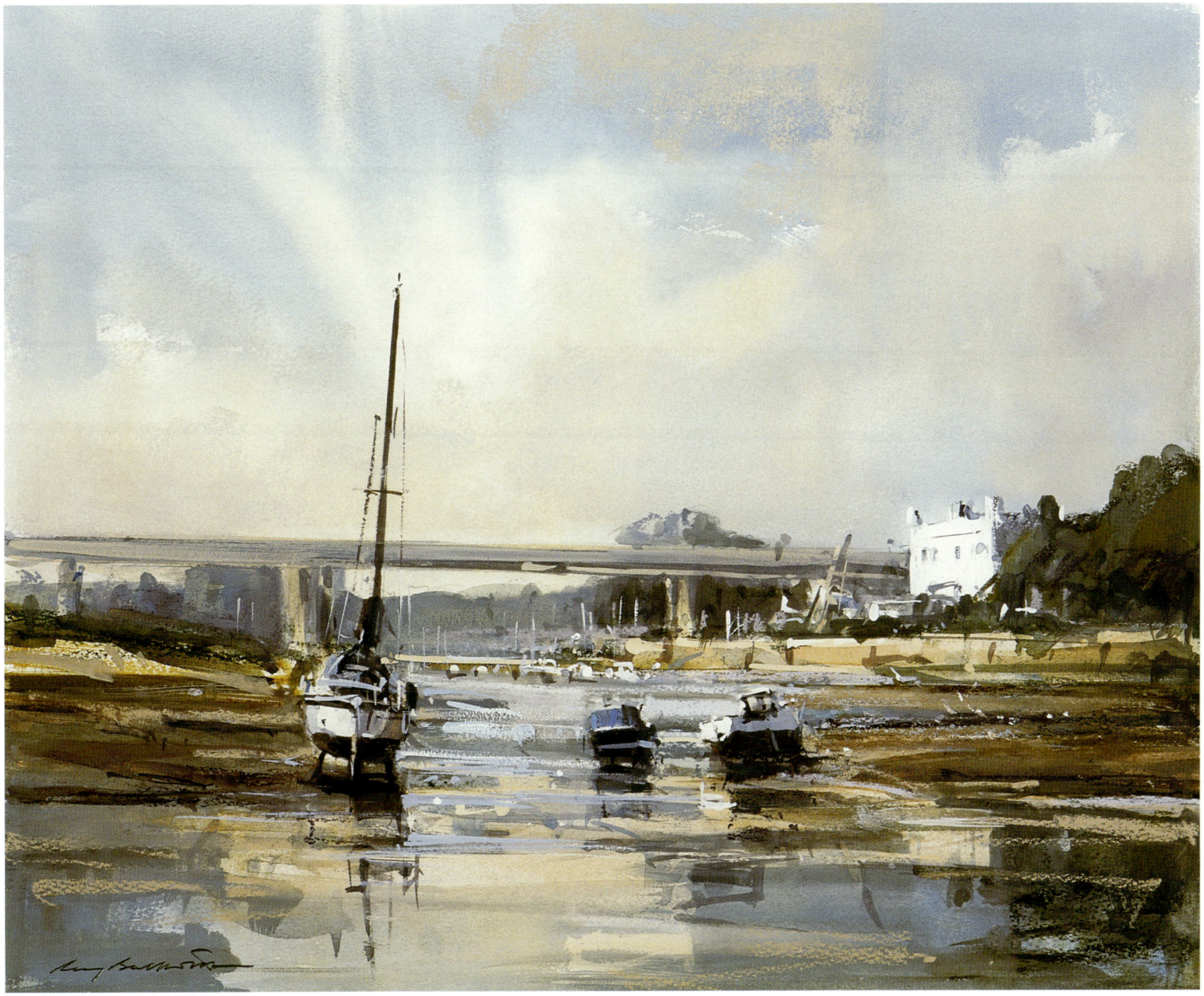

Retreat House, Topsham
Mixed Media 13.5x16.5in (34x42cm)

Now somewhat dominated by the bridge that carries the M5 motorway over the river, Retreat House, with its white façade is still a landmark for miles around. It was converted from a sugar store into an imposing house for Sir Alexander Hamilton in the mid eighteenth century. The walk beside the Retreat was known as 'Under Sir Alex's', but over the years has been corrupted to 'Serallick's Walk'.

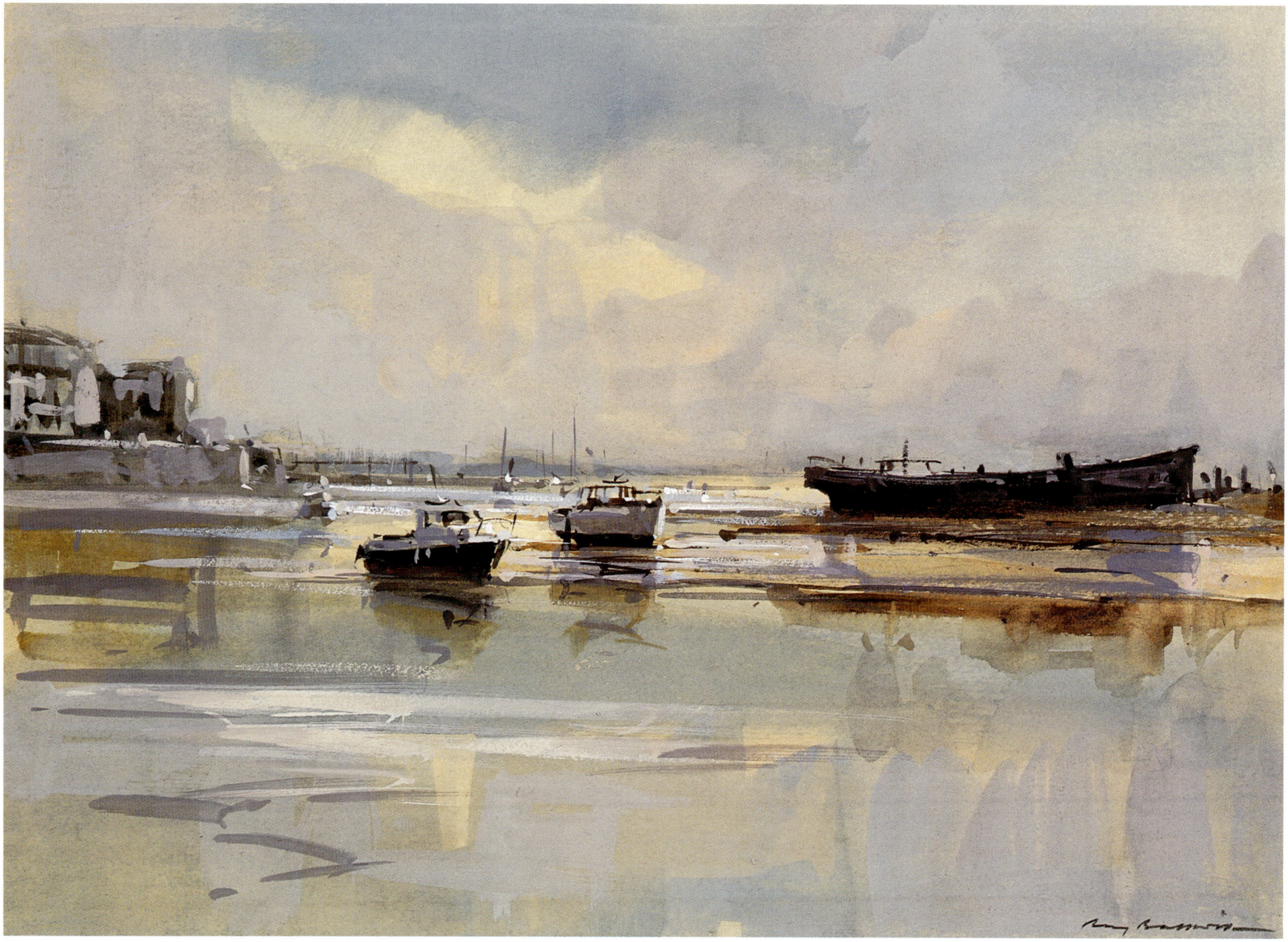

Sun Breaking Through at Topsham
Watercolour/Gouache 10x14in (25x36cm)

I find that the translucency of watercolour is the perfect medium for a subject like this. *'A flat wash,'* the great watercolourist John Varley used to tell his pupils; *'is like a silence in which you can hear the faintest whisper.'*

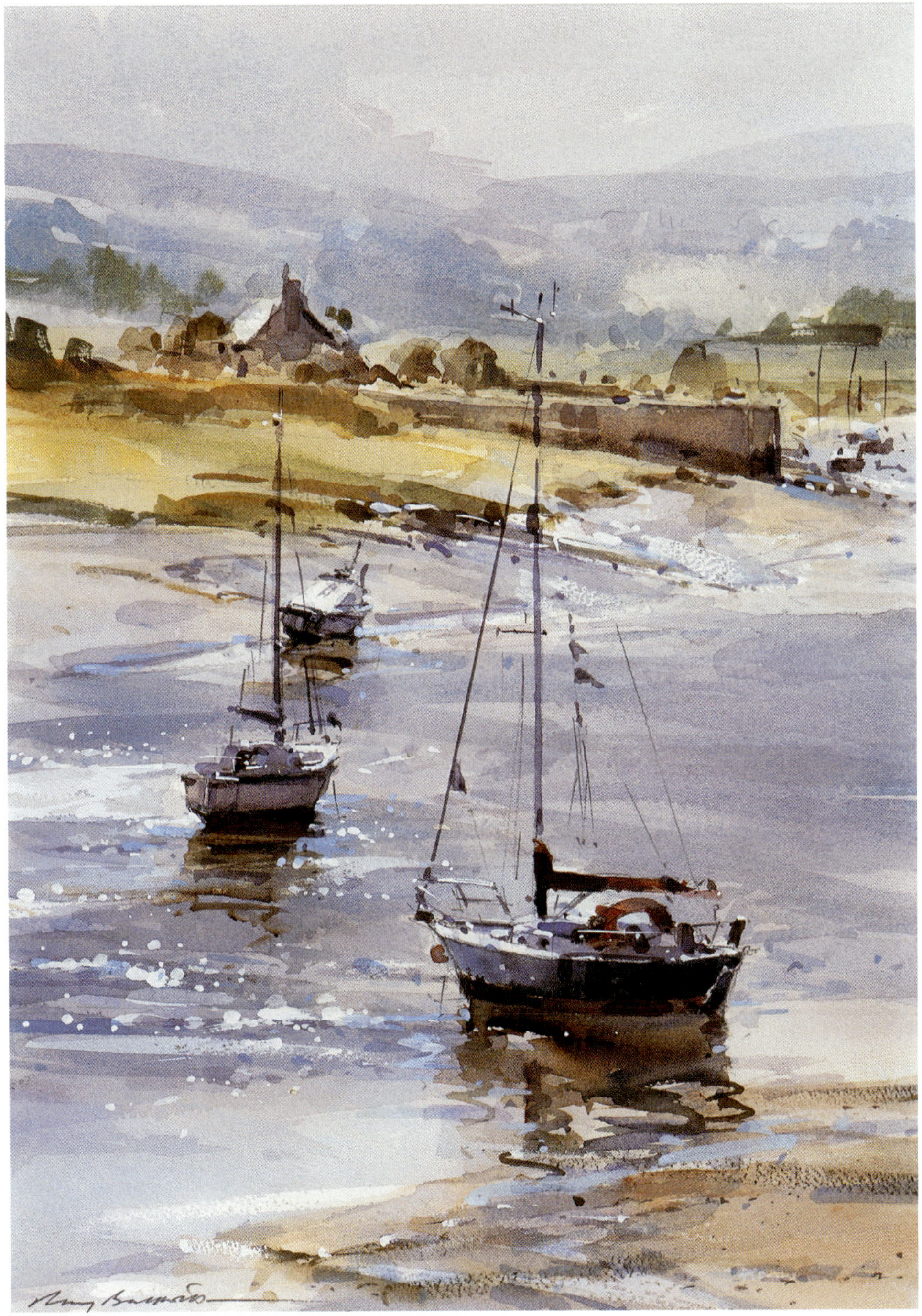

Sunlit Water, Topsham
Watercolour 14x10in (36x25cm)

This view is from St Margaret's Church and it is perhaps apt to quote the Victorian novelist Geoge Gissing, who lived in Exeter for a time and said: *'A long ramble ended at Topsham, where I sat on the churchyard terrace and watched the evening tide up the broad estuary. I have a great liking for Topsham; and that churchyard, overlooking what is not quite sea, yet more than a river, is one of the most restful spots I know.'*

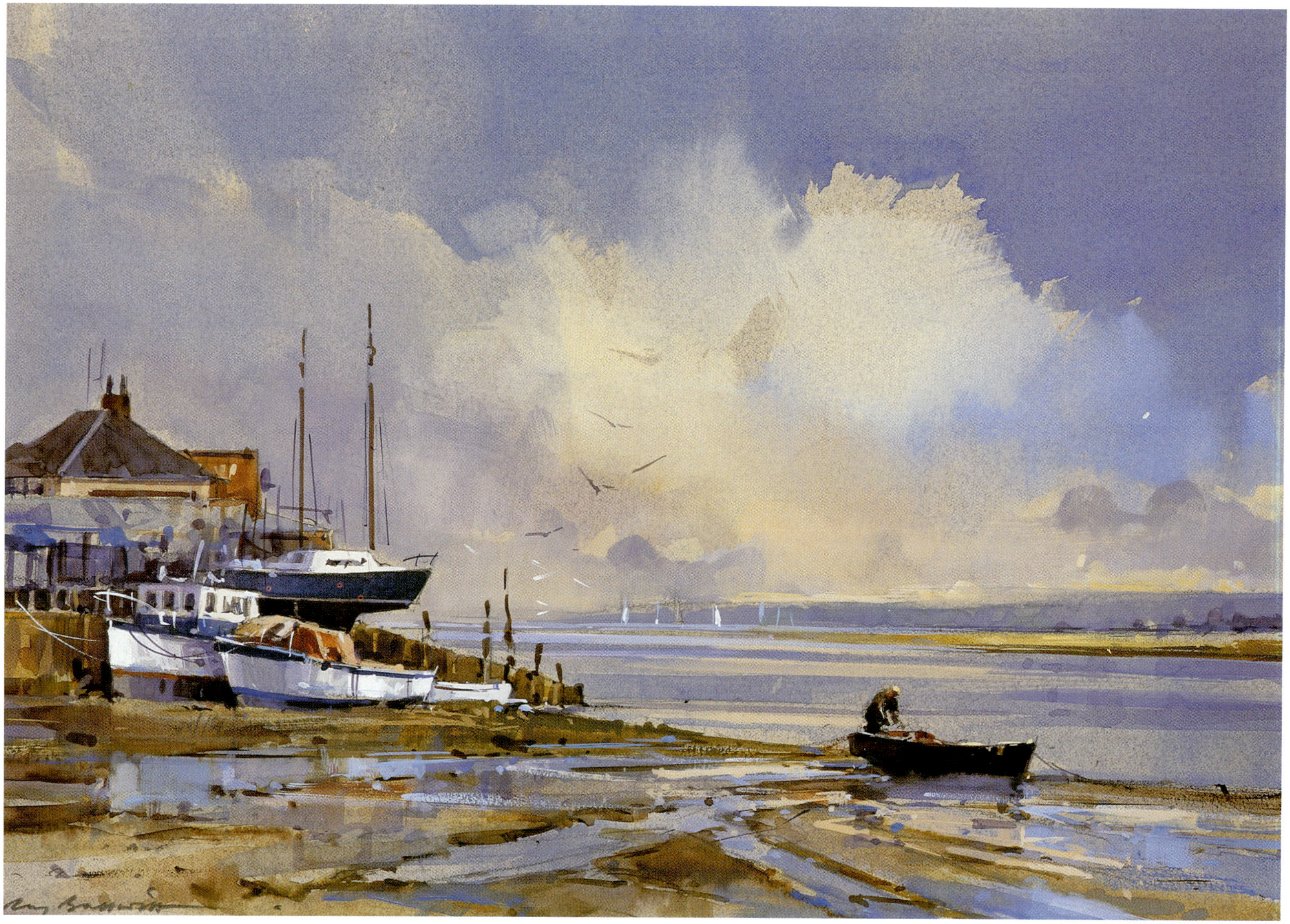

Down River, Topsham
Watercolour/Gouache 10x14.5in (25x37cm)

This view shows Trout's boatyard which was first established in 1902 by Daniel Trout who made salmon boats. The Trout family continue the tradition of repairing and building boats to this day. Beneath the quay are two vessels, a Brixham trawler *The Rescue,* and a former ammunition barge from Plymouth, both brought aground to form the quay's foundations.

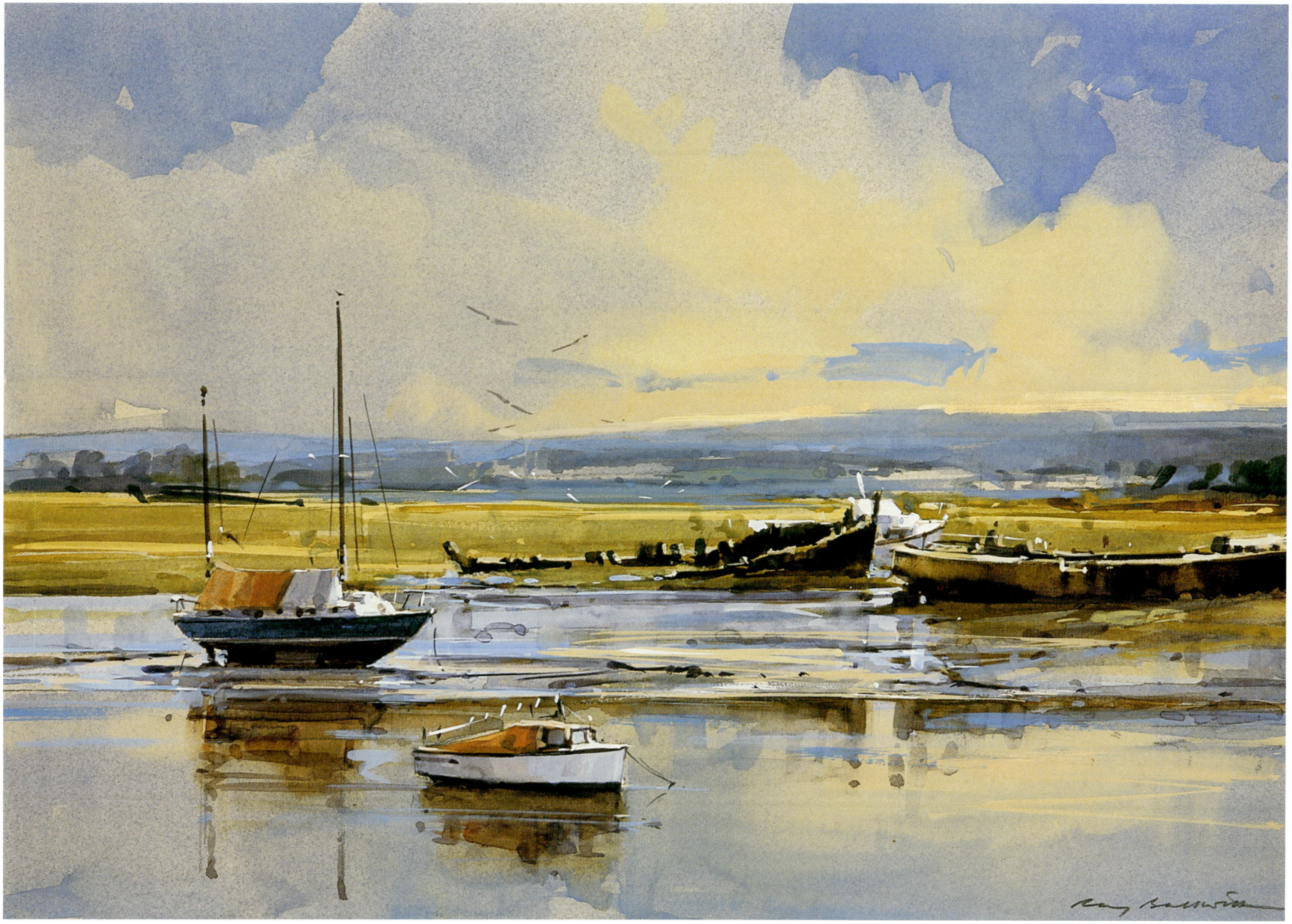

Setting Sun, Topsham
Watercolour/Gouache 10x14in (25x36cm)

The sea pushes up to meet the river at Topsham twice a day and Thomas Hardy once said: *'It is where the Exe scents the sea'*.

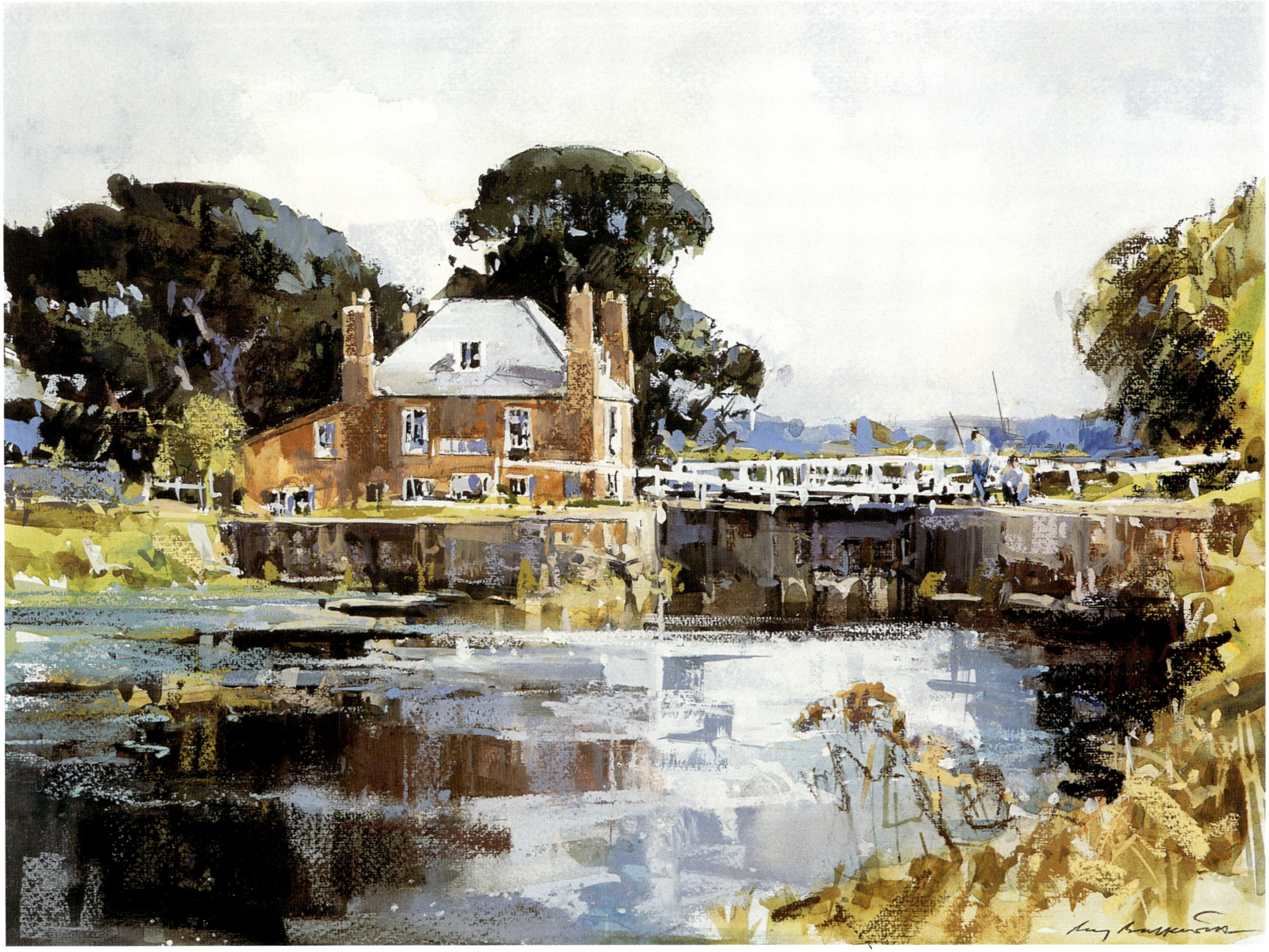

Summer Day at Double locks
Mixed Media 12x16in (30x41cm)

I have fond memories of the trips made here with my grandfather back in the sixties, as we watched the coasters navigating the locks. This popular inn was built in the early eighteenth century from 'clinkers', bricks that were made in Holland and carried back as ballast on trading ships.

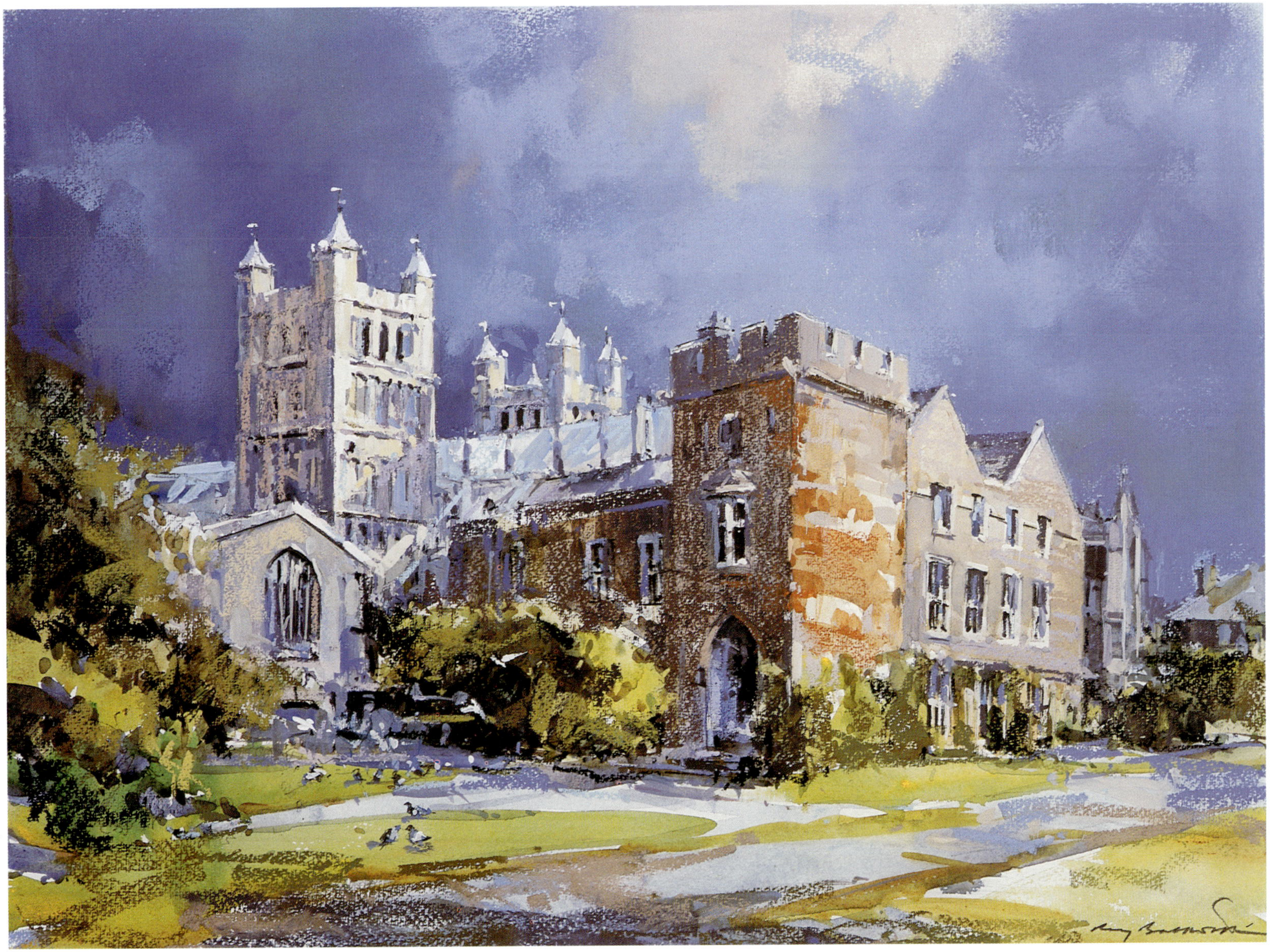

Cathedral and Bishop's Palace, Exeter
Mixed Media 13.5x18in (34x46cm)

The magnificent cathedral is Exeter's greatest jewel and according to experts the Gothic vaulted interior is unsurpassed in England. Although the cathedral was hit during the Blitz in the Second World War, miraculously it escaped major damage, allowing us to continue to cherish what our forefathers have left us.

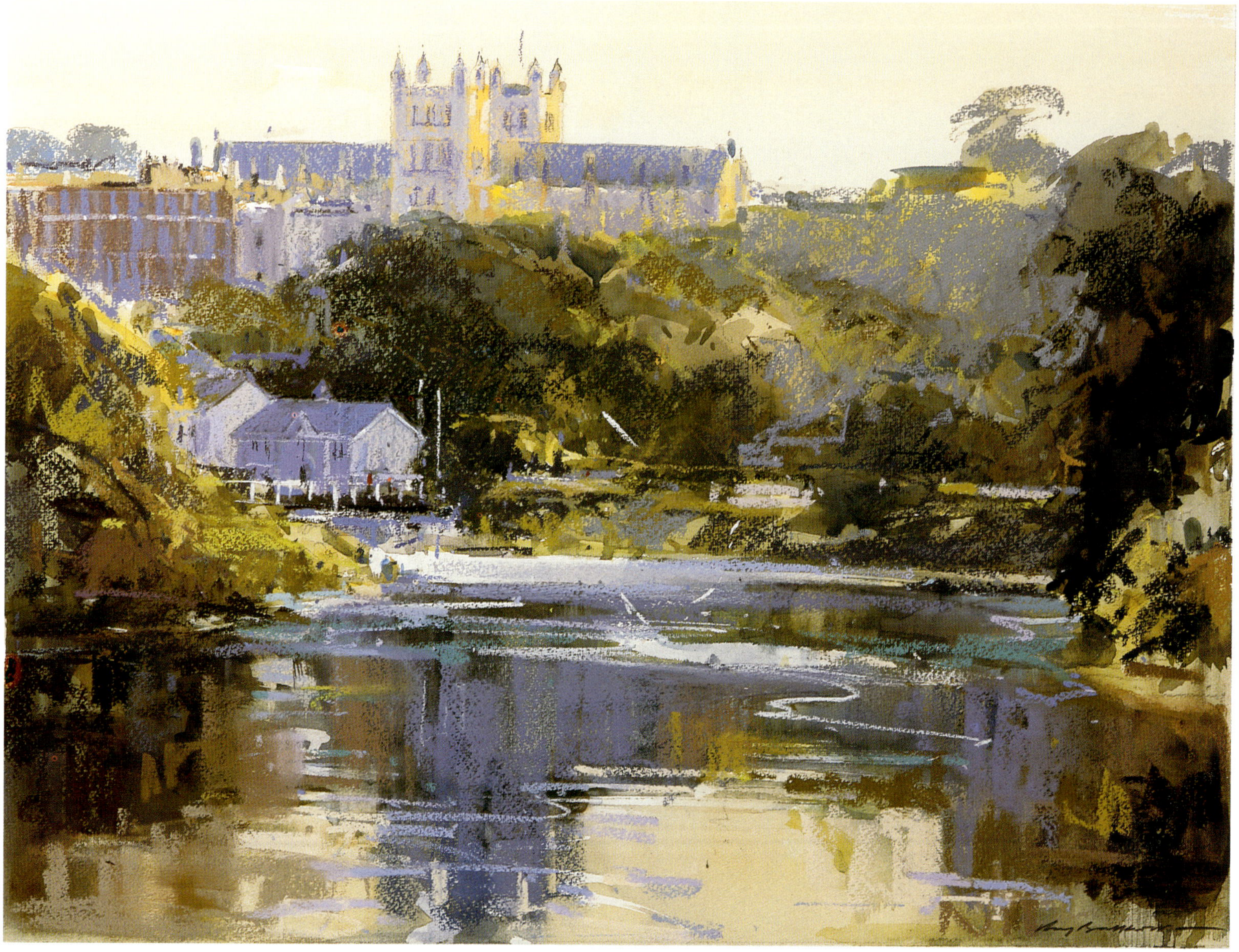

Exeter Cathedral from the Canal
Mixed Media 13.5x18in (34x46cm)

Crowning the whole city, the cathedral with its silvery roof and twin Norman towers, can be seen for miles around. Paintings of the city from the river and canal have always been popular with artists over the centuries including Turner and De Wint, and this is one of my favourite views of the cathedral.

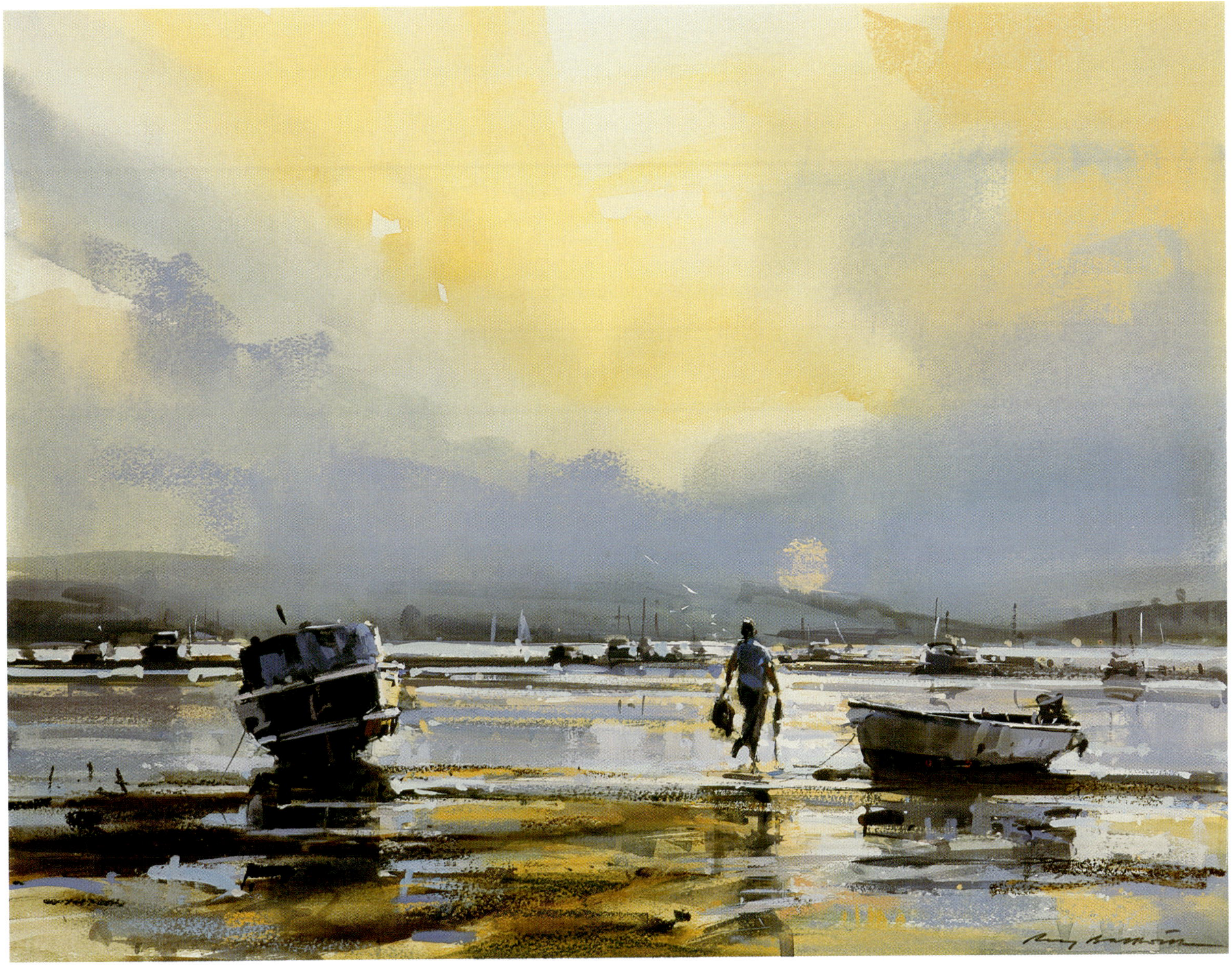

Going Home
Mixed Media 13.5x17in (34x45cm)

Another day ends as the mustard-seed sun descends behind the Haldon hills at Exmouth. The salty flats at the edge of the open sea can always be depended upon to send me home with something worthy of these moments; when earth, sea and sky seem suspended in thin air to encompass, as one, the true spirit of the Exe estuary.

BIBLIOGRAPHY

Books featuring the Exe estuary

Barber, Chips. *Around and about the Haldon Hills,* Obelisk Publications, 1982
Bush, Robin. *The Book of Exmouth,* Barracuda Books, 1978
Cattell, Raymond B. *Under Sail Through Red Devon*
Clark, E.A.G. *The Ports of the Exe Estuary 1660–1860,* The University of Exeter, 1960
Delderfield Eric R. *The Raleigh Country,* 1992
Derounian, J. and Smith, C. *Changing Devon,* Tabb House, 1988
Everitt, Rev. William. *Memorials of Exmouth,* T. Freeman, 1885
Gosling, Gerald. *Exe to Axe – The Story of East Devon,* Alan Sutton Publishing Ltd, 1994
Insull, Mary E. *Lympstone Heritage,* Caldicotts Ltd, 1965
Lawrence, Rod. *The Exe – A River for Wildlife.* Ex Libris Press, 1991
Thomas, Peter and Davis, Stan. *The Exe Estuary – Wildlife in Camera,* Barracuda Books Ltd, 1984
Wills Graham. *Devon Estuaries,* Devon Books, 1895

Books featuring painters associated with the Exe

Baker, C. Jane. *A Vision of Dartmoor,* Victor Gollancz Ltd, 1988
Ellis, Elizabeth. *Conrad Martens Life & Art,* State Library of New South Wales Press, 1994
Gray, T. and Rowe, M. (eds) *Travels in Georgian Devon* (Volumes 1-4) Devon Books, 1997
Greenacre, Francis. *Francis Danby 1793–1861,* Tate Gallery, 1988
Hunt, Peter. *Payne's Devon,* Devon Books, 1986
Jacobs, Michael and Warner, Malcolm. *Art in The West Country,* Phaidon Press Ltd, 1980
Le Messurier, Brian. *Dartmoor Artists,* Halsgove, 2002
Smiles, Sam and Pidgley, Michael. *The Perfection of England – Artist Visitors to Devon c.1750–1870,* University of Plymouth, 1995

Articles on Hester Frood

The Studio, Arthur Reddie, March 1926
Watercolours & Drawings, Felicity Owen RSW Publications, Spring 1990

FURTHER READING

Art and Instruction Books featuring Ray Balkwill's work:

Balkwill, Ray. *Watercolour Plus…,* David & Charles, 2002
Bulgin, Sally. *The Artist's Practical Problem Solver,* Collins, 2003
Hosegood, Betsy. *Paint! Seascapes and Waterways,* RotoVision, 2001
Jelbert, Wendy and Sidaway, Ian. *The Encyclopedia of Watercolour,* Lorenz Books, 2003
Jennings, Simon. *Art Class,* Collins, 1999
Jennings, Simon. *Artist's Colour Manual,* Collins, 2003
Le Messurier, Brian. *Dartmoor Artists,* Halsgrove, 2002

Articles by Ray Balkwill

The Artist Magazine

1995 December – *'Painting Estuaries and Harbours in Watercolour'.*
1997 May – *'Adventures in Mixed Media'.*
July – *'Sketching Boats and Harbours'.*
August – *'On the Waterline: Boats and Harbours in Watercolour'.*
1998 April – *'Painting Skies in Pastel'.*
October – *'First Impressions in Oils'.*
1999 January – *'Irish Skies and Italian Colour'.*
2000 July and August – *'Painting Seascapes in Mixed Media'.*
2001 April – *'Changing Light in the Landscape'.*
2002 June – *'Tide Lines – Boats and Harbours'.*
2003 March – *'Painting Skies'.*
September – *'Out in the Wilderness'.*
2004 October – *' A Sense of Place – The Exe Estuary'.*

International Artist Magazine

1998 June – *'Painting Seascapes in Mixed Media'.*
1999 June – *'Masters of the Media'.* by Ron Ranson.

Pastel Artist International Magazine

2000 May – *'United Kingdom Showcase'.*

Exe Estuary Prints

For details of Limited Edition Prints of some of the paintings featured in this book visit: www.raybalkwill.co.uk

An art instruction film with Ray Balkwill painting on the Exe Estuary is available from: APV Films. Tel: 01608 641798